Discovering Ayrshire

Peter Robertson
26 Kingsway Barshare
Cumnock.

Already published:
Discovering Galloway
Discovering Lewis and Harris
Discovering West Lothian

Forthcoming:
Discovering Aberdeenshire
Discovering East Lothian
Discovering Fife
Discovering Inverness-shire

Discovering Ayrshire

JOHN STRAWHORN
and
KEN ANDREW

Photographs by Ken Andrew

JOHN DONALD PUBLISHERS LTD
EDINBURGH

ISBN 0 85976 199 1

Phototypeset by Newtext Composition Ltd., Glasgow.
Printed in Great Britain by Bell & Bain Ltd., Glasgow.

Acknowledgements

Many people are due thanks for help in the preparation of this book. Chapters 1-11 obviously owe much to experts who have generously supplied specialist information over a long period of years. To a list of those previously and elsewhere acknowledged may be added the names of Robert Kirk and Jim Mair for details included in Chapter 11. In the preparation of Chapters 12-22, numerous churches were visited at irregular times – clergy and laity were almost invariably welcoming and helpful; gratitude is recorded to those churches mentioned in the text, with regret that much useful information has had to be omitted. Thanks are also due to Frank Beattie, Bill Bennett, Rob Close, Annie Joss, George McNaughton, T.G. Ovens, R.M. Pepper, Irvine Development Corporation, Nobels Explosives Company Limited, the Sisters of St Joseph of Cluny, and many informants met casually in the field. Both authors are indebted to Cumnock and Doon Valley District Council, Cunninghame District Council, Kilmarnock and Loudoun District Council, Kyle and Carrick District Council, their officials, their planning departments, and especially their Library services.

This book is the work of two equal partners, and the only reason why one name precedes the other is because of the order in which their chapters appear.

JOHN STRAWHORN
KEN ANDREW

Contents

Introduction

This book should appeal to a variety of readers. Tourists passing through Ayrshire will find it a handy guide. Those spending a holiday will discover just how much this area has to offer. The quite considerable number of incomers who have chosen to make their homes here will surely enjoy exploring Ayrshire. Those who have grown up in the county will be reminded of places they know and often be amazed at what they hadn't noticed. Exiles who have left Ayrshire will want to have this reminder of their native haunts.

John Strawhorn, who has written the first eleven chapters, is author of a number of books on Ayrshire and its history. But this is not a potted history of the county, full of old forgotten far-off things. Instead he has selected a series of topics which should interest most readers by supplying a view of both past and present.

Ken Andrew, author of the other eleven chapters, has written several books popular with visitors and especially hill walkers. Here he takes readers on a series of tours which draw attention to places worth visiting. On his way he has taken those photographs which illustrate *Discovering Ayrshire*.

The index gives references to the principal places and topics, and indicates where one author's information is supplemented by the other. Our simple route plan (page x) requires to be complemented by the appropriate Ordnance Survey maps, and not only to locate those places for which Map References are given.

Some other advice should be heeded. The fact that a place is mentioned in this book does not imply that the reader has open access. If in doubt seek permission. Also, some places can be dangerous. Accidents can too easily occur in ruined castles or abandoned quarries. And hill walking requires adequate preparation and equipment. But taking all necessary care, you can enjoy 'Discovering Ayrshire'.

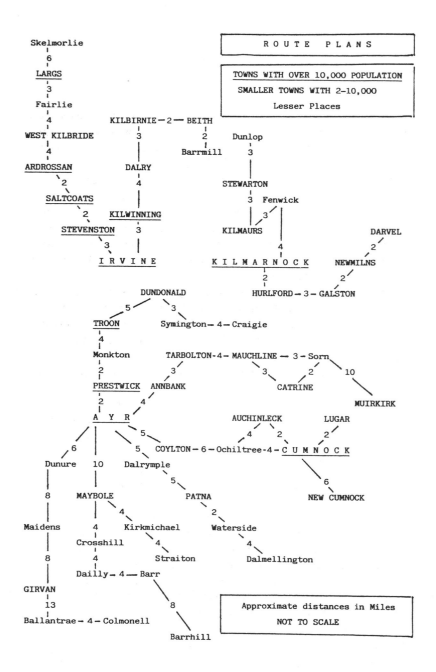

ROUTE PLANS

TOWNS WITH OVER 10,000 POPULATION
SMALLER TOWNS WITH 2-10,000
Lesser Places

Skelmorlie
6
LARGS
3
Fairlie
4
WEST KILBRIDE
4
ARDROSSAN
2
SALTCOATS
2
STEVENSTON
3
IRVINE

KILBIRNIE — 2 — BEITH
3   2   Dunlop
        Barrmill 3
DALRY
4   STEWARTON
        3 Fenwick
KILWINNING   3
3   KILMAURS

DARVEL
2
4   NEWMILNS
KILMARNOCK   2
2
HURLFORD — 3 — GALSTON

DUNDONALD
5   3
TROON   Symington — 4 — Craigie
4
Monkton   TARBOLTON - 4 - MAUCHLINE — 3 - Sorn
2   3   3   2   10
PRESTWICK ANNBANK   CATRINE
2   4   MUIRKIRK
A Y R   AUCHINLECK   LUGAR
5   4   2   2
6   5   COYLTON — 6 — Ochiltree - 4 - CUMNOCK
Dunure 10 Dalrymple
        5   6
8   MAYBOLE   PATNA   NEW CUMNOCK
        4   2
Maidens 4   Kirkmichael Waterside
        Crosshill   4   4
8   4   Straiton   Dalmellington
        Dailly — 4 — Barr
GIRVAN
13   8
Ballantrae — 4 - Colmonell
        Barrhill

Approximate distances in Miles
NOT TO SCALE

x

CHAPTER 1
The Ayrshire Scene

Imagine a great natural amphitheatre facing westwards towards the sea. This is Ayrshire, in the south-west of Scotland. From the eastern boundary on the upland moors beyond Glenbuck there is a descent of 26 miles towards Troon on the Firth of Clyde, with magnificent views over the water to the sun setting behind the mountain peaks of Arran. The northern extremity on the coast is at Skelmorlie, less than an hour's drive from the centre of Glasgow. 63 miles to the south, or 85 miles by road through varied coastal scenery, brings you to Glenapp on the border of Galloway, with Ireland just 30 miles distant across the North Channel.

The highest parts of the encircling hills are to the south, rising to Shalloch on Minnoch at 2522 feet (769 m). Just over the county boundary is the Merrick, at 2770 feet (843 m) the highest point in the Southern Uplands. These Carrick hills are also the oldest, formed of hard Ordovician and Silurian rocks which reach down to the sea, and the road from Girvan to Ballantrae follows a scenic route along old sea cliffs. The rocky shoreline is a haven for marine biologists, botanists, searchers for gem stones, and for geologists following in the path of James Hutton, the Scottish founder of their science, who came here exploring in 1786.

The great Southern Uplands Fault extends from Girvan inland through New Cumnock towards the east of Scotland. Most of Ayrshire lies north of it, forming a basin of younger and softer rocks. On the upland rim of the county, to east and north, there are some Silurian and Old Red Sandstone rocks, the latter obvious on the rocky northern coast from Ardrossan to Largs. The lower-lying land of central Ayrshire rests on Carboniferous strata with extensive beds of coals and limestones, which dip down to sea level where gently-shelving sandy beaches attract bathers to the central part of the coast between Ardrossan and Ayr. The youngest rocks of all, the red Permian sandstones found around Mauchline, were once quarried for house-building locally and even for export across

1

the Atlantic.

The geological pattern is complicated by widespread faulting throughout the area, and volcanic activity contributed spreads of lava in some places and intrusions of igneous rocks in others. Little enough of this subterranean system is obvious to the view, apart from sills of hard igneous rock along the coast and on river beds, and the cores of three extinct volcanoes which survive as impressive monuments of the geological past – Loudoun Hill east of Darvel; the Heads of Ayr; and the island Ailsa Craig off Girvan. The basic rocks are however almost universally covered by soils which were produced by the Ice Age. The glaciers which covered most of Britain seriously eroded the earlier rock surfaces – portions of Ailsa Craig granite have been found in North Wales! – and crushed the stony materials into boulder clay which, as the glaciers melted, was left behind as a soil covering. On the uplands of Ayrshire this remains as a thin layer, but lower down there are thick deposits and an irregular surface of ridges, hillocks, and valleys which would give the later landscape its distinctive and interesting character. Only for a few miles along the central part of the coast is there anything resembling a flat plain. And all along the shores of the Firth of Clyde recession of the sea following the Ice Age has left well-marked raised beaches. Behind the coastal strip are to be seen remains of old sea caves, to the north between Ardrossan and Largs, to the south between Girvan and Ballantrae.

Since the period of glaciation the present river system has established itself. To the south the Stinchar and the Girvan Waters flow through fault lines which had cracked the old resistant rocks. To the north the Garnock, the Irvine, and their numerous tributaries converge, cutting valleys through the boulder clay. In the central part of the county, the Doon and the Ayr both cut deep channels, the former through 'the banks and braes of bonnie Doon' of Robert Burns's song, the latter gouging its way through the soft Permian sandstone to form a deep and spectacular gorge in its middle course, so that there is no real Ayr valley. All these rivers flow towards the Ayrshire coast and into the Firth of Clyde. The River Nith however has reversed its original westward course, and with the Afton Water, also famed in song, finds its way through a gap in the

The scenery of the Ayrshire coast ranges from broad sandy beaches to rocky shores as at Culzean in Carrick. Behind the coast, farmland rises to upland moors, more quickly here than in the busier heart of Ayrshire.

upland rim to turn southwards through Nithsdale and Dumfries and into the Solway Firth.

The rains which feed the rivers have eroded the uplands and left behind badly-drained areas of moorland. Only peat, moss, the coarsest of grasses, and some bog-loving plants will grow in acid soils with a short growing season and an annual rainfall of up to 100 inches (2.5 m). On the lowlands, however, there is less rain, a longer growing season, and generations of liming and draining and hard work by farmers have made Ayrshire a noted agricultural region. Visitors, though, are less concerned about the climatic prospects for crops than about what the weather forecasts may have to offer them. The rain, which contributes to the attractive greenery of the Ayrshire landscape, may be expected throughout the year. While the months from April to July can be drier, August is often quite wet. Rainfall in Ayrshire is less than in most parts of the west of Scotland, and on the coast averages 30 inches (0.76 m) per year. The prevailing wind is a warm south-west, and fog is so rare on the coast that Prestwick Airport is seldom affected. As far as temperatures are concerned, the July average of 58°F (15°C) is of course often exceeded, and when it does the sandy beaches provide good, safe bathing. The sea, which keeps things cool in summer, has a similar modifying effect in providing Ayrshire with mild winters, so mild indeed that palm trees may be found growing at Culzean Castle and other sheltered spots along the coast. The December average temperature is 41°F (5°C), and often when the rest of Britain is stricken with heavy winter snowfalls, Ayrshire remains green.

Ayrshire is a land of small towns. The two largest have each around 50,000 of a population. Ayr, an old royal burgh, is the county town with 49,500 inhabitants according to the 1981 census. The younger industrial town of Kilmarnock has 52,100. Both are well-equipped as shopping centres, and have other attractions as later pages will show. So too has Irvine, originating as a royal burgh, with a present population of 32,900 plus another 22,400 within that area which is now designated as Irvine New Town. On or near the coast is a string of sizeable towns – Largs (9,800), West Kilbride (4,200), Ardrossan (11,300), Saltcoats (12,800), Stevenston (11,300), Kilwinning (16,200, included in Irvine New Town), Troon (14,300), Prestwick (13,500), Girvan (7,900). The coast resorts have attracted holiday visitors, and more permanent residents who can enjoy seaside life with Glasgow only an hour or so away by train. Inland, apart from Kilmarnock, the biggest local centre is Cumnock (9,600), with Kilbirnie (8,700) and Stewarton (6,400) next in size. There is a score of smaller townships, each with its own distinctive character, usually a pride of identity, and often with something quite special for the interested visitor. There are as many more villages and hamlets, mostly off the main traffic routes, and sometimes

When Burns wrote 'Flow gently, sweet Afton, among thy green braes' he was obviously describing the lower reaches of the river. Here in its early stages it passes Craigbraneoch Rig. In such territory rise all Ayrshire rivers.

quite charming.

Though the townsfolk are dependent for their livelihood upon industries, these are seldom intrusive enough to spoil the environment. Townsfolk and countryfolk are close neighbours, and the Ayrshire farms are situated amid green fields bounded by thorn or beech hedges and shelterbelts of trees, the rolling landscape punctuated by stretches of woodland against a backdrop of the moorlands beyond. Ayrshire's 375,000 people live together in the lowlands and adjoining valleys, which occupy just about half of the county area of 1,132 square miles (otherwise 724,251 acres or 293,100 ha). The empty moors and hills which surround the county on its landward sides almost entirely segregate Ayrshire folk from their neighbours in adjoining counties. This means that Ayrshire has retained its sense of identity despite the legislative changes of 1975 which abolished Ayr County Council as a unit of local government, and incorporated the area in the massive Strathclyde Region, with only 15 elected representatives among the total of 103 on the Regional Council, and major public services like education administered from headquarters in Glasgow.

The same reorganisation of local government sadly involved the abolition of the burghs, some of them with a tradition of municipal independence dating back seven centuries or more. Local patriotism however has survived the transfer of local services like housing to four District Councils centred in Irvine (Cunninghame D.C.), Kilmarnock (Kilmarnock and Loudoun D.C.), Ayr (Kyle and Carrick D.C.), and Cumnock (Cumnock and Doon Valley D.C.). Oddly enough the process of modernisation which required the legislative abolition of the shire of Ayr (which had been created as a sheriffdom in the 13th century) and its county council (formed in 1890) revived the names of those even more ancient provinces of Cunninghame (north of the River Irvine), Kyle (in the middle), and Carrick (south of the River Doon) – which had been combined seven centuries before to form Ayrshire. Simultaneously the parliamentary constituencies were unnecessarily renamed Cunninghame North (formerly North Ayrshire and Bute), Cunninghame South (formerly Central Ayrshire), Kilmarnock and Loudoun (Kilmarnock Burghs), Ayr (Ayr Burghs), Carrick, Cumnock and Doon Valley (formerly and more simply South Ayrshire). The Labour Party has a firm hold on Kilmarnock, Central, and south Ayrshire seats, and gained North Ayrshire in 1987, while Ayr remains in Conservative hands. It is perhaps a sign of good choice of candidates that William Ross, M.P. for Kilmarnock, became Secretary for State for Scotland in two Labour administrations; in a subsequent Conservative government that post was held by George Younger, M.P. for Ayr, until he became Minister of Defence. All the Ayrshire seats have from time to time produced some well-known backbenchers.

Ayrshire has retained its sense of identity despite the obvious efforts of certain faceless bureaucrats to eliminate the name. The sense of local identity has been sustained, to some degree, by the local newspapers. Most now belong to the Guthrie Newspaper Group which prints in Ardrossan the *Ayr Advertiser* (founded in 1803); *Ardrossan and Saltcoats Herald; Largs and Millport Weekly News; Irvine Times;* and the *Cumnock Chronicle.* Scottish and Universal Newspapers Ltd. print in Irvine the *Ayrshire Post; Kilmarnock Standard;* and the *Irvine Herald.* Once upon a time these weeklies provided comprehensive coverage of local events, problems, and achievements. Modern tabloid presentation of items considered newsworthy, and the publishers' dependence on advertising revenue means that the traditional weeklies (and the free-issue advertising news-sheets now competing with them) are less effective in revealing the interests and spirit of the communities they serve. But it is still the case that a good way to become acquainted with a place is to buy a local newspaper. At the very least it will advertise forthcoming events and attractions.

Of course if you are a visitor and want to find out just what the locality has to offer in the way of entertainment and places to visit, then you should head for one of the main tourist offices: Ayrshire and Burns Country Tourist Board, 39 Sandgate, Ayr; Ayrshire Valleys Tourist Board, 62 Bank Street, Kilmarnock; Cunninghame Information Centre, The Promenade, Largs. And listen to the local commercial radio – Westsound – on medium wave 290 m (1035 kHz), or VHF/FM 96.2 MHz (Girvan area 97.1 MHz). Westsound is another agency which keeps its listeners informed of local events and presents some interesting feature programmes within the inevitable and predominant diet of pop music.

The serious searcher after knowledge about Ayrshire will find a way to the public library, and will be best served at one of the four district library headquarters: Carnegie Library, Main Street, Ayr; Dick Institute, London Road, Kilmarnock; Cunninghame District Library, Princes Street, Ardrossan; Cumnock Library, Bank Glen, Cumnock. A request for books on local history may well be followed by a spell browsing in the library's files of local newspapers, which better than anything else can bring the past to life. The staff in these libraries we have always found able and willing to supply helpful advice – though it may be necessary to offer a reminder that they are busy people and cannot be expected to undertake for you detailed investigations like searching out for you your Ayrshire ancestors.

As visitors will constantly be reminded, there is widespread pride in the fact that this was the homeland of Robert Burns, Scotland's National Poet and one of international renown. The Burns Trail will be explored in Chapter 8. Those who are historically aware will recall also that it was from Ayrshire that centuries earlier Wallace and Bruce led their campaigns in the Wars to secure Scottish Independence. A select list reveals how many Ayrshiremen have won fame:

William Wallace (c.1270-1305), born at Elderslie, Renfrewshire, or perhaps (as local patriots suggest) at Ellerslie, Riccarton, where he organised his first guerrilla forays against the English occupying forces.

Robert Bruce (1274-1329), son of the Earl and Countess of Carrick, is presumed born at Turnberry; enthroned as King Robert I in 1306, he won victory at Bannockburn in 1314.

George Lockhart (c.1485-1547), born in Ayr, became Prior of the College of Sorbonne in Paris and a philosopher of international reputation.

Sir Hew of Eglinton (died 1380), Alexander Montgomerie of Hessilhead (1545-1611), Walter Kennedy of Cassillis (born c.1460), Quintin Schaw from Straiton (1450-1505), Mark Alexander Boyd of Penkil (1563-1601) were Makars – poets of the Renaissance period.

James Dalrymple (1619-1695) from Stair, author of the celebrated *Institutions of the Laws of Scotland*.

David Dale (1739-1806) began herding cattle as a lad near Stewarton, and became a wealthy Glasgow businessman with interests in banking and especially in cotton manufacture.

James Boswell (1740-1795) – born in Edinburgh but his home was at Auchinleck – the great biographer who wrote the *Life of Dr Johnson*.

William Murdoch (1754-1839), born at Lugar, engineer and inventor who introduced gas-lighting and pioneered steam locomotion.

John Loudon McAdam (1756-1836), born in Ayr, returned from New York to live at Sauchrie from 1787 till 1798; as a member of the Ayrshire Turnpike Trustees constructed the first 'macadamised' roads.

Robert Burns (1759-1796), born at Alloway, whose Kilmarnock Edition of *Poems Chiefly in the Scottish Dialect* was published in 1786.

William Maclure (1763-1840) emigrated from Ayr to Philadelphia to become wealthy businessman, philanthropist, radical thinker, and 'father of American geology'.

John Galt (1779-1839) was born in Irvine, scene of several of his novels.

Alexander Macmillan (1818-1896), born in Irvine, founded the famous London publishing firm.

Johnnie Walker, the Kilmarnock whisky blender, 'born 1820, still going strong'.

John Boyd Dunlop (1840-1921) from Dreghorn invented the pneumatic tyre.

James Keir Hardie (1856-1915), born in Lanarkshire, came to Cumnock in 1879 to organise the Ayrshire Miners Union and in 1893 founded the Independent Labour Party.

Andrew Fisher (1862-1928), a coalminer from Crosshouse, emigrated to Australia in 1885 to become Labour Party leader and Australian Prime Minister 1903, 1910-13, 1914-15.

George Douglas Brown (1869-1902) from Ochiltree, whose novel *The House with the Green Shutters* introduced a new era in Scottish literature.

John Boyd Orr (1880-1971), born in Kilmaurs, biologist, nutritionist, and first director of the United Nations Food and Agricultural Organisation.

Alexander Fleming (1881-1955), born on a farm near Darvel, discoverer of penicillin.

Ayrshire is noted not only for such famous persons but for some of its products. From the country come Ayrshire early potatoes, the Ayrshire breed of dairy cattle, and Dunlop cheese (now marketed as Scottish cheddar). From the towns come a range of manufactures including Irvine Valley machine lace, Mauchline curling stones, Johnnie Walker whiskies. Many visitors from overseas arrive in Scotland's international airport at Prestwick, and some stay to play on the championship golf courses at Turnberry, Prestwick and Troon.

Some who read these words will belong to that welcome band of people who have come to work and reside here. Those from abroad, and even English people from south of the border, find certain features of Scottish life a little strange. The natives are friendly, it is true, but their accents and idiom may occasionally be a trifle difficult to interpret. In north and central Ayrshire, West Mid Scots is spoken, with South Mid Scots a somewhat different Scots dialect in that part of the county nearest to Galloway. Most of the older Scots vocabulary has disappeared – and even Ayrshire folk need to refer to a glossary when reading the poems of Burns! Only in some corners will you find people regularly speaking broad Scots. But even the most sophisticated local residents who believe they are speaking pure English use expressions which are in fact standard Scots. 'Going for the messages' means going shopping – and in the butcher's shop the cuts of meat will have different names. A 'carry out' is the Scots version of a take-away. At home 'a chap at the door' should be translated as a knock at the door. Confusion over times may be avoided if it is remembered that 'half two' means half-past two o'clock – though it is best to check, for in a few places locally the Germanic practice is followed and there 'half two' means half-an-hour before two! Those who when here plan to get married, divorced, draw up a will, or commit a crime will discover that the Scottish legal system and its terminology are in many respects different from the English. Similarly with education. Nearly all children attend public schools – and here that means local authority schools, not private schools as the name implies in England. Most of the primary schools (incoming parents may be delighted to discover) continue the traditional Scottish emphasis on the 3 Rs of reading, 'riting, and 'rithmetic. In secondary schools (now all comprehensive) able pupils will be preparing for O grades (instead of English O levels) and then their 'Highers' in Scottish

In the remotest corner of Ayrshire south of Loch Doon, accessible only on foot, Gala Lane flows past Mullwharchar (on right), one of Ayrshire's biggest hills.

Certificate of Education examinations. Within the schools some peculiarly Scottish names will be found. Here the school caretaker is 'the janitor', more colloquially 'the jannie'; and the teachers and pupils call the exercise books 'jotters'.

For those who find fascination in language, *The Scots Word Book*, 1977, by William Graham (of Ayr) has English-Scots and Scots-English vocabularies and notes on pronunciation, spelling, grammar, and idiom. This can be supplemented by the excellent *Concise Scots Dictionary*, 1985, edited by Mairi Robinson. For local history, John Strawhorn's *Ayrshire, The Story of a County*, 1975, gives a brief but comprehensive account of how the county has developed right up till recent time. Those books are still in print, as are others listed in a 'Current Catalogue of Books and Pamphlets relating to Ayrshire' compiled by the Ayrshire Federation of Historical Societies. The main libraries can advise on what local histories are available, and the study of any community can best be approached through the *Statistical Account of Scotland 1791-1799*, Vol. VI on Ayrshire reprinted 1982; the *New Statistical Account*, Ayrshire volume 1842; and the *Third Statistical Account*, Ayrshire volume 1951, the most recent and detailed account of our way of life.

CHAPTER 2

Old Forgotten Things

Writers of guide books seem to think that their readers have an avid interest in the detail of everything that happened in the past. We, however, do not believe that readers of this book feel an urgent need at this moment for a potted history of Ayrshire, chronologically arranged, complete with dates for every important event that occurred within the bounds of the county. We do not believe, for example, that there is any point in describing the Battle of Mauchline Muir of 1648, for there is nothing to be seen on the site but an empty field. If anyone happens to be interested in identifying the religious factions contesting the issue by combat on that occasion, that like many other specialised subjects may be read up in the series of *Ayrshire Collections* published by the Ayrshire Archaeological and Natural History Society.

What is planned in the chapters immediately ensuing is to select certain themes which may appeal to people of various interests. Each topic will be looked at from the point of view of the present-day observer, whose attention will be drawn to places worth a visit, with note of anything surviving from the past which seems to deserve mention. If you prefer, you can skip these chapters just now and go straight to the second part of this book which will take you on a number of tours around the county, with some information about the places you may visit on your trips.

In this chapter we will bow to convention and give some account of the 'old forgotten, far-off things, and battles long ago', offering a broad view of the local past, with digressions to consider some aspects of Ayrshire's tradition.

The first inhabitants were mesolithic hunters and fishermen who arrived here around six thousand years ago, following the coast in search of a bare livelihood in what was then an Arctic climate. Archaeologists have discovered microliths – little stone-made knives, harpoon heads, and the like – in considerable quantities near Irvine at Ardeer and Shewalton, at Ballantrae to the south, with lesser finds elsewhere along the coast. But nothing remains for the casual observer to remark upon, and the same is true of later settlers of the Neolithic and Bronze Ages. Pottery and other objects have been unearthed – examples can be inspected in the Dick Institute, Kilmarnock – which indicate a more widespread settlement by the later immigrants. Here and there on farm fields can be seen an isolated standing stone which may date from these prehistoric times. Near the beginning of the Christian era the Iron Age is marked by hill forts, and traces of such artificial features can often be noted by observant passers-by. In the same era were constructed crannogs or lake dwellings, as in the little loch beside the farm of Lochlea where Robert Burns lived. There is some evidence that the Romans occupied this corner of Caledonia. The sites of marching stations have been located near Largs and Girvan, but there are no substantial remains; and their great fort opposite Loudoun Hill has been wiped out by sand quarrying. If you want to know more about prehistory, you will find that John Smith's *Prehistoric Man in Ayrshire* published in 1895 is sadly out of date, but for several local areas lists of *Archaeological Sites* have been produced by the Royal Commission on the Ancient and Historical Monuments of Scotland, and the annual issues of *Discovery and Excavation* may be consulted.

In the first ten centuries of the Christian era the Welsh-speaking Britons who inhabited this area were joined by Gaelic-speaking Scots from Ireland and Argyll, and Viking settlers from Scandinavia – all of whom have left their mark in the place names of the county. It has been argued that the counting-out rhymes that children still use sometimes in their playground games – 'Zeenty, teenty, figgery fell . . .' – have their origin in the numerals of the earliest of these peoples. Anglian farmers from the east also arrived, who began clearing the lowland forests and naming many of our modern farms. Because so little is known of this period it has been called the Dark Ages. Legends of this and later times are recounted in still-popular old books like William Robertson's *Historical Tales and Legends of Ayrshire*, 1889, and John Macintosh's *Ayrshire Nights' Entertainments*, 1894. There is, for instance, the story of Coilus who gave his name to the province of Kyle and may have been the original Old King Cole of the nursery rhyme. Kyle lay between the Rivers Irvine and Doon, with Cunninghame to the north and Carrick to the south. These three ancient provinces were part of a kingdom of Strathclyde, which was incorporated into the kingdom of Scotland in the 11th century. The Kings of Scots from the 12th century onwards made Ayrshire part of their feudal kingdom. Anglo-French barons were imported who acquired control of great landed estates. A civilising influence was exerted by incoming priests and monks. To encourage trade, burghs were established. The first was at Prestwick, established sometime between 1163 and 1173. Then came the royal burgh of Ayr, dating from 1205; Irvine, created about 1230 and made a royal burgh in 1372; and Newton-upon-Ayr in the 14th century. Merchants from abroad settled in the two royal burghs which became important places because they had the privilege of foreign trade. From the 13th till the 16th century there was a series of wars against England. In the initial struggle for independence the Ayrshire exploits of William Wallace made him a sort of folk hero, so that there are two statues of him within Ayr; Robert Bruce who won the struggle has never engendered any similar enthusiasm, so that he is commemorated only by Bruce's Well in Prestwick, where at Kincase he sought relief from his leprous condition.

In the 16th and 17th centuries, the Reformation was followed by conflicts involving the Protestant church, and throughout the county are to be found numerous memorials to the Covenanters of the late 17th century who died as martyrs for their beliefs. During this time there was progress, with the establishment of burghs of barony throughout the county. In these centres manufacturing was developed, in some cases with contributions from Flemings and other refugees from the Continent who introduced improved crafts. Most of the early Ayrshire burghs (which were important as places where markets and fairs were held) survived to become in the 19th century, along with some of the newer industrial townships, local authorities responsible for providing public services, and continued as such till these burghs were abolished in 1975. But, as a curious anomaly, Tarbolton continues as Scotland's solitary surviving burgh. It received a charter in 1671; it never became a local authority as it might have done under 19th-century legislation; but it continued, as it still does, to hold its annual

A Standing Stone at Drybridge. No one can tell with certainty when it was erected, by whom, or for what reason. Though most place names are similarly ancient and obscure, Drybridge got its name in the 19th century after the construction of the Kilmarnock-Troon railway.

Yule meetings by virtue of its charter grant, and elect a burgh council which operates as a voice of the community though with no statutory powers.

In the 18th and 19th centuries Ayrshire participated in the tremendous economic and social developments which transformed the lowlands of Scotland. The county population increased from less than 60,000 in 1750 to 84,000 at the first census in 1801, reaching 190,000 by 1851 and 154,000 by 1901. In the 18th century the improving landlords began the agricultural revolution which brought into being our modern commercial farming. People displaced from the land found their way into the growing industrial towns, or emigrated, as many of them did in subsequent generations to Canada, the

United States, Australia, and New Zealand, often planting new settlements abroad with Ayrshire names. The expansion of the cotton industry in the 18th century absorbed some immigrants from the Highlands, and the massive developments in coal and iron in the 19th century brought a flood of others from further afield. A principal contribution came from Ireland – in 1851 11% of the Ayrshire population were Irish-born. In the later 19th century others were brought in to work – sometimes as strikebreakers – so that groups of families may still be identified who came from places like Cornwall (Galston), Lithuania (Annbank) and Spain (Muirkirk).

Before the United Kingdom was formed in 1707 the Scottish Parliament had made valiant attempts to realize John Knox's 16th-century dream of a school in every parish. The Education Act of 1696 was effective enough to provide Ayrshire in the following century with a system of schools which provided most children with a basic literacy and allowed the 'lad o' pairts' the opportunity for self-advancement. It is no accident that Scotland in the 18th and 19th centuries produced so many notable and innovative men – as the list of famous Ayrshiremen in Chapter 1 shows. They, and others of lesser fame, are remembered by statues, busts, and plaques in appropriate places. Robert Burns, of course, has precedence, as the 'Burns Trail' indicates. In Auchinleck the old church has been converted into a Boswell Museum which preserves relics not only of the great biographer but of William Murdoch who also came from that parish. Alexander Fleming, who had his first lesson in a little one-teacher school before travelling by foot and train daily to Kilmarnock Academy, has his bust in Hasting Square in the centre of Darvel – alongside the 'Dagon Stone', a monolith which some prehistoric people erected nearby long centuries before.

In the 20th century, despite the decline of heavy industries, and the demise of many traditional crafts, Ayrshire's population has continued to grow from 254,000 in 1901 to 375,000 by 1981. Emigration continues, but the annual net loss, to other parts of Britain and abroad, is, in the latter part of the 20th century, counted in hundreds as compared with the thousands each year a century before. To compensate, numbers have been augmented and the population diversified by new groups of immigrants. Italians who came to provide fish suppers and ice cream are now accepted members of the community, and in process of integration are the more recent Chinese and Indians who have opened restaurants and the Pakistanis serving in their little grocery shops. Much more numerous are recent immigrants from England who with a few from Europe and America are involved as specialists or managers in new business enterprises. A recent census showed around 5% of the Ayrshire population as born in England and Wales, less than 1% who were Irish-born, a mere 2% immigrants from abroad. Nearly 20% had come from Glasgow and other parts of Scotland to stay in Ayrshire, joining the 73% of the population who are native-born Ayrshire folk.

CHAPTER 3
Castles and Cottages

Ayrshire's castles are many and varied. Most magnificent is
certainly Culzean Castle, a National Trust for Scotland
property, whose architecture, furnishings, gardens, woodland,
and coastal views attract about 300,000 visitors throughout the
year. But if that place must be awarded three stars for
excellence, there is a range of others, less well-publicised, which
merit one or two stars as worth a visit. Not all the buildings to
be mentioned are open to the public. Some are privately-
owned, which may offer occasional access. Some may be viewed
only from a discreet distance which does not intrude upon
anyone's privacy. Remember that even abandoned ruins may
be on private property upon which it may be injudicious to
trespass without permission.

Apart from prehistoric hill forts, castle-building locally began
in the 12th century. The Kings of Scots brought in Anglo-
French warrior barons to whom they allocated lands and who
required fortified homes. These were wooden structures
erected upon huge artificial mounds called mottes. Nothing
now survives of the wooden castles, but samples of prominent
motte hills may be easily viewed in Tarbolton and
Dalmellington.

Ayrshire's first stone-built castles date from the 13th and
14th centuries. Most survive as impressive ruins as at Dunure,
Dundonald, Portencross, and Loch Doon. Elsewhere, as at
Sundrum, the original old stone tower is contained within
building of later centuries.

Despite extravagant claims for greater antiquity sometimes
put forward locally, most of Ayrshire's castles belong to the
15th and 16th centuries. With 29 built in the 15th and 38 in the
16th century, this must have been a busy time for stone
masons. These were stormy times with many of the leading
families engaged in bitter feuds, so that there was still a need for
defensive structures. But economic advances were being made
(how else could so many lairds have afforded new buildings?)
and the tower houses were designed to provide a greater

18

Many tower houses survive only as impressive ruins. Portencross Castle has since the 14th century guarded what was once an important though tiny harbour.

degree of domestic comfort than was hitherto available. Many survive only as empty shells in the fields or in quiet corners of old towns. But some of these substantial keeps are still occupied as comfortable homes and it may be possible on occasion to visit such castles as Kelburn, Hunterston, Sorn, Blairquhan, and Penkill – this last with the additional attraction that it was later a holiday home for 19th-century Pre-Raphaelite artists. Perhaps the most impressive example is Dean Castle, Kilmarnock, which was begun in the 15th century, now set within a country park and open to the public.

By the 17th century few castles were being built, with one remarkable exception. When Cromwell invaded and occupied Scotland he ordered the erection of five great citadels, one of them at Ayr, constructed in 1652. A walk around the streets south of the harbour reveals remains of its strong walls and defensive ditches, with the main gateway half-buried in a lane behind Ayr Academy. Do not, however, be misled by that little watch tower overlooking the harbour. This was constructed in the 19th century by John Miller to add to the Citadel whose grounds he had bought.

Blair House near Dalry originated as a tower house, one of several which have been adapted and extended by successive owners to provide a modern residence.

In the 18th century the great landowners commenced those improvements which historians have entitled the Agricultural Revolution. They also beautified their estates by planting woodlands, laying out parks and gardens, and constructing new mansion houses either in the classical style or as Gothic-style castles. The Adam brothers, the most celebrated architects of the 18th century, were commissioned to design several in Ayrshire. They built Dumfries House near Cumnock for the Earl of Dumfries, and this remains a private residence of the Marquess of Bute. They took over for Richard Oswald, a successful merchant with American connections, the construction of Auchincruive House, now occupied by the West of Scotland College of Agriculture, and with an attractive Adam Teahouse in its grounds. Robert Adam then undertook for the Earl of Cassillis the transformation of the old tower house of Culzean into a castellated mansion, perched romantically on a sea cliff, and approached through a specially-designed mock-ruined archway. As already noted, it is now a National Trust for Scotland property, set within a Country

Park, and with the Adam-designed home farm reconstructed as a visitors' centre. On a much smaller scale are the mansion houses built by prosperous Ayr merchants in the environs of the town. Those most accessible are Craigie House (now part of the College of Education), Rozelle (which houses an Ayr burgh museum and art gallery), and Belleisle (hotel restaurant set within a public park).

Many of the mansion houses built in the 18th and 19th centuries have not survived the break-up of most of the great estates and the crippling taxation of the 20th century. Michael C. Davis, in *The Lost Mansions of Ayrshire*, 1984, gives details of sixty which have had to be demolished and another eight currently at risk. He lists another score which have been saved by conversion for public or commercial purposes. Among those lost was the grandiose Loudoun Castle near Galston. It was once known as 'the Windsor of Scotland' but was destroyed by fire in 1941 – yet even the ruins remain impressive. Equally grand was Eglinton Castle near Kilwinning, scene of a celebrated mock-medieval tournament in 1839, but left in 1925 to fall into ruin. Only a single tower remains, restored by Clement Wilson, a local manufacturer who converted the grounds into a country park and donated them for public recreation. To assess all that has been lost you must turn again to the public libraries to browse through the pages of Robert Bryden's *Castles and Mansions of Ayrshire*, and the five volumes of MacGibbon and Ross, *Castellated and Domestic Architecture of Scotland*.

If the castles and mansions which survive can recapture for us the wealth and power of the landed gentry of former days, there is little surviving to recall our medieval towns. None of the Scottish burghs could of course rival the magnificence of some of their Continental counterparts, so that hardly anything has been thought worth preservation. In Ayr the modest Loudoun Hall has been rescued as a sole solitary surviving example of a 16th-century town house, and the Auld Brig remains as a sample of early municipal enterprise. But Ayr's old market crosses have disappeared, remembered only by paving stones inserted in the road surface. Little 'mercat crosses' remain at places like Newton-upon-Ayr, Prestwick, Ochiltree, Cumnock, and Kilmaurs – in the last case beside an

Several Ayrshire villages are attractive places with pleasing rows of unspoilt 18th and 19th-century vernacular building, as at Barr beside the Water of Gregg.

old tolbooth or council house. Much of the municipal past was swept away with the renovation of towns which accompanied the industrial expansion of the 18th century. From the beginning of the 19th century Ayr laid out Wellington Square and adjacent streets in obvious imitation of Edinburgh's New Town. That century saw the construction of many attractive public buildings in Ayr, Kilmarnock, Irvine, and even some of the smaller towns. The 20th century, alas, has fewer comparable examples to offer. Indeed the principal shopping streets of the main towns have been defaced by modern shop frontages. But if you can halt on the busy pavements and look upwards you are often rewarded with interesting glimpses of the urban architecture of earlier ages.

What used to be called 'the lower orders' are too often ignored by historians, and it is never easy to discover how they lived. The traditional ordinary Ayrshire house was the two-roomed 'but and ben', the 'ben' being the single room where the family lived, while in the 'but' the cattle were kept or the

A vanished era is recalled by the 'Steamie' or communal laundry at Glenburn by Prestwick. The houses provided here for the coal miners were unusually substantial. The array of chimney pots reminds of times when coal was cheap.

craftsman worked. Some such but and bens of the 18th century or even earlier are to be found in the country or in rows in several of the smaller towns and villages, with interiors modernised and exteriors (sometimes) tastefully conserved. Some such have been rescued at Dalmellington to provide the Cathcartson centre where handloom weaving and other traditional aspects of local life may be inspected. Elsewhere the fact that a number of buildings associated with Robert Burns have been preserved offers people (who may not be particularly interested in the National Poet) the opportunity to inspect some humbler dwelling places. Burns Cottage at Alloway was built in 1757 as a farm house before it became a drinking place and then a kind of shrine. Souter Johnnie's house at Kirkoswald shows how a village shoemaker lived. Glasgow Vennel in Irvine, the Bachelors Club in Tarbolton, the Burns House in Mauchline, and the Tam O' Shanter Inn museum in Ayr High Street are similarly worth visiting. In the

B

19th century Ayrshire acquired a new type of dwelling with the miners' 'raws' which were thrown up all over the county wherever coal was worked. Those often-isolated and squalid **rows** of cottages have been swept away by 20th-century local authority re-housing programmes. It is a pity a typical example was not retained as a museum of mining life. To ascertain what living conditions were like for many people not that long ago, a survey of *Ayrshire Miners' Rows in 1913* has been reprinted.

At the beginning of this century, according to the 1901 Census Report, 19% of all Ayrshire families lived in 'single-end' one-room homes, and 41% in two-roomed houses, nearly all rented from private property-owners. In the period since there has been a housing revolution. By 1971 Ayrshire local authorities had built over 70,000 houses, providing up-to-date accommodation for 62% of the population. Private building also expanded, with an increase to 29% owner-occupiers by 1971. Perhaps some far-seeing conservationist will purchase a council house and a bungalow and preserve them with their furnishings as examples of typical 20th-century homes, for inspection by curious visitors of a distant future.

CHAPTER 4
Holy Places

The oldest Christian relic in Ayrshire is a slab of sandstone with a cross inscribed, which was found at Cambusdoon near Alloway and is now on display within Loudoun Hall. One expert has dated it as from sometime between the 4th and 6th centuries; another as between the 8th and the 12th. At any rate it marks the spread of Christianity northwards from Whithorn in Galloway where there seems to have been a community of converts in the 4th century even before the time of Ninian. Certainly there were churches in this south-western corner before Columba crossed from Ireland to Iona in 563, and before Augustine arrived at Canterbury in 597 to begin converting the heathen English. It is accepted that many of the place names with *kil–* as a prefix were named after early preachers who established 'cells' or primitive churches. These are especially common in south Ayrshire. But not all places whose names begin with *kil–* have necessarily a religious origin. Kilmarnock, for example, has been interpreted as 'the church of St Marnock' but there is doubt as to whether there was ever anyone called Marnock; definitely not a recognised saint; the name almost certainly means something else, though just what no one can be quite sure, as with most place names.

Though there must be doubt about origins, there is certainty about the establishment, under royal patronage, of an organised church system in the 12th century. The Kings of Scots who brought barons into the county brought also churchmen. Indeed the territorial awards of baronies can be associated with the creation of parishes.

In the course of the Middle Ages from the 12th till the 16th centuries each of the 45 parishes was equipped with its small stone-built parish church. Some of these survive as ruins, as at Alloway and Prestwick. One has continued intact at Symington, interesting to inspect, though its interior has been altered and adapted for Protestant worship. The two royal burghs of Ayr and Irvine had, of course, more elaborate town churches, which must have been quite magnificent structures before their

25

demolition in the 18th century. Slezer's 'View of Ayr' of 1696 shows the great Church of St John, of which now only the Tower survives as a reminder of the building where the Scottish parliament met in 1315.

Besides the system of parish churches, Ayrshire in the Middle Ages also accommodated various religious orders of friars and monks. Within the royal burgh of Ayr there were Black Friars and Grey Friars. The former, of the Dominican order, arrived here about 1250 and Blackfriars Walk beside the river marks the place where they served for three centuries. The Franciscan Grey Friars operated locally for less than a century after 1474, on the spot where Ayr's Auld Kirk now stands. At Irvine there were Carmelite White Friars who came in the 14th century to the place still called Friars Croft. The Trinitarian Red Friars has a house at Fail not far from Tarbolton and from the 13th century raised money for the redemption of captives from the heathen Turks. The ruins of their little abbey survived till the present century, when, thoughtlessly, its stones were removed to bottom roadways around the new airport at Prestwick. All that remains of them is a rhyme of unsubstantiated authenticity:

> The friars of Fail, they made guid kale,
> On Fridays when they fasted,
> And they never wanted gear enough,
> As long as their neighbours' lasted.

Even more prominent were the monastic orders who were among Ayrshire's greatest landowners. To the Cistercian monks of Melrose was awarded in the 13th century that great tract of land extending eastwards from Tarbolton as far as the county boundary at Glenbuck, with the headquarters of this Kylesmuir estate at Mauchline, whose castle is still known as Abbot Hunter's Tower. Earlier about the year 1187 a monastery of the order of Tiron was set up at Kilwinning, with extensive possessions in north Ayrshire. The ruins of Kilwinning Abbey stand impressively in the middle of the modern town. In a more remote location is south Ayrshire, in open country beside the Maybole-Girvan road, are the remains of Crossraguel Abbey. This Cluniac monastery was founded

A visit to Crossraguel Abbey near Maybole makes clear what a medieval monastery was like. The ruined central buildings of the abbey are enclosed by the Abbot's Tower (right), the Gate Tower (left) and the Doocot (in the foreground) where pigeons were kept.

sometime near the beginning of the 13th century, and anyone who wishes to find out just how a medieval monastery was laid out should certainly spend some time exploring this site. There is a good guide book; Professor Ian Cowan has produced an up-to-date historical study of *Ayrshire Abbeys,* 1986; and the libraries have older and ponderous tomes containing plans and charters.

How important was the role of the church in medieval Ayrshire can be indicated by mentioning some other holy places. Near Monkton at Ladykirk was a chapel (no longer surviving) where King Robert III married Elizabeth Mure of Rowallan in 1347, and a place to which pilgrims from all over Scotland once came seeking miracles and mercy. At St Leonard's in Ayr and Kincase in Prestwick were 'spittals', at the latter of which is Bruce's Well where lepers sought relief. Throughout the county were nearly a hundred properties belonging to the crusading military order of Knights Templars, many retaining names like Templehouse, Templands, Templehill. William Dillon's *Catholic Ayrshire*, 1958, published by the Catholic Truth Society of Scotland, is a little booklet which will fascinate even those who are not of that faith.

The Roman Catholic Church in Scotland was overthrown by the Protestant Reformation of 1560. Long before that it had its critics in Ayrshire. There were the Lollards of Kyle who faced trial for their heretical beliefs in 1494. Early in the 16th century Murdoch Nisbet of Loudoun produced a *New Testament in Scots*, a manuscript which has been printed by the Scottish Text Society. John Knox, the leading figure of the Reformation, came to preach in Ayrshire, and indeed in 1564 as a 50-year-old widower found here a second wife in 17-year-old Margaret Stewart of Ochiltree. Not all, of course, favoured the new doctrines. George Lockhart, a native of Ayr who became Prior of the Sorbonne in Paris, defended the traditional faith as dean of Glasgow until his death in 1547. Quintin Kennedy, last abbot of Crossraguel, in 1564 spent three days in public debate with Knox at Maybole. Yet the majority accepted the Reformation. Some churchmen became protestant parish ministers, and those who didn't – like two Black friars at Ayr – were allowed peacefully to retire on a pension. In the whole of Scotland only one Catholic was martyred. The Reformation indeed was largely a political affair, with Scottish lords seeking an English alliance against threatened French domination during the reign of Mary Queen of Scots. Inflation had forced the church already to dispose of most of its estates to laymen, so there was no major upset in 1560. Many tenants of Kilwinning Abbey, for example, became owners of their own farms, so that Ayrshire acquired that numerous class of small landowners whom later generations would call bonnet lairds – though they owned a little land, they could not afford hats other landowners wore, but wore bonnets for they were no better off than tenants.

That the Scottish Reformation was accomplished without major disturbance is further shown by the fact that all the churches continued in use, though the interiors were adapted for protestant worship. Images were removed, altars replaced by communion tables, and sometimes the chancel was converted into a school room. The sermon, in which Calvinist

In this 18th-century Dailly Parish Church there have worshipped together local landowners (like the Fergussons of Kilkerran) and local coal miners (like John Brown who was entombed underground for 23 days).

theology was propounded at length, became the principal part of the church service. Family worship in the home was insisted upon, and because of this the parish church, required only for Sunday services, could be kept closed most of the time – as they still are, a feature which some visitors may find disconcerting. Another unusual feature of Scottish protestantism is that holy days were abolished, on the doctrinal grounds that since all days should be devoted to God and kept holy, to specify only certain days as holy was a blasphemy. Thus over a period it was actually illegal to celebrate Christmas and Easter in Scotland. Only during this present century has Christmas become a popular festival in Scotland, and even today Easter is not a public holiday as in other Christian countries.

The first purpose-built Protestant church in Ayrshire was erected in 1655 – the present Auld Kirk of Ayr, between High Street and the river. The burgh's Church of St John and its Tower had been requisitioned by Cromwell's army to be incorporated within the Citadel, so the townspeople (with a subsidy from the army) built this new church. It is worth seeing inside, particularly to admire the woodwork of the pulpit and the galleries. The graveyard contains a number of interesting tombstones (and here may it be noted for the benefit of searchers after ancestors that the main libraries should be able to tell you which local cemeteries have had their burial places catalogued). The entrance to the Auld Kirk from High Street is through the Kirk Port, whose archway was built in 1656, and beside it may be seen 'mortsafes' which were required in the early 19th century to deter the resurrectionists who stole bodies to sell for dissection by anatomy students.

From the 17th century date other 'holy places'. After the Union of the Crowns of Scotland and England in 1603, efforts of successive Stuart monarchs to bring the Church in Scotland under royal control and organise it on an episcopal basis with bishops (as in England) resulted in a National Covenant in 1638 pledging resistance to such innovations. Later in the century there was armed rebellion, with one notable victory for the Covenanters in 1679 at Drumclog just beyond Loudoun Hill over the Lanarkshire border; and a final defeat a year later at Aird's Moss near Muirkirk. During this period illegal church services called conventicles were held, often in moorland places. When royal troops were sent to enforce the law, a number of Covenanters were martyred during these 'Killing Times', about three dozen from Ayrshire and as many more from Galloway. Those who then died for their faith are commemorated on tombstones and memorials throughout the area, reverently maintained by the Scottish Covenanters' Memorials Association. The presbyterianism that they died for was officially recognised in 1689, and is required to be guaranteed by royal oath at the accession of each successive monarch.

By the 18th century all the old pre-Reformation church buildings required replacement or extensive renovation. At St Quivox near Ayr the little old church was retained, and the interior as redesigned in 1767 has been little altered since, so affording a nice impression of what an 18th-century church was like – with its box pews, long-handled collection boxes, its central pulpit with sounding board, overlooking the precentor's place – the precentor being the person, usually also the parish schoolmaster and clerk to the kirk session, who led the

This is Dundonald Church, strikingly similar in appearance to several other parish churches of the early 19th century, characterised by austere simplicity both outside and in.

congregation in singing psalm tunes. Also near the front (though now removed from all churches) would be the 'cutty stool' or seat of repentance where at times of service would be exposed to public censure and humiliation those whom the kirk session had found guilty of offences, usually sexual ones.

Most of the churches built in the 18th and early 19th centuries are without architectural distinction – externally great box-like structures surmounted by steeples, internally stark and bare until the later 19th century where there was piecemeal installation of organs, stained glass windows, and new seating. Just how many places of worship were built it would be difficult to compute, for as well as parish churches there were those erected by dissenters who formed their own congregations – seceders of the 18th century who themselves split into separate sects, and the Free churches built after the Disruption of the Church of Scotland in 1843. In 1847 the majority of the 18th-century seceders agreed to form a United Presbyterian Church which in 1901 combined with the Free Church to form a United Free Church, which in 1929 participated in a reunion with the established church to create the present Church of Scotland. Such amalgamations resulted in a surplus of places of worship, particularly in the centre of larger towns. Many of the old box-like churches have been demolished or converted to other purposes without many tears from conservationists.

The 19th century witnessed a pleasing improvement in church design. Stern Calvinism was superseded by more humane sentiment, and beauty was no longer considered always a devilish distraction. So from the churches the cutty stools were removed and pipe organs installed. New churches were built which were graceful as well as functional. The best illustration locally is surely the Trinity Church in Irvine. Built in 1863 as a United Presbyterian Church, it was designed by an unorthodox Edinburgh architect, T.F. Pilkington, in Venetian Gothic style with variegated colour in the stone and altogether a most ornate structure. Though closed as a place of worship in 1966, it was mercifully rescued from demolition to be converted into a centre for community activities.

The 19th century saw the re-establishment in Ayrshire of Roman Catholic places of worship, to serve the growing number of Irish immigrants. Pastoral work was begun between 1802 and 1811 by Abbé Francis Nicholas, a refugee priest who taught French in Ayr Academy. A chapel was established in Ayr in 1826, in Kilmarnock in 1847, and by the end of the century in a score of mining and industrial centres, many of them erected with generous aid from the third Marquess of Bute. Quite unique is St Sophia's in Galston, built in 1885 of red brick in Byzantine style, an exotic transplantation from Constantinople on to Ayrshire soil. During the 19th century a variety of other religious denominations established themselves in the county, most of them with small and undistinguished meeting places save for the Holy Trinity Church in Ayr, built in 1898 by adherents of the Scottish Episcopalian Church. The 20th century has seen a further proliferation of sects, with nearly 30 different denominations recorded in mid-century by the Third Statistical Account, but (a sign of increased secularism) only a half of the adult population claiming membership. Of the churches' continuing vitality evidence is found in the building of new churches for new needs. In 1957, for example, the Cathedral of the Good Shepherd was built in a new housing area in Ayr, as seat of the Bishop of Galloway, under whose care are the 12% of the Ayrshire population who belong to the Roman Catholic Church. The principal denomination remains, of course, the Church of Scotland, with about 33% of the adult population in its membership, and building as necessary in new housing areas. Witness the new St Andrew's Church in Irvine, where a Church of Scotland congregation began worshipping in 1957 in a wooden hut until there could be built a modern church – which is shared with the local Episcopalian congregation in pleasing ecumenical amity.

CHAPTER 5
Some Tales and Legends

Some incidents in history have become memorable – for a variety of reasons.

William Wallace, hero of the struggle for Scottish independence, is remembered for the Burning of the Barns of Ayr. Those of you who have heard the story will guess that its long-continuing local popularity reflected an equally long and bitter memory of the 13th-century English army of occupation. Most if not all readers will nowadays agree that Wallace's actions on that occasion did him little credit, and classify him as blood-brother to those objectionable 20th-century 'freedom fighters' who rely on terror, brutality, and butchery to advance their ends. The best that can be said is that it is uncertain when the incident took place, what alleged treachery inspired it, and how far the events were embroidered by later chroniclers. The actual location is equally doubtful, though the Barns were probably wooden storage sheds beside the river at Mill Street. English troops were billeted there, and Wallace and his adherents surrounded the Barns at midnight, and set them alight. Escape routes were barred and the entire body of English died by sword or fire. A number of English soldiers were lodged in the nearby house of the Blackfriars. The friars patriotically collaborated with Wallace and put their guests to the sword in what became known as the Friars' Blessing.

Bloodthirsty hatred is found too in the stories of the Ayrshire feuds, here combined with fierce pride in the honour of the family. The first of the great Ayrshire feuds was in north Ayrshire between the Cunninghams of Kilmaurs and the Montgomeries of Eglinton; the second mainly in Kyle between the Campbells, Craufords, and other adherents of Loudoun, and their rivals the Kennedys; the third and most bitter in Carrick between the Kennedys of Cassillis and those of Bargany. Early in the 16th century the Craufords of Kerse (near Dalrymple) looked across the River Doon into Kennedy territory. From time to time cattle-rustling parties crossed the river; from time to time there were affrays. At length some of the Kennedys issued a challenge: at Lammas they would cross the river at Skeldon and – the ultimate insult – tether a sow on Crauford land. Both sides prepared for a set battle, the Kennedys massing a force of the men of Carrick, the Craufords collecting recruits from all parts of Kyle. Old David Crauford of Kerse was no longer fit to ride, but had to stay at home when his sons went off to battle, to flit (remove) the sow that the Kennedys had brought. At length a messenger returned to Kerse with news of the battle's outcome. 'Alas, your son John is dead.' 'But is the sow flitted?' 'Ay, sir, the sow's flitted and five score Kennedys drowned in Doon.' 'My thumb for Jock,' cried old Crauford, 'My thumb for Jock. The sow's flitted!' The honour of the family was more important than the welfare of its individual members.

The feuds involved the assassination in 1527 by Hugh Campbell of Loudoun, sheriff of Ayr, of the 2nd earl of Cassillis, ambushed as he travelled homewards through the sandhills at Prestwick. In 1586 the 4th earl of Eglinton was ambushed near Stewarton and shot by a party of Cunninghams. In south Ayrshire the bitter conflicts between the adherents of Cassillis and of Bargany originated in 1570 with the Roasting of the Abbot of Crossraguel by Gilbert Kennedy, 4th earl of Cassillis. The victim was not really an abbot, for the monastery had ceased to function as such by the Reformation of 1560, though its last real abbot, Quintin Kennedy, brother to the 4th earl, continued to hold that office till his death in 1564. Thereafter the earl took possession of the monastic buildings. In 1565 the crown appointed Allan Stewart from Renfrewshire as commendator to take charge of the Crossraguel estates. This was resisted by the earl of Cassillis, by the scholar George Buchanan who had been promised an income from Crossraguel in 1564, and by the laird of Bargany to whom Buchanan leased his claim. In 1570, to secure his interests, the earl kidnapped Stewart, incarcerated him in the Black Vault of Dunure Castle, and tortured him by roasting over a fire till Stewart signed away his rights to the earl. Stewart was rescued by Thomas Kennedy of Bargany who took Dunure Castle, the privy council required the earl to compensate Stewart, but the bulk of the estate remained in the hands of the earl of Cassillis.

From the 17th century comes another tale of violence, this time one incident in the religious conflicts. Those Covenanters known as 'Cameronians' or 'hillmen' refused to accept any compromise with the episcopal church as royally established. John Graham of Claverhouse and his dragoons rounded up suspects who would not 'take the test' acknowledging the king as supreme in church and civil matters; and refusal to swear not to bear arms against the king could mean arbitrary execution. In 1685, in pursuit of the hill preacher Alexander Peden, Claverhouse came to the farm of Priesthill beyond Muirkirk. John Brown, 'the Christian carrier', had been giving Peden refuge. He refused to take the test, or to adjure the treasonable declarations of the Cameronians. John Brown was condemned to death by Claverhouse and shot before his cottage in presence of his wife and children. 'What thinkest thou of thy husband now, woman?' Claverhouse is reputed to have asked. 'I thought ever much good of him and as much now as ever' was the reply of the martyr's widow. So the story goes, as told by those for whom the Covenanters were heroes. Others, however, will argue that the 'hillmen' were not innocent victims of ruthless persecution but a fanatical minority of extremists themselves committed to violence. Decide where truth lies between the version given above and that presented by Claverhouse himself in a report dated 3 May 1685. 'On Friday last, amongst the hills betwixt Douglas and the Ploughlands, we pursued two fellows a great way through the mosses and in the end seized them. They had no arms about them, and denied they had any. But being asked if they would take the abjuration, the eldest of the two, called John Brown, refused it, nor would he swear not to rise in arms against the King, but said he knew no King. Upon which, and there being found bullets and matches in his house, and treasonable papers, I caused shoot him dead; which he suffered very unconcernedly.'

These tales concern identifiable persons, involved in incidents which certainly occurred, however dubious may be the details. We now cross the ill-defined border into the realm of legend where characters, who seem to be fictional, are involved in incidents which often seem quite incredible.

A number of ballads survived to be collected by James

Maybole Castle, scene of conflict between the Kennedys in the bitter 16th-century feuds; and where the legendary Countess of Cassillis was imprisoned after her elopement with the gipsy Johnnie Faa.

Paterson in his *Ballads and Songs of Ayrshire*, 1846. 'Johnnie Faa' tells of an unidentified Countess of Carrick who eloped with the gipsy king. 'May Colvin' tells how she escaped the clutches of the false Sir John of Carleton. 'The Lass of Lochryan' made a fruitless search for a lost husband. 'Loudoun Castle' was attacked and burned, and its lady died in its defence. 'Kellburn Braes' tells of a termagant wife who was taken away by the devil but returned to the husband by the devil who had realised for the first time what hell was like. 'The Laird of Changue' sold his soul to the devil, who on claiming it was told to 'Go to hell' – which he did. All these tales are widespread, and versions from other parts of the world have been recorded in F.J. Child's classic study of *English and Scottish Popular Ballads*.

These Ayrshire ballads, like some other legends, have some interesting features. Nearly all are located in Carrick, the southern part of the county. There are some notable heroines, especially May Colvin: False Sir John had already disposed of seven wives by disrobing them and throwing them into the sea;

but May claimed to be modest and when Sir John's back was turned threw him into the sea. Another feature of Ayrshire legend is that the Devil when he appears is far from all-powerful, and indeed in many respects very human. Much more likeable than the cannibal Sawney Bean, a legendary figure who occupied a cave north of Ballantrae and with his family preyed upon passing travellers, capturing, killing, and eating them. The Carrick coast boasted other personalities. Also by Ballantrae, near the mouth of the River Stinchar a mermaid used to sing each night, seated on a black stone. The mistress of nearby Knockdolian Castle found this serenade kept her baby awake and had the black stone destroyed. The lyrical mermaid cast a spell:

> Ye may think on your cradle, I'll think on my stane;
> And there'll never be an heir to Knockdolian again.

Soon after the cradle was overturned, the baby died, and in due course the family became extinct. More fortunate was the laird of Culzean (originally known as Cove or Co') who was kind to a little fellow who asked for ale for his sick mother, even though mysteriously it took more than half a cask to fill the can. Years later the laird was a prisoner in Flanders, condemned to death; when the dungeon doors flew open, the dwarf appeared, saying, 'Laird of Co', Rise and go!' Then, on the dwarf's shoulders he was transported through the air and deposited at Culzean with a farewell message:

> Ae guid turn deserves anither,
> Tak ye that for being sae kind to my auld mither.

North and central Ayrshire have noticeably fewer legendary characters. There was a Sir Fergus Barclay known as the Deil of Ardrossan because of a secret compact with the Devil who awarded him an enchanted bridle with which he won horse races all over Europe! Also at some early time in Ardrossan Castle there resided one Michael Scott, warlock child of a mermaid, and also possessed of a flying horse.

In these parts of Ayrshire witches featured more prominently. With this we are returning to the border where fact and fiction meet. For in the 16th and 17th centuries persons were accused, tried, and executed as witches. Contemporaries, relying on scripture, had no doubt that these were persons who derived supernatural powers from the Devil. Evidence in certain trials that groups of witches met in covens has suggested the possibility that there was in fact some type of organised witch cult. At any rate more than twenty persons from various parts of Cunninghame were executed in Irvine as witches; and possibly as many more from Kyle suffered the usual tortures, trial, and burning in Ayr. If you dip into the *Ayr Burgh Accounts*, edited by George Pryde, 1937, you will find listed, for example, the 'expensis sustenit in the burning of the witche of Barnweill', which included coals, timber, barrels of pitch, resin, and heather. Ayr's most notorious witch, Maggie Osborne, does not appear in any such records. One tradition has it that she was the natural daughter of a warlock laird of Fail. By day she kept a tavern in Ayr; by night she practised sorceries, causing shipwrecks and other disasters, till she was betrayed by a servant-maid. Others have it that Maggie Osborne was the daughter of a prominent merchant family; when her parents died she lived alone in a house opposite the Fish Cross long afterwards known as Maggie Osborne's House; brain fever and delirium brought her to the attention of the kirk session; she was subjected to torture by the witch-finder, and ultimately to execution.

A more curious and better-documented case was that of Bessie Dunlop from the north Ayrshire parish of Dalry who in 1576 was tried before the High Court of Justiciary and found guilty of charges of 'Sorcerie, Witchcraft, and Incantation, with Invocation of Spirits of the Devil'. She admitted an association with one 'Thomas Reid who died at Pinkie' (i.e. in that battle of the year 1547). He advised her on medicinal cures, enabled her to detect lost and stolen property. He tried to persuade her 'if she would deny her Christendom' and introduced her to twelve persons who were fairy-folk 'in the Court of Elfame, who came there to desire her to go with them'. The sentence was 'Convict and Burnt'.

That the witch cult, or at least belief in its existence, survived well into the 18th century is clear from the evidence at Alloway. Robert Burns knew of 'many Witch Stories I have heard relating to Alloway Kirk'. That church was abandoned as a

place of worship only after 1690, so that any tales of witch
gatherings there must be more recent than that. At any rate
Robert Burns persuaded Francis Grose to include a drawing of
Alloway Kirk in his book *Antiquities of Scotland* by promising
him some witch stories. He was in fact inspired to write his
great poem on 'Tam O'Shanter', but before so doing he sent
Grose three witch stories relating to Alloway, including the one
which formed of the poem. This prose version of 'Tam O'
Shanter' forms a fitting close to this chapter.

'On a market day in the town of Ayr, a farmer from Carrick,
and consequently whose way lay by the very gate of Alloway
kirk-yard, in order to cross the river Doon at the old bridge,
which is about two or three hundred yards farther on than the
said gate, had been detained by his business till by the time he
reached Alloway it was the wizard hour, between night and
morning.

'Though he was terrified with a blaze streaming from the
kirk, yet as it is a well known fact, that to turn back on these
occasions is running by far the greatest risk of mischief, he
prudently advanced on his road. When he had reached the
gate of the kirk-yard, he was surprised and entertained,
through the ribs and arches of an old gothic window which still
faces the highway, to see a dance of witches merrily footing it
round their old sooty blackguard master, who was keeping
them all alive with the sound of his bagpipe. The farmer
stopping his horse to observe them a little, could plainly descry
the faces of many old women of his acquaintance and
neighbourhood. How the gentlemen was dressed, tradition
does not say; but the ladies were all in their smocks; and one of
them happening unluckily to have a smock which was
considerably too short to answer all the purposes of that piece
of dress, our farmer was so tickled that he involuntary burst
out, with a loud laugh, "Weel luppen, Maggy wi' the short
sark!" and recollecting himself, instantly spurred his horse to
the top of his speed. I need not mention the universally known
fact, that no diabolical power can pursue you beyond the
middle of a running stream. Lucky it was for the poor farmer
that the river Doon was so near, for notwithstanding the speed
of his horse, which was a good one, against he reached the
middle of the arch of the bridge, and consequently the middle

Each summer Tam O'Shanter rides again! Tam is impersonated leaving (soberly and in daylight) the museum which was once an inn (following a modern route to Alloway Kirk and the Brig O'Doon).

of the stream, the pursuing, vengeful hags were so close at his heels, that one of them actually sprung to seize him: but it was too late; nothing was on her side of the stream but the horse's tail, which immediately gave way to her infernal grip, as if blasted by a stroke of lightning; but the farmer was beyond her reach. However, the unsightly, tail-less condition of the vigorous steed was to the last hours of the noble creature's life, an awful warning to the Carrick farmers, not to stay too late in Ayr markets.'

CHAPTER 6

Getting Around

'Discovering Ayrshire' necessarily involves you in travel, by private or public transport, unless you have the time and energy for a great deal of walking. Such travel for recreation and sightseeing had a very limited clientele before the present century. Even travel on business was not all that common. Less than 50 years ago one could point to old north Ayrshire farmers whose furthest trips were weekly visits to Kilmarnock market, and who never had seen the sea. But this does not mean that the further back in history you go the less travel there was.

What modern minds find it difficult to realise is that for most of human history the easiest form of travel, as well as the most convenient means of transporting loads, was by sea. It was by sea that the earliest settlers arrived here. Prehistoric finds bear witness to items brought from Ireland, England, and from the Mediterranean. In the Middle Ages the royal burghs of Ayr and Irvine traded regularly with Europe, bringing in cargoes from as far afield as Scandinavia and Spain. By the 17th century their little sailing ships were venturing across the Atlantic to trade in sugar and tobacco. In the 18th century the creeks and sands all along the Ayrshire coast were busy as the 'free traders' landed cargoes of smuggled tea and brandy. By the beginning of the 19th century two modern ports had been created at Troon and Ardrossan to cope with an increased traffic in coal and general cargo. The old harbours of Ayr and Irvine continued busy; like the smaller creeks, they still maintained their own fishing fleets; and steam packet boats provided coastal passenger services. Angus Graham's *Old Ayrshire Harbours,* 1984, lists and describes what are now in many cases abandoned ruins. Ayr, Troon, and Ardrossan continue as minor cargo ports. Ayr is the only place where fish are now landed. Ardrossan is the only passenger port (with a service to Brodick in Arran when it isn't too windy), apart from a Largs-Millport ferry. Yet the waters of the Firth of Clyde are busier than ever with private pleasure craft, which have their

The turbine steamer *Duchess of Hamilton*, shown here, called regularly at Ayr during the Clyde cruising season before her role was taken over by paddle steamers *Caledonia* and then *Waverley*. Although Ayr has a narrow harbour, it is a busy fishing port and has a thriving international trade.

requisite facilities in marinas as Troon, Irvine, Fairlie, and Largs.

Travel by land was, until comparatively recently, more awkward, in the absence of made thoroughfares. The Romans in their incursions into Caledonia necessarily constructed military roads, but how long these survived is uncertain, and locally their routes can only be conjectured. Later invaders like Edward I of England made use of the southern approaches by Nithsdale or up the Doon Valley. By the Middle Ages there was a well-marked series of routes radiating from the county town of Ayr. That by way of the Irvine Valley to Edinburgh was used by magistrates, merchants, and messengers riding from the county town. Those routes from north to south were used by pilgrims trudging towards the holy shrine of Ninian at Whithorn in Galloway. From time to time the royal household arrived, to stay awhile at a royal castle like

Dundonald, or within a royal burgh like Ayr and Irvine. What was due to the king in cash and kind could be collected and consumed. Departure followed when the local larder was emptied (or earlier if the dry closets were filled). For the convenience of such travellers, bridges were erected to span the major rivers – like the surviving auld brigs over the Ayr and Doon – and even by the 17th century over minor streams, as is shown on the fascinating maps of Cunninghame, Kyle and Carrick from Blaeu's Amsterdam *Atlas* based on the surveys of Timothy Pont. Though there were no made roads, the tracks were sufficient for the limited traffic. They were not yet suitable for wheeled vehicles. In 1619 the 6th earl of Eglinton who had acquired a coach required six of his ablest tenants to assist it on journeys to Glasgow.

Traffic however was beginning to increase in the 17th century. In 1642 a royal postal service was introduced on several major routes including that from Edinburgh to Portpatrick via Hamilton, Ayr, Girvan, and Ballantrae, supplemented in 1662 by another to Ireland via Glasgow and Kilmarnock. Private postal services to Edinburgh were also organised by the town councils of Ayr (1663) and Irvine (1665). There was, however, apparently no great urgency, for until the middle of the 18th century the postmen went on foot. One from Ayr, for example, left on a Monday and returned from Edinburgh on Saturday. Increased road traffic required Irvine council in 1692 to erect a signpost 'for directing strangers'. By that time the Carters Society of Irvine (a body still in existence) had been formed to meet a new demand. Transatlantic imports landed at Irvine were transported overland to Glasgow (which was still an inland town on a shallow river). Such caravans of pack-horses were making the unmade tracks increasingly difficult to negotiate. The Scots parliament passed a series of acts (1617, 1661, 1669, 1686, 1696, 1698) which had limited success in persuading justices of the peace to call out tenants and others for up to six days' compulsory 'statute labour' in repairing highways.

By the middle of the 18th century new developments in industry and agriculture involved increased transportation of goods and heavier demands on the roads. John Galt, whose novel *The Annals of the Parish* so graphically and amusingly depicts the social changes in Ayrshire at that time, indicates how legislation for road improvement now seemed urgent:

The king's highway, as I have related in the foregoing, ran through the Vennel, which was a narrow and a crooked street, with many big stones here and there, and every now and then, both in the spring and the fall, a gathering of middens from the fields; insomuch that the coal-carts from the Douray moor were often reested in the middle of the causey, and on more than one occasion some of them laired altogether in the middens, and others of them broke down. Great complaint was made by the carters anent these difficulties, and there was, for many a day, a talk and sound of an alteration and amendment; but nothing was fulfilled in the matter till the month of March in this year, when the Lord Eaglesham was coming from London to see the new lands that he had bought in our parish. His lordship was a man of a genteel spirit, and very fond of his horses, which were the most beautiful creatures of their kind that had been seen in all the country side. Coming, as I was noting, to see his new lands, he was obliged to pass through the clachan one day, when all the middens were gathered out, reeking and sappy, in the middle of the causey. Just as his lordship was driving in with his prancing steeds, like a Jehu, at one end of the vennel, a long string of coal-carts came in at the other, and there was hardly room for my lord to pass them. What was to be done? His lordship could not turn back, and the coal-carts were in no less perplexity. Everybody was out of doors to see and to help; when, in trying to get his lordship's carriage over the top of a midden, the horses gave a sudden loup, and couped the coach, and threw my lord, head foremost, into the very scent-bottle of the whole commodity, which made him go perfect mad, and he swore like a trooper that he would get an act of parliament to put down the nuisance – the which now ripened in the course of this year into the undertaking of the trust road.

Copying those in other counties, leading Ayrshire landowners obtained from parliament Ayrshire Turnpike Acts in 1767 and 1774. Powers were granted to a committee of Ayrshire Turnpike Trustees to construct roads, the expense being recouped by tolls collected at gates called turnpikes. Within a generation it could be written that 'There are probably few districts in Scotland, where so many excellent roads have been made, within so short a period'. Much of the credit was due to John Loudon McAdam, a native of Ayr who as a child went to live in New York. In 1783 he returned to become laird of

Sauchrie, for the next thirteen years was an active member of the Ayrshire Turnpike Trust, then went south to win fame for bringing English roads up to Ayrshire standards. 'Macadamised' roads formed of compacted layers of small stones of fairly uniform size were relatively cheap and easily repaired, which made them so popular.

The new roads (and new wider bridges) accommodated carts bringing farm produce to market, transported industry's raw materials and manufactures, and carriers provided regular services for goods throughout the county – no fewer than nine were operating as far as Edinburgh by 1786. Passenger traffic was augmented with private coaches of the gentry and public coaches plying for hire. By the end of the century there was a thrice-weekly service between Glasgow and Ayr via Irvine, and others linking up with Kilmarnock and also Dumfries and Edinburgh. By 1813 there was a daily mail coach between Glasgow, Kilmarnock, and Ayr. Horse posts continued along the route to Stranraer. Foot posts from Kilmarnock took the mail to Stewarton, Irvine, and Cumnock.

The heavy loads of coal and other minerals required special provision. Canals, which were so successful in England, proved less viable here. In 1772 Robert Reid Cunningham of Auchenharvie constructed a 2½ mile Saltcoats canal (which was first in Scotland); later there was a mile-long canal at Muirkirk ironworks; that was all, for the 12th Earl of Eglinton's proposed canal from Glasgow to Ardrossan begun in 1807 was abandoned after three years with only eleven miles (outwith Ayrshire) between Port Eglinton and Johnstone. Greater success was achieved with railways. Various wagonways were constructed in the 18th century to transport coal to the harbours of Irvine and Ayr from nearby pits. Harry Broad's *Rails to Ayr*, 1981, gives appropriate details. Something much more ambitious was initiated in 1808 by the future 4th Duke of Portland whose wife Henrietta Scott had acquired extensive properties in Ayrshire. From Kilmarnock where coal was extensively worked a railway was projected to the coast at Troon where the duke planned a new harbour. The duke's Kilmarnock-Troon line can claim to be the first real railway in Scotland. It was the first to be constructed under act of parliament, necessary since it was to cross several properties in

The world's oldest railway bridge, crossing the River Irvine on Scotland's first real railway, initiated in 1808 between Kilmarnock and Troon. Horses pulled wagonloads of coal, and by 1814 passengers as well.

its 9½ miles. It was double-tracked, with iron-flanged rails laid on stone blocks, with a 4-foot gauge. On its way it had to cross Shewalton Moss; also the River Irvine, by a four-arch stone bridge which survives in ruinous condition; and it was itself crossed by a bridge at that place appropriately called Drybridge. Coal and other merchandise in wagonloads up to 12 tons were hauled by horses. And on summer Saturdays the wagons were scrubbed out to convey Kilmarnock people down to the coast on pleasure trips, so that this can claim to be one of the earliest passenger railways. In 1816 a steam locomotive built by George Stephenson was tried but soon abandoned.

The railway age really reached Ayrshire in 1840. Glasgow, Paisley, Kilmarnock, and Ayr Railway Company opened the line from Ayr (north harbour) to Irvine in August 1839. This was just in time to provide excursions to the 13th Earl of Eglinton's celebrated Tournament – an odd combination of the modern steam train becoming involved with celebration of a vanished feudal past. The main line from Glasgow to Ayr was opened in 1840, by 1843 a link line from Dalry reached Kilmarnock, in 1847 the old Kilmarnock-Troon line was taken over, and branch lines extended to serve the coalfield and industrial towns. The company pressed on with its plans for a main line to the south via Nithsdale, linking up with Dumfries and Carlisle in 1850. A more direct route from Glasgow via Beattock had been completed in 1848 by the rival Caledonian Company. But the Nithsdale line was and remains a notable engineering achievement, witness the great viaducts at Kilmarnock, Hurlford, and Cumnock, and near Mauchline the Mossgiel tunnel and the massive masonry arch spanning the River Ayr at Ballochmyle. The Glasgow and South Western Railway Company as constituted in 1850 extended its lines throughout Ayrshire and Galloway, incorporated in the London, Midland and Scottish Railway Company in 1921, and becoming part of British Railways in 1948. To recapture the flavour of the old railway days, you must read David L. Smith's books, then make contact with the Ayrshire Railway Preservation Society, either through their magazine *The Duke* or at an open day at their railway museum near Dalmellington.

The original Glasgow-Ayr line remains the busiest segment of the now truncated railway system, with electrification introduced in 1986. The northern part of the coast is served by the link from Kilwinning to Largs, also busy and electrified. South of Ayr the line extends to Stranraer to connect with the ferries for Larne and Belfast, though now these take cars and lorries rather than railway traffic. The other main line from Glasgow through Kilmarnock and Dumfries still carries direct trains from London. It remains a useful alternative route, especially for goods traffic, which probably has saved it from closure; the re-opening of abandoned passenger stations, some argue, would prove a profitable experiment.

In the 20th century the roads have come into their own again. When registration of motor vehicles was introduced in 1903, Ayrshire had 25 cars, including the Marquess of Ailsa's numbered 'SD 1'. By mid-century the number had increased to 10,000, but the most spectacular rise followed over the next twenty years. By 1972 the number for Ayrshire was 72,000, and most families now had a car, some more than one, used for

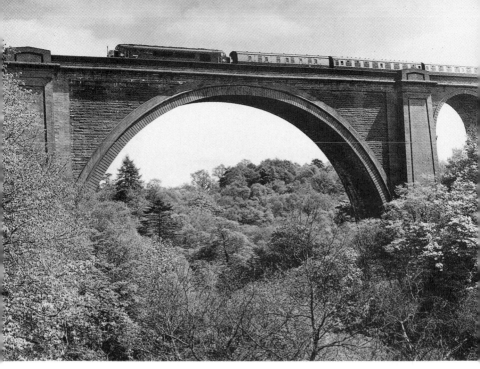

A north-bound 'Peak' class locomotive pulls its train across the River Ayr on Ballochmyle Viaduct, Britain's highest railway bridge and the one with the greatest masonry span. It was built by 400 navvies in 19 months and since 1848 has carried traffic on the Kilmarnock-Dumfries line.

travel to work and during the extended leisure hours. Public road transport by motor bus began in the early years of the century, and the colourful story of enterprise and expansion can be followed in *The Western Way* by Neil Macdonald, 1983, and *Dodds of Troon* by William Macgregor, 1985. Municipal electric tramways in Ayr (1901-31) and Kilmarnock (1904-26) proved a failure but make a fascinating story in Ronald Brash, *The Tramways of Ayr*, 1983, and Brian T. Deans, *Green Cars to Hurlford*, 1986. Motor buses superseded trams and more generally most local passenger railway services. In mid-century queues at bus stops were a regular feature as people travelled to work, shops, and the cinemas. Fewer buses are now required with the great increase in private cars. Bus services throughout the county and beyond are provided by Western S.M.T., from depots at Kilmarnock, Ayr, and Cumnock. AA Buses provide an alternative service between Ayr and Ardrossan, and A1 between Kilmarnock and Ardrossan. The tremendous increase in traffic has required improvement of Ayrshire's 1,500 miles of public highways. The roads as engineered by McAdam were composed entirely of road metal taken from small roadside quarries. Cars in 1901 travelling at the stipulated general speed limit of 12 miles per hour could raise clouds of dust, and 'Stoorie Aggie' was the appropriate nickname for an early bus. Less obvious was the impact on the road itself. Roads had now to be treated with 'tar-macadam' – a process invented in 1882 of laying a surface of small stones intermixed with tar. Such a use for tar McAdam himself had never envisaged, though he was a partner in a company manufacturing coal tar at Muirkirk, which ironically failed to find a profitable market. As well as the necessary and continuous repair of road surfaces, increasing traffic forced other improvements. The first major undertaking was in the thirties when, to relieve unemployment, the road from Kilmarnock to Glasgow was reconstructed. War and postwar problems postponed further schemes till the sixties when Prestwick and Ayr were by-passed with a dual carriageway which dwindles to a three-lane then two-lane on its way south. This is linked by new dual carriageway to Kilmarnock, where a bypass of motorway standard was opened in 1973, but continuing towards Glasgow by the road as designed in the thirties. The last decade, the eighties, has seen more roads of near-motorway standard extending up the coast as far as Kilwinning, with a link between Irvine and Kilmarnock. But only minor improvements have been made or are proposed for the routes linking Ayrshire with the outside world. Local industrialists feel disadvantaged. And the enjoyment of tourists driving along pleasant rural roads is spoiled by speeding heavy lorries. Similarly in the towns – though this is not a local problem – traffic congestion continues despite by-passes, ring-roads, one-way systems, pedestrianised areas, multi-storey car parks, and traffic wardens.

One last tentative paragraph. The 20th century has brought Ayrshire into closer contact with the wider world through Prestwick Airport. There was a grass flying strip in 1935. In 1940 runways were constructed to provide for 20,000 wartime planes to be ferried across the Atlantic to this accessible and

Prestwick Airport – before its modern terminal was provided in 1964. Its situation proved admirable for wartime transatlantic flights, so Prestwick was appropriately designated an international airport in 1946. The photograph shows some of the wartime buildings still in use, and the former control tower curiously perched on the roof of Orangefield House.

virtually fog-free spot. Appropriately, after 1946 Prestwick was designated an international airport, equipped to handle the largest aircraft, provided in 1964 with a modern terminal able to cope when necessary with 3,000 passengers in an hour. The railway from Glasgow passes the airport, and improved communications by road make Prestwick convenient for most of the west of Scotland – closer than most international airports are to their customers. But nasty local rivalry intervened. Glasgow Corporation insisted that the prestige of that City required it to have its own airport, so one was constructed at Abbotsinch to which were channelled all internal flights and those to Europe, leaving Prestwick to handle transatlantic flights but without any internal links. So for many the most convenient route into Scotland is via London's Heath Row. Prestwick languishes; and if further money is spent equipping

Abbotsinch to cope with larger transatlantic planes, then the closure of this most excellent airport seems certain. A sad note with which to end a chapter, but there still remains the possibility of a happier ending to be included in a future edition.

CHAPTER 7
The Farm Scene

The casual observer of the countryside will note the ever-changing seasons but presume that from year to year there is a permanence about things. Even country folk take for granted that farms and fields have always been more or less as they are. Yet however natural the countryside may appear, the landscape as we know it is largely an artificial creation, product of the enterprise of generations of hard-working farmers.

Take a look at any Ayrshire farm. The fields that you see today are an invention of the 18th-century Improvers. Before that there were strips of arable land which were seldom enclosed. From about 1750 landlords began to lay out with the help of surveyors those rectangular fields with which we are familiar, and enclose them with hedges or dykes. Hedges of hawthorn or beech were most popular, some still thriving after two centuries of care, others replaced by fences when mass production of wire in the 19th century made this cheaper than replanting. In the uplands and on some exposed parts of the coast where hedges would be more difficult to grow, plenty of stones were conveniently available for dry-stane dyking – that highly-skilled craft that is almost a forgotten art. Throughout Ayrshire landowners who could afford it planted shelter belts of trees. After two hundred years of growth many of these have been felled – especially those alongside roads – and they are rarely replaced.

But land divisions and hedges, you say, are incidental. The important features are the fields and what is grown on them. Yet the fields of today are the result of generations of intensive care. For at least four centuries the sour acid soils of Ayrshire have been 'sweetened' with lime, quarried locally and burned with coal from adjacent seams, in now-abandoned lime kilns. Cultivation has benefited from the improved ploughs and other implements of the last two hundred years. The land has been made much more productive since the introduction of tile-draining in 1825. The soil has been enriched by dung from the herds of improved well-fed dairy cattle; and by artificial fertilisers now mainly imported but first manufactured locally at Newton-upon-Ayr in 1860. Contrast the fields of a typical farm with the occasional unimproved undrained patch in valley or upland. Notice how often the words bog or moss or moor in the names of lowlands farms commemorate former conditions. The grass in Ayrshire is greener now that it ever was, and the banks and braes are bonnier than they used to be, thanks to the improvements in soil husbandry.

The crops grown are based on rotations which have been long tested as suitable for local climatic conditions. In the late 18th century Alexander Fairlie of Fairlie near Dundonald devised what became known as the Fairlie Rotation which is still, with modifications, the basis of modern local systems. For long enough oats was the principal grain crop, quite recently superseded by varieties of barley which are easier to harvest and suitable for silage. Potatoes and turnips, first grown locally as a field crop in the later 18th century, are in continued use. Sown grasses, once grown as hay and often ruined by a wet summer, are now harvested green for silage. Fairlie's rotation was two years of oats, a year of a root crop, a year of hay, followed by five or six years of grass – and this emphasis on grass continues, for ever since Fairlie's time Ayrshire farmers have specialised in dairy farming.

The Ayrshire breed of dairy cattle originated in the 18th century and became renowned for their output of milk. No one is sure who first bred them – if you wish to investigate this and the 18th-century agricultural revolution, consult articles on these topics in *Ayrshire Collections*, especially volumes 1 and 3. Throughout the 19th century the brown and white horned cattle were almost the only type known to Ayrshire farmers. An Ayrshire Cattle Herd Book Society was formed which still records the pedigree of the specimens which were specially bred with increased milk yield, some of which were exported to different parts of the world. Until early in the present century most of the milk was converted into cheese on the farms by the farmers' wives – Dunlop cheese was another of Ayrshire's creations. Now the liquid milk is collected from the farms by tankers of the Scottish Milk Marketing Bord for sale in liquid form or processed into butter and cheese at one of their creameries. The 20th century has seen a change of a different

Modern dairy farming in Ayrshire owes its origin to the 18th-century Improving Lairds who not only popularised the Ayrshire Breed of cattle but created the farms with their hedges and sheltered belts, as shown in this typical landscape at Garfield near Mauchline.

sort with the Ayrshire cattle. They are now de-horned – as was suggested by the poet Robert Burns who is quoted on the subject in the first Board of Agriculture Report for Ayrshire, written by Colonel William Fullarton in 1793: 'In order to prevent the danger arising from horned cattle in studs or straw yards, the best mode is to cut out the budding knob, or root of the horn while the calf is very young. This was suggested to me by Mr Robert Burns, whose general talents are no less conspicuous, than the poetic powers, which have done so much honour to the county where he was born'. Another 20th-century change is that many farmers have been successfully experimenting with foreign breeds and cross-breeds to establish herds which will produce beef as well as milk.

Having looked at the fields and what they contain, let us turn now to the farm buildings. First of all note where these are located. Quite often you will find farm buildings at the far end of a road leading off the public highway, where they are conveniently situated in the middle of that farm's fields. Such farms were part of one of the great estates of the 18th century, whose wealthy landowners could afford to employ expert land surveyors to replan completely the layout of farms with new buildings centrally located. By contrast other farm buildings you will notice are situated on the roadside (where they always were) because their owners could not afford rebuilding on a new site. Nowadays many farms are owner-occupied, since the early part of this century when Lloyd George's death-duties forced the break-up of most of the estates both great and small. Some of the roadside farms can nowadays be as prosperous as those set back, though on the latter additional buildings can usually be more conveniently located. On a few farms it is possible to examine successive stages of building, just as a geologist can identify the successive strata in the rocks. Occasionally a wall in undressed stone can be attributed to a century earlier than the 18th, on a roadside farm. Many and perhaps most farm houses can be traced back to an 18th-century origin, though little of their first stage remains visible.

The typical steading was built just about two hundred years ago as a cottage with attics, raised to two storeys in the 19th century, containing living quarters and the dairy. In front is a courtyard, on one side of which are the byres where the cattle are housed in winter and milked twice daily throughout the year; on the other the barns and stables where the horses used to be kept. The interiors have vastly changed in the course of this century. Farmhouses used to be bare and sparsely furnished, with floors of stone slabs or, occasionally still, dirt; now they are as luxurious as any town dwelling. Similarly the byres have been transformed into milk parlours where the cows are hygienically machine-milked and the product refrigerated and stored for collection, untouched by human hand. At the side of some farmyards may be noticed mysterious circular or hexagonal buildings. These were locally known as mill rinks, and they housed horse gins, so called because horses were used to go round in circles grinding corn – at the time of the Napoleonic Wars when high grain prices persuaded farmers even in Ayrshire to plough up their grass to grow oats and wheat. Nowadays these old buildings survive only as toolsheds. More prominent are the tall silage towers of

Along the Ayrshire coast it is drier, and the lighter soils are suitable for arable farming. The cultivation of early potatoes is the speciality of Carrick shore farms. This view looks past Culzean Castle to Ailsa Craig.

the last 25 years, which are anything but picturesque, but serve as a reminder that 20th-century Ayrshire farmers are involved in an industry which is modernised and highly mechanised. In 1930 there were fewer than a hundred tractors in use on Ayrshire farms; half a century later there were more than three thousand. A search in 1972 discovered only two horse teams still being used for ploughing.

There are of course variations in the type of farming practised in different parts of the county. Near the coast where it is drier and the soils are lighter a higher proportion of the farm land is devoted to crops, and indeed all along the coast there are farmers who specialise in the cultivation of early potatoes. Planting takes place in February and March and the crop is ready for lifting from mid-June until late July. Seasonal workers are required on the potato farms which traditionally employ gangs of itinerant Irish tattie-howkers (-lifters). Further inland the amount of cropping decreases as the soils become

57

heavier, the rainfall increases, and conditions become cooler at higher elevations. This is the heartland of dairying, with a 10 to 15-year rotation, and most of the land in grass. The typical farm is from 100 to 150 acres with a herd of 35 cows plus followers. The farmer's wife and family are necessarily involved in the unbroken routine of attending to the cattle morning and evening every day throughout the year – not only milking, but feeding and watering them when indoors from October to April, plus the calving each spring. On the edge of the moors mixed farming is practised. One such farm contains 80 acres arable, 150 rough grazing, and 900 moorland, and maintains a small herd of dairy cattle plus 180 blackfaced ewes which, mated with Border Leicester rams, will produce in a fair season as many cross-bred lambs. In the recesses of Carrick are large hill sheep farms, with the lonely steadings in the deep valleys where a few crops can be raised in the short growing season. Here lambing does not commence till April; the flocks are maintained on the hill grazings through the summer. After the sales of August and September, the remaining ewe flocks are brought down to rented pasture on lowland dairy farms.

Strangers to the area might notice with interest how busy Ayr can be on Tuesdays, when farmers come to town for the sales of cattle conducted by the long-established local firm of Messrs James Craig, auctioneers, at the market beyond Burns Statue Square. Besides these weekly sales there are other special auctions in spring and autumn. Watch the local press also for Open Days at the West of Scotland Agricultural College at Auchincruive and the nearby Hannah Dairy Research Institute. The enthusiastic local Young Farmers' Clubs sometimes have demonstrations and shows, and there are meetings of the branches of the Scottish Women's Rural Institute. Throughout the county in the summer months long-established local cattle shows are held, and each April – a highlight of the year – the three-day Ayrshire Agricultural Association Show at the Racecourse in Ayr. For a nostalgic view of the farm scene as it used to be, visit Dalgarven Mill on the Kilwinning-Dalry road for the Museum of Ayrshire Country Life and Costume.

CHAPTER 8
The Burns Trail

All round the world, each year the anniversary of Robert Burns's birth on 25 January is celebrated by Burns Suppers where the poet's Immortal Memory is toasted. All year round the Burns Federation keeps in touch with its 350 affiliated Burns Clubs found everywhere from Bangkok to Niagara Falls. Every year thousands of overseas tourists come in pilgrimage to Burns's birthplace at Alloway. Burns's poems have been translated into German, French, Danish, Russian, Japanese – and even into English. Those readers who are familiar with Burns's work will need no further introduction. But for those who are puzzled by the Burns Cult, it may be helpful to try to explain his appeal.

I suppose a reason why some people are interested in Burns is his life story. Here was a poor boy who won fame, the local lad who made good. To many of his contemporaries (as well as some still) he was 'this heaven-taught ploughman' who miraculously could produce marvellous poetry – ignoring the facts that he was not a hired ploughman but the son of a proud tenant farmer, and that he had benefited from several years of schooling and wide reading. For some later admirers Burns was the tragic hero whose greatness was cut short by an early death at the age of 37. For others there is a romantic fascination in the details of his life and loves.

Anyone who enjoys music can appreciate Burns's songs. They can be presented as art songs by professional singers with piano or orchestral accompaniment. Some prefer them as folk songs, unaccompanied or with a backing of strings, taking the traditional tunes to which Burns added his words. Most of his songs and many of his poems are really in English, even though they may sound best in a Scots accent. His one great narrative poem, 'Tam O' Shanter' (whose story is given among the legends near the end of Chapter 5), is typical in that English-speaking foreigners can enjoy it, with only occasional words, phrase, and idioms requiring explanation. Admittedly some of Burns is difficult – even for Scots! – when he lapses into a dense vernacular in making one of his humorous satiric attacks. **But even so it is possible to catch the spirit, as in his disparagement of Willie's ugly wife:**

> Auld baudrans by the ingle sits,
> And wi' her loof her face a washin;
> But Willie's wife is nae sae trig,
> She dights her grunzie wi' a hushian . . .

For many people who are not particularly interested in poetry, Burns makes an appeal because of his ideas. Not because of their originality, but because he could express so aptly the feelings, moods, fears, and hopes he shared with people of his time and of ours. Here is the poet of liberty, equality, and brotherhood:

> The rank is but the guinea's stamp,
> The man's the gowd for a' that.

Here is the rebel who protests against oppression:

> Poor tenant bodies, scant o' cash,
> How they maun thole a factor's snash;
> He'll stamp an' threaten, curse an' swear,
> He'll apprehend them, poind their gear,
> While they maun stand, wi' aspect humble,
> An' hear it a', an' fear an' tremble!

Here is a poet who can mock the Unco Guid and satirise the hypocrisy of religious bigotry. How cleverly he makes Holy Willie pray in this damning definition of Calvinist theology:

> O Thou that in the heavens does dwell!
> Wha, as it pleases best thysel,
> Sends ane to heaven and ten to hell,
> A' for thy glory!
> And no for ony gude or ill
> They've dune before thee.

We are all creatures of different moods, Burns like the rest of us. Sometimes we wish we were carefree as the Jolly Beggars:

> What it Title, what is Treasure,
> What is Reputation's care?
> If we lead a life of pleasure,
> 'Tis no matter how or where.

We can enjoy the pleasures of life, singing with Burns that

> The sweetest hours that e'er I spend
> Are spent amang the lasses O.

There are occasions when we can boldly declaim that

> Freedom and whisky gang thegither.

At other times Life's cares crowd in on us when

> The best laid schemes o' Mice an' Men,
> Gang aft agley,
> And lea'e us nought but grief an' pain,
> For promis'd joy!

We can become melancholy when

> Man's inhumanity to Man
> Makes countless thousands mourn!

None of us is without fault:

> O wad some Pow'r the giftie gie us
> To see oursels as others see us.

We must try to be forgiving:

> Then gently scan your brother man,
> Still gentler sister woman;
> Though they may gang a kennin wrang
> To step aside is human.

Within ourselves we know where the true contentment must lie:

> It's no in titles nor in rank;
> It's no in wealth in London Bank,
> To purchase peace and rest . . .
> Nae treasures, nor pleasures
> Could make us happy lang;
> The heart ay's the part ay,
> That makes us right or wrang.

We can have our hopes and dreams of better and happier times for humanity:

> Then let's pray that come it may,
> As come it will for a' that,
> That Sense and Worth o'er a' the earth
> Shall bear the gree and a' that.
> For a' that and a' that,

It's comin yet for a' that,
That Man to Man the world o'er,
Shall brothers be for a' that.

For those who wish to sample more of Burns there are numerous editions of his works for sale, various records and cassettes containing his songs, and a biographical novel by James Barke in five paperback books. The libraries have scholarly biographies (especially Hecht's and Snyder's), studies of the poetry (by Crawford and by Daiches), and annotated collections of his works (poems edited by Kinsley, letters by Ferguson or Ross Roy).

Here we wish to take our readers on a tour of the Land of Burns, following the Burns Trail to places associated with the poet. It is a trip through some of the most attractive parts of Ayrshire and worth taking for that reason alone. Burns enthusiasts should take with them Andrew Boyle's *Ayrshire Book of Burn Lore*, 1985, which is a convenient and comprehensive compendium of local places and persons associated with Burns. Here we shall note the places of interest, with a much briefer commentary, and before doing so provide a handy summary of Burns's life.

1759-1766 at Alloway: Robert and other three children born here to William Burnes from north-east of Scotland and Agnes Broun from Kirkoswald.

1766-1777 at Mount Oliphant: at this nearby farm other three children born; Robert attended schools at Alloway, Dalrymple, Ayr, and Kirkoswald; in 1773 wrote his first song, 'Handsome Nell'.

1777-1784 at Lochlea: in Tarbolton parish, Robert joined a dancing class, founded a Bachelors' Club, enrolled as a freemason, spent some months in Irvine learning flax-dressing; after a lawsuit over tenancy of the farm, the father died.

1784-1788 at Mossgiel and Mauchline: the family rented nearby farm; thereafter came Robert's association with Jean Armour, Highland Mary Campbell, and others; also an outburst of poetic composition; in 1786 the *Poems* were published at Kilmarnock; instead of emigrating he visited Edinburgh as a celebrity, made various tours; belatedly married Jean Armour and set up house briefly in Mauchline.

It may be odd to see Tam O'Shanter (with police escort) on a summer ride past the Cottage where Burns was born on 25 January 1759. Some will find it as odd that the world's first Burns Supper was celebrated in the summer – at the Cottage in 1801.

> *1788-1796 in Dumfriesshire:* with wife in Ellisland farm, also travelling around as an exciseman; then moved into Dumfries as a full-time excise officer; Scots songs were now his principal interest; his early death at the age of 37 followed a recurring illness attributed to the hardship of his childhood.

The Burns Trail begins at Alloway. Two hundred years ago this was a little group of cottages two miles distant over a barren moor from the county town. William Burnes was employed as overseer of gardens and policies of new estates nearby. In 1756 he purchased seven acres and in preparation for his marriage built what is now famous as Burns Cottage. In this 'auld clay biggin' Burns was born on 25 January 1759 –

> Twas then a blast of Janwar wind
> Blew hansel in on Robin.

Here Robert spent his first seven years, in the rooms you can now inspect. Here he had some of his first lessons from John

Murdoch, whom William Burnes and some neighbours hired as a teacher. Within the grounds of the Cottage is a Museum, portraying the Poet's Times, His Life, and His Work, plus a collection of original manuscripts.

Beside the Cottage is Greenfield Avenue which William Burnes laid out for Ayr town council in 1756, this contract earning him sufficient to buy the land and build the cottage. Only a few hundred yards along is Alloway Kirk, already a ruin in Burns's time. The wall round the kirkyard was rebuilt by William Burnes and here he was brought from Lochlea to be buried, and the tombstone bears an inscription penned by his poetic son. Later in his life Robert Burns would recall

> Alloway's auld haunted kirk . . .
> Where ghaists and houlets nightly cry.

He would be inspired to write the story of how Tam O' Shanter encountered the witches dancing in the ruined church and escaped from them over the Auld Brig O' Doon. But Maggie, the mare Tam rode, was less lucky:

> Ae spring brought off her master hale,
> But left behind her ain grey tail:
> The carlin caught her by the rump,
> And left poor Maggie scarce a stump.

From that old bridge over the River Doon you can (unlike Tam) admire the view of the 'banks and braes of bonnie Doon'. They are overlooked by the Burns Monument erected in 1820, whose gardens provide a restful retreat. A little way back along the road is the more recent Burns Interpretation Centre, whose visual displays will effortlessly present to you the eventful life of Robert Burns and show you scenes you will want to visit.

Alloway can conveniently be reached by public transport, and it is an easy walk to the various places of interest. It is possible to make a series of expeditions by bus to some of the other places associated with Burns. More satisfactory is a leisurely trip by car through the countryside.

A tour into Carrick will present the other scenes of his

childhood. Carrick is that part of Ayrshire south of the River Doon, while the area to the north is Kyle. So Burns, born in Alloway, could refer to himself thus: 'There was a lad was born in Kyle'; and recall (also in song) that when they lived at Mount Oliphant 'My father was a farmer upon the Carrick border'. To reach Mount Oliphant take the A77 road heading towards Maybole. From Alloway this means going up Doonholm Road, which is almost opposite Burns Cottage, passing the Doonholm estate some of whose trees were planted by William Burnes. Turn right at the main (A77) road. Immediately afterwards turn left off the A77 and look out for the sign for Mount Oliphant, which is on your right. At Mount Oliphant there is a car park opposite the farm, which has recently been converted into a restaurant. You may sardonically recall that here the Burns family 'lived very sparingly. For several years butcher's meat was a stranger in the house'. Gilbert Burns also remembered that 'all the members of the family exerted themselves to the utmost of their strength, and rather beyond it'. It was in a harvest field at Mount Oliphant that 15-year-old Robert composed a song to Nellie Kilpatrick – 'Thus with me began love and poetry'.

Continue past Mount Oliphant to reach the B703 and turn left for Dalrymple where Robert and Gilbert Burns had some schooling in 1772. In the centre of this pleasant village take the right-hand road to the bridge over the River Doon. Now you are in Carrick where his mother came from, with its traditions which 'had so strong an effect upon my imagination'. The B742 from Dalrymple passes Cassillis House (on the right). Burns knew the old ballad of an unidentified Countess of Cassillis who eloped with the gipsy Johnnie Faa. He had also heard that on the hill across from Cassillis House, 'Fairies light, On Cassillis Downans dance'.

This is the road Robert Burns would take on his way in 1775 to Kirkoswald. He would reach Maybole where the Kennedys used to feud. On – again following the A77 – past the ruins of Crossraguel to Kirkoswald. Here he studied surveying in Hugh Rodger's school, but 'a charming filette who lived next door to the school overset my Trigonometry, and set me off on a tangent from the sphere of my studies'. In Kirkoswald too he learned 'to look unconcernedly at a large tavern bill', perhaps

in the company of Kirkton Jean with Douglas Graham of
Shanter farm, smuggler and prototype of Tam O' Shanter.
Statues of Tam and his bosom friend can be found in the
grounds of Souter Johnnie's Cottage in Kirkoswald. This is a
National Trust for Scotland property, where once John
Davidson cobbled shoes. The graves of Tam and the Souter,
and relatives of the poet's mother are to be found in the old
churchyard.

When Burns was in Kirkoswald 'the contraband trade was at
that time very successful', so if you have time continue along
the A77 to Turnberry or by one of the hill roads to the coast
near Maidens. This is longer than just returning to Ayr direct
by the A77, but the coast road is especially attractive. So 'for
Collean the road is ta'en', and north of Culzean take the sharp
left turn to continue along the A719 past Dunure, identifying
the numerous convenient spots where you can imagine the
18th-century smugglers landing their brandy and tea in what
was then called 'the free trade'. And so back to Ayr.

In Ayr with its modern shops and traffic it is difficult to
recapture the atmosphere of the little town of three thousand
people that Burns knew:

> Auld Ayr wham ne'er a town surpasses,
> For honest men and bonnie lasses.

Burns Statue Square – centred on a statue of the Poet erected
in 1891 – was then a cattle market on the outskirts of the old
royal burgh. Down High Street is that former Tam O' Shanter
inn, now a museum, where it is claimed Tam and his cronies
'had been fou for weeks thegither'. In Sandgate a plaque marks
the house of John Murdoch with whom Burns lodged when
learning French in 1773; behind in Fort Street in the grounds
of Ayr Academy stood the old burgh school which he attended
for these three weeks. Down at the harbour is the Ratton Quay
he noted in his poem 'The Brigs of Ayr'. The New Bridge of
1878 replaces the one which ninety years before had been
prophetically addressed in that poem by the Auld Brig: 'I'll be
a brig when ye're a shapeless cairn'. Each June in Ayr there is a
Robert Burns Festival with concerts, exhibitions, and a mock
'Tam O' Shanter Ride'.

A Tarbolton scene, with the building on the left where the Bachelors' Club met. The 19th-century church replaces an older one in which the Burnes family worshipped.

Perhaps another day, another trip to follow the trail. Head for the bypass and at the Whitletts roundabout take the B758 road towards Mauchline. After a mile turn right before the Agricultural College to visit the Leglen Monument. Burns 'chose a fine Sunday, the only day my life allowed, and walked half-a-dozen miles to the Leglen Wood'. For there William Wallace, the 13th-century Scots patriot, had sought refuge, and Burns's 'heart glowed with a wish to be able to make a song on him'. So later, 'Scots wha hae wi' Wallace bled' opened his stirring poem which has become a sort of Scottish national anthem. Appropriately the Leglen Monument is dedicated jointly to Wallace and Burns.

Returning to the main road, continue through Mossblown on the B758, then branch off by the B744 into Tarbolton. This was the centre of Burns's social life in his formative years from 18 till 24. Here he worshipped in the parish church (now replaced). Here, in a building maintained by the National Trust for Scotland, he joined a dancing class, he formed the Bachelors' Club, and he joined the freemasons in 1781, becoming Deputy Grand Master of the lodge three years later. In the upstairs room the 18th-century scene can vividly be imagined.

From Tarbolton you may decide to take the B730 road and travel as Burns did in 1781 the 10 miles to Irvine: 'I joined a flax dresser in a neighbouring town to learn his trade. This was an unlucky affair'. Irvine has commemorated Burns's short stay with a statue on the Moor, and a Burns Club Museum (open Saturdays or as arranged by telephone) which has some interesting manuscripts. An additional attraction is the recently restored Glasgow Vennel. The whole little street has been expensively refurbished to give it a period atmosphere, including the heckling shop where Burns worked, and the attic where he lodged.

It may be decided to keep Irvine for a separate visit, and from Tarbolton continue towards Lochlea. The direct route is the B744, the back road 'round about the hill, And todlin down on Willie's mill', then after three miles taking a left turn. Or you may go by the B730 to join the A719 to pass Adamhill where lived Burns's friend John Rankine and then take the second turning on the right. Lochlea is a working farm in private hands, but it is worth stopping here. For here began this prolific output of verse. From Lochlea came the rollicking 'Corn Rigs' when

> I kiss'd here owre and owre again,
> Amang the rigs o' barley.

Or the haunting echoes of the plaintive 'Mary Morison':

> Yestreen, when to the trembling string,
> The dance gaed thro' the lighted ha',
> To thee my fancy took its wing,
> I sat, but neither heard or saw.

William Burnes died in 1784 and was carried back to Alloway for burial. Robert (who about this time adopted the simpler local spelling of his surname) became head of the family and they were able to secure another farm at Mossgiel just a few miles away.

If you travelled from Tarbolton by the B744 road you will have to return to it, then follow the signs towards Mauchline. This road twists along the crest of a ridge, with the fine views familiar to Burns. To the south are 'the distant Cumnock hills'; to the north on a clear day you can see the distant Highlands when 'winds frae off Ben Lomond blaw'; to the east in front may be seen 'The rising sun, owre Galston muir'. As you breast the hill, Mauchline lies before you, and you approach the farm (now called East Mossgiel) where Burns flitted in 1785. A modern farmhouse replaced the one that was occupied then, so there is nothing to see apart from a hedge in front of the house said to have been planted by Robert and Gilbert; to the east of the farm the field where Robert ploughed up the mouses's nest; to the north that other field where the daisy was ploughed up to produce another of his best-known poems. But though the farmhouse is new, the fields more productive, and the landscape altered, this is a place to pause, remembering that in his four years here Burns wrote most of his most famous works and was able to have them published at Kilmarnock.

Just beyond Mossgiel is the tower of the Burns Monument, overlooking the schemes of houses of old folk, also inaugurated in 1896. 'Better a wee bush than nae bield' was a motto Burns invented for himself, 'bield' meaning shelter. So it is appropriate that he is here commemorated by what is now called sheltered housing for old people, long before that term was invented, and indeed pioneering the concept of special housing for old people. The original houses of 1896 (fully modernised now of course) plus others built later form the scheme of twenty managed by the National Burns Memorial and Cottage Homes, while another eleven Jean Armour Burns Houses were the creation of Glasgow and District Burns Association.

Down into Mauchline turn right at the traffic lights to reach a large and convenient car park. Through a hedge and beside

Mauchline Tower can be seen a private house once occupied by Gavin Hamilton, the poet's friend and patron. Take the path alongside the Tower to reach Mauchline Burns House Museum. This is where Burns set up house with Jean Armour in 1788 before they departed from Ayrshire as a married couple into Dumfriesshire. This sandstone dwelling house once provided accommodation for four families. In the renovation of the interior the single apartment they rented has been restored to suggest their humble abode; there is a display illustrating Burns's stay in Mauchline; and there is also a local folk museum downstairs. The narrow Castle Street (once the main road through the town) contains also the house of Dr John Mackenzie, another of the poet's friends. Opposite was Nanse Tinnock's tavern. In the kirkyard are buried four of the poet's children and many of his associates. Across the road is Poosie Nansie's inn, where the Jolly Beggars caroused, still open for custom as licensed premises. So too is the Loudoun Arms, down the street beside the car park – there Burns and some of his friends met as a Reading Club.

From Mauchline there are various possibilities. You may wish to explore some of the places in the immediate neighbourhood. You may choose to make the long trip that Burns made through Cumnock and New Cumnock and leave Ayrshire towards Ellisland and Dumfries. You may decide to return to Ayr. Or you may travel, as you must sometime, to Kilmarnock.

To Kilmarnock from Mauchline take the A76, going back up the hill, passing the Monument on your left. Drive straight into Kilmarnock town centre where there are various parking places. Not much remains of 'the streets and neuks o' Killie', for most of the 18th-century town has been obliterated by modern urban developments. In the pedestrianised area find the covered Burns precinct, where there is a plaque marking the spot where stood John Wilson's printing shop in the Star Inn Close. There in 1786 was published the *Poems Chiefly in the Scottish Dialect* which have become world famous. Take the exit leading by an underpass to London Road for a quite short walk. After crossing the Kilmarnock Water, beyond the bridge on the right-hand side, uphill stood the house of Tam Samson, one of his many local associates. Quite soon you reach the Dick Institute which is the headquarters of the international Burns

The Burns House Museum in a corner of Mauchline which retains an 18th-century atmosphere. Here in Castle Street, then the main thoroughfare, Robert Burns set up house with Jean Armour in 1788.

Federation formed in 1892. The Dick Institute houses an important collection of Burns manuscripts which may be inspected by arrangement. Not far away, across London Road, is the Kay Park with its Burns Monument and Statue. Each summer Kilmarnock commemorates its links with Burns with a parade and appropriate ceremonies.

If you decide to leave the visit to Kilmarnock for another day, return from Mauchline to Ayr by the B758. But stop at Failford. Here there is a simple column commemorating Robert Burns's last parting on a Sunday in May 1786 from his mysterious and beloved Highland Mary Campbell, who would soon afterwards die tragically at Greenock before their planned emigration to Jamaica. From Failford you can get a fine view of the River Ayr as it cuts its way through its sandstone gorges. All along its banks are places mentioned in Burns's poems and other places of interest, but to be reached only by minor roads or on foot, for the main B758 road leaves the river at Failford and does not meet it again till Ayr is reached.

CHAPTER 9
Industrial Past and Present

Once upon a time before Industrial Archaeology was invented, tourists were gently steered away from broken-down factory areas, and any artefact older than yesterday was designated junk. True, anything prehistoric or medieval was worth preserving, but it is only in recent years that more modern things have been deemed historical, and certain mundane objects of an industrial nature have been elevated into the category of tourist attractions. Ayrshire has been noted for the variety of its industries. Some have disappeared, leaving little or no trace. Other long-established businesses have survived, though often operating in modern premises. Anyone intent on 'Discovering Ayrshire' will want some details about the county's industrial past and present without a full-blown historical account or an analysis of the economy at the time of writing. Perhaps the best approach is just to make an annotated catalogue of the various types of industry, and hope that will not be as boring as it may seem.

Mining and Quarrying

There are some references to coal being worked locally from the 15th century, but exploitation on a significant scale did not occur till the 18th century. The main demand was by farmers for use in lime-burning (to improve the productivity of the acid soils). Much of it was exported, hence the sinking between Saltcoats and Irvine and at Newton-upon-Ayr of early coal pits. No trace of these remains, though at Stevenston the remains have been preserved of the engine house (257414) where a Newcomen steam pump was installed as early as 1719. Throughout the 19th century the north Ayrshire coalfield was intensively worked by small companies who sank a succession of small pits and left behind a litter of pit bings, most of which are now covered with grass, and not too obvious a memorial to the former workings. Coal from north Ayrshire required construction of harbours at Troon and Ardrossan, and the network of railways was initiated by the Duke of Portland's wagonway of 1810 from Kilmarnock to Troon. Its route may still be traced, crossing the River Irvine by a bridge (383369) near Gatehead; and on the branch line at Caprington by Kilmarnock there is a signalbox (417352) often mistaken for a ruined castle! Ayrshire's coal production reached a peak around 1901 when 14,000 miners produced four million tons for industrial and household use and for export. Most of that came from north Ayrshire, which was left with only nine small pits fifty years later. In central Ayrshire there were extensive workings of coal and ironstone during the 19th century and the construction of a series of isolated miners' rows. The remains of small 18th-century bellpits can be traced south of Muirkirk on the moorland (693255). In the 20th century production in this field was increased, by Baird and Dalmellington Ltd. before 1947 and by the National Coal Board for a period after nationalisation. Here at the Barony Colliery (528219) was a shaft of 617m, the deepest in Scotland; not far off was Beoch No. 4 (515095) with its pithead 325m above sea level, the highest in Scotland; and Glenburn Colliery (367258) worked coal from under the sea. In south Ayrshire there is only a small and isolated coalfield near Dailly, particularly memorable for a seam which went on fire in the 18th century and continues to burn, reputedly providing underground heating for certain farm fields in Kirkoswald parish. In 1950 Ayrshire still had more than forty pits where 11,500 miners produced over three million tons annually. Since then the industry has contracted; Barony Colliery alone survives, apart from several small private pits and large-scale opencast operations.

Once Ayrshire produced ironstone, and at various periods smaller quantities of other minerals such as lead, copper, graphite, and antimony from the New Cumnock area to fireclays including Ayrshire Bauxitic Clay from north Ayrshire. There is a long-established little industry located near Stair (435234), described in the booklet *Ayrshire Honestones,* by Gordon Tucker, 1983. But the vast Ballochmyle sandstone quarries near Mauchline are filled in, local clays are no longer worked for Cumnock pottery or the manufacture of field

When the National Coal Board was formed in 1947 it operated 37 large pits in Ayrshire. The sole survivor is Barony Colliery, Auchinleck, which extracts coal from seams nearly half a mile deep.

drains, and most of the lime the farmers need is imported. The only major quarrying enterprises that remain are those for lime near Beith and near Girvan, and for road metal at Hillhouse by Dundonald.

Iron and Engineering

It is hard to believe that a hundred years ago Ayrshire was a major producer of iron with over forty furnaces in blast in various corners of the county, making use of local ores, and manned largely by immigrant Irish labour. Roy Campbell's article on 'The Iron Industry in Ayrshire' in Volume 7 of the *Ayrshire Collections* tells in detail the story of its rise and fall. The Muirkirk iron works is particularly noteworthy since it operated for 136 years from 1787 till 1923. But little evidence of its existence survives, the result of measures to remove

unsightly installations and landscape the site, laudable enough
though regretted by industrial archaeologists. The same is true
of the other major iron works at Lugar, Kilwinning, and
Stevenston, which survived till the 1920s using imported ores;
and Glengarnock which continued alone as a steel-making
plant till its closure a decade ago. At Waterside in the Doon
valley something remains of the works which closed in 1921,
and efforts are afoot to conserve these. One other site which
survives is of an iron forge at Terreoch which operated as early
as 1730. It can be viewed through binoculars from Townhead
of Greenock (642272) on the B743 between Muirkirk and
Sorn, several hundred yards downhill on the other side of the
River Ayr, accessible only to enthusiasts willing to wade across
the river, or walk from the A70 over a mile of moorland. While
little remains of Ayrshire's erstwhile iron industry, there is
more evidence of the associated engineering trades by virtue of
the fact that a number of businesses large and small continue to
operate. Examples of the diversity are found in Kilmarnock
(Glenfield and Kennedy for water valves, Andrew Barclay for
locomotives, Glacier Metals for metal bearings), Ayr (the
Stamp Works making car parts), and Irvine (Ayrshire Metal
Products Ltd making rolled steel prefabricated structures). At
Irvine lorries are built (by Volvo), at Prestwick aircraft are
constructed (by British Aerospace), while at Troon the older
trade of shipbuilding is continued (by Ailsa Perth). At Irvine
harbour former engineering premises have been appropriately
adapted to become part of the Scottish Maritime Museum.

Textiles and Clothing

Textiles were for a long time Scotland's principal
manufactured product, the country's main contribution to
international trade in the 18th century when industrial
expansion began. Demand was so great for woollen and linen
cloth that the farm folk who did much of the spinning and
weaving in the winter months could not cope. Nor could the
craftsmen of the burghs. Villages and towns were extended
and indeed new ones formed – with cottages built where full-
time handloom weavers could set up in business. The supply of
wool and flax proved insufficient, so exotic fibres were

The iron industry was one of Ayrshire's principal businesses from the opening of Muirkirk Iron Works in 1787 till the closure of Glengarnock Steel Works in 1985, this latter a sad loss to the Kilbirnie area.

imported, and during the first half of the 19th century the export of cotton manufactured goods became Scotland's principal industry. Factories with power-operated spinning machines were followed by others containing power looms for weaving. But most of the cotton was woven on handlooms till the trade was ruined by the shortage of cotton supplies during the American Civil War. The handloom weavers were famed for their radical views, and though they depended upon the South for their cotton, they sympathised with the North and advocated the abolition of slavery. Abraham Lincoln's acknowledgement of this support from Newmilns weavers is commemorated by a flag in the church. Some handloom weavers working in fine fabrics which the power looms could not handle continued into the present century, working in their two-apartment but-and-bens, with the handloom in the but and living in the ben. The Cathcartson Centre at Dalmellington provides a display. Many weavers' cottages are still occupied, some over two centuries old. None of the textile factories has survived that long. Catrine Cotton Works had to be demolished after a fire in 1963. This was a great pity, for the original buildings contained the spinning mill set up in 1787, to which power-loom weaving was added in 1805, a bleachworks in 1824, and the massive Catrine Big Wheels – 50 feet (15m) in diameter – to provide increased water power in 1827. These have all gone, but some of the adjoining buildings survive.

Following the closure of the new factory in 1968, the only continuing branch of the cotton industry is the Irvine Valley lace industry, though even here synthetic fibres have been substituted. Factory production of lace curtains began in Darvel in 1876, and a range of premises there and in Newmilns display a variety of architectural styles. Cotton did not entirely oust the traditional textiles. The linen industry remained, concentrated in the Garnock Valley, where one firm still continues. William and James Knox in 1788 began as bleachers, then spinners of linen thread, using local then imported flax and hemp, and in the present century the firm has successfully converted to the manufacture of fishing nets. Several firms in the woollen industry also continue. These include carpet manufacture, especially at Kilmarnock, and knitwear produced in the hosieries centred in Stewarton.

In America's colonial days and afterwards when the frontier was being extended westwards, some of the pioneers were dressed in Ayrshire linen shirts, woollen Tam O' Shanter bonnets, and boots perhaps also exported from Kilmarnock. For leather was another material suitable for use in expanding local manufacturing. In the 18th and early 19th centuries tanneries were busy, and shoemakers were at work all over the county. When mechanisation was introduced, factories were set up in Maybole, Kilmarnock, and Ayr. But as demand for heavy boots declined, the Maybole factories closed, and the long-established firms which made shoes in Kilmarnock and Ayr found it no longer profitable to do so in the last quarter of the present century. Shoes are still made, like Bata shoes at Cumnock, but the tradition of local craftsmen working on local materials has disappeared.

Food and Drink

The traditional diet was based on what could be produced locally. Oatmeal was used to make porridge, brose, bannocks, and special dishes like haggis and sowens. Kale was the principal vegetable in Scotch broth. Milk was mostly converted into cheese. Most farmers and their families had to subsist on these items. Part of their produce of course had to be handed over to the landlord as kind, and the laird could dispose of part of that in the burgh market to purchase luxury imports. For most people meat was a rarity, and not till the 18th century did sugar, tea, and potatoes become widely known. In that century farming was revolutionised, not only to provide raw materials for weavers and shoemakers, but to produce an augmented supply of foodstuffs for the inhabitants of the growing towns. In north Ayrshire, which even before that time had specialised in dairy products, Dunlop cheese was produced, a sweet milk cheese from a recipe reputedly first used by Barbara Gilmour of that parish. Until the early years of the present century every dairy farm in Ayrshire made its own cheese, abandoning the practice only when it became easier to store liquid milk and transport it more speedily for sale. The Scottish Milk Marketing Board and others found it profitable to continue converting some milk into cheese in their creameries. But when they tried to export it to England under the name of Dunlop cheese, customers were influenced by the name to find it rubbery, till it was renamed Scottish Cheddar. During the period when the farmers' wives made their own cheese, the whey by-product was used to fatten pigs – which until then had been unpopular in Ayrshire because of the Biblical story of evil spirits being cast into swine. Ayrshire bacon is a distinctive type which continues to be cured even though the carcases now come from piggeries rather than dairy farms. Some other meat from pigs and cattle finds its way into tinned products which are manufactured in several local factories, and local mutton fills the succulent Scotch pies. But most meat is now imported into Ayrshire – though Ayrshire veal was once a popular delicacy in Glasgow. Similarly grain meal is imported – for the making of bread and bakery products. Whisky, that other grain product, associated with Johnnie Walker of Kilmarnock since

1820, was never distilled here, but blended and bottled; though distillation is now carried on locally by other firms. Aerated waters also continue to be manufactured locally. In July and August the products of the coastal potato farms go on sale. Market gardens provide seasonal crops of fruit, vegetables, and flowers. Seasonal too are Ayrshire's fish harvests – salmon and trout from the rivers, and sea fish landed at Ayr.

Chemicals and Science-based Industries

The chemical industry has long and diverse connections. Along the coast there used to be saltpans where sea water was evaporated with the aid of local coal. At Saltcoats only the name survives as a reminder, but at Prestwick and Newton-upon-Ayr there are a few relics. In the 18th century tar works were set up beside the iron works at Muirkirk with John Loudon McAdam as one of the partners; it failed because it was being superseded by copper for bottoming ships; and its use on macadamised roads had to await the 20th century. Also in the 18th century William Murdoch of Lugar was carrying on those experiments in the distillation of gas from coal which led in 1792 to his invention of gas lighting. He is commemorated at Bello Mill (597216, on the A70) where he grew up, with the caves where he made his experiments on the bank of the Lugar Water nearby. He is given a corner in the Boswell Museum at Auchinleck, for he belonged to the same parish as the biographer. But the gas works which many of the 19th-century towns established have all disappeared since the arrival of piped natural gas from the North Sea, and most of the gasometers have gone which dominated the skylines of some towns. After 1873 the chemical industry in Ayrshire could be summed up by the name Ardeer. For in that year the Swedish inventor of dynamite chose the sand dunes of Ardeer as a suitable site for manufacturing the explosives that would eventually finance the Nobel Prizes. The Nobel Works, now operated by ICI, grew during two World Wars into a vast complex, providing in peacetime explosives for industrial use and other chemicals. The county has also a remarkable range of other chemical and science-based businesses such as petroleum (Ardrossan), medical products (Dalry), glass bottles (Irvine), fertilisers (Ayr), asphalt (Ayr), and alginates (Girvan).

Beyond the ancient dry-stone dyke are Hunterston 'A' and 'B' nuclear power stations. From 1964 Hunterston has been feeding electricity into the grid. The 'A' station is of the Magnox type and the 'B' of the advanced gas-cooled reactor variety.

It is probably no more than coincidence that most of these are, like Ardeer, sited by the coast. And industrial estates at Ayr and Irvine have attracted firms specialising in electronics and computer parts, while at Irvine the New Town has also Beecham's pharmaceutical products and a new papermaking plant. Many of the new firms are foreign-owned, but it is to be hoped that some of them will become as long-established as Ardeer.

Power

The elder of your present co-authors can remember when cooking was done on an open fire or on a gas ring, when gas lighting was being superseded in some homes by electricity, and when radio reception was difficult, for the wireless set was powered by wet batteries that had to be taken somewhere to be recharged weekly. Outside there were petrol-driven buses now providing regular services, but goods vehicles were drawn by horses. Children ran after steam-powered traction engines and rushed out to see the rare sight of an aeroplane. That was in the 1920s. Few private houses then had telephones. Kilmarnock's first phone was installed in Johnnie Walker's in 1881. In 1896 the Burgh of Ayr inaugurated a local electricity supply and in 1904 Kilmarnock followed with its coal-driven generating plant which after the formation of the Ayrshire Electricity Board in 1924 extended lines throughout the county. Now that is superseded by the South of Scotland Electricity Board's two nuclear power stations at Hunterston. The first of these began feeding power into the grid in 1964; a quarter of a century later the safety of such installations is more widely questioned; the critical and the merely curious are equally welcome to conducted tours round the premises at Hunterston. Fifty years ago there were bus tours to inspect the dams being constructed at Loch Doon in connection with the Galloway hydro-electric scheme, then a novelty. Surviving remnants of earlier types of power can be traced by anyone particularly interested. Windmills at Saltcoats and Irvine have long disappeared, but the tower of one survives in a field at Monkton (362281). Steam power, not so long ago universal for looms, machines, pumps, and railway locomotives, has now to be hunted for, and rescued by conservationists. Horse power is remembered only in pictures of horse ploughing and by abandoned mill rinks beside farm steadings. The oldest form of power, lest we forget, is manpower. Look at any historic building, and indeed at some not so ancient. Consider for example the massive Ballochmyle railway viaduct, whose stone was hewn by hand from the quarries, raised 50m above the River Ayr, and laid on a temporary cradle of 1,200 logs to form a masonry arch of 55m plus six auxiliary arches of 15m span – this with embankments, cuttings, and tunnels, all formed by teams of Irish navvies equipped only with spades, ropes, and levers.

CHAPTER 10

Some Ayrshire Worthies

In Chapter 1 there were listed those persons associated with Ayrshire who are famous enough to be well known by name and whose biographies can be easily found in reference books. There are also, as in most communities, some persons with no such pretensions to celebrity but who are remembered locally for their eccentricity or some other special feature of their life. Three dowager countesses of the 18th century deserve passing mention. Lady Margaret Dalrymple, daughter of the first Earl of Stair, married the third Earl of Loudoun and after his death in 1731 lived in widowhood till 1779, dying aged 99 at Sorn Castle – an estate which she improved to earn the praise of Andrew Wight the agriculturalist. 'There perhaps does not exist in the world such another woman', he wrote after a visit in 1778. A second notable figure was the Dowager Countess of Eglinton. Susannah Kennedy, daughter of the wicked Sir Archibald Kennedy of Culzean, was a renowned beauty, and a patroness of literature, to whom Allan Ramsay in 1725 dedicated his play 'The Gentle Shepherd'. She became third wife of the 9th Earl of Eglinton and mother of 11 children, including the 10th Earl who was murdered and the 11th Earl who succeeded him. In her widowhood she lived at Auchans House from 1772 till her death in 1780 at the age of 91. There she was visited by Dr Samuel Johnson who found 'her reading extensive and her conversation elegant'. She preserved her complexion by daily washing her face in sow's milk, and for sport tamed and made pets of the rats which abounded in the old mansion. The last of the trio was Elizabeth McGuire, the daughter of a Newton-on-Ayr carpenter who played the fiddle. Her father had befriended a poor boy called James Macrae who made a fortune in India and returned to enrich the members of the McGuire family. So the lowly-born fiddler's daughter was wealthy enough to be wooed and wed in 1744 by the Earl of Glencairn. It was not a happy marriage, but she contrived to outlive him by 26 years as Dowager Countess of Glencairn till her death in 1801.

Moving among the gentry was the owner of a small estate, the Laird of Logan. He was well-known as a wit in his lifetime. His anecdotes were published in Glasgow in 1835, and were so popular that numerous editions followed, and one far-sighted merchant took the opportunity of naming a blend of whisky after him, and this 'Laird of Logan' blend is still marketed. The Logan estate outside Cumnock is now built over with council houses, and nothing remains of Logan House where Hugh Logan was born in 1739. He was a younger son but he loathed study and told his father that 'I've made up my mind, faither, to follow nae trade but your ain'. In fact his two elder brothers died young and Hugh succeeded to the estate in 1759. His guardians sent him to Edinburgh University where he lodged with Ayr-born Professor Robert Hunter, but learned little beyond convivial drinking with his fellow-students John Hamilton of Sundrum and Hugh Montgomerie of Coilsfield, later 12th Earl of Eglinton. Hugh Logan's estate was small, and he had to sell it off in 1798 and move to the smaller Wellwood House near Muirkirk where he died a bachelor in 1802. But he was always a welcome guest among the highest ranks of Ayrshire society. In 1784, for example, the celebrated James Boswell travelled from Edinburgh to Ayrshire with Logan, and 'Logan's continual flow of ideas, no matter what, entertained me all the way'. He often dined at Eglinton Castle. On one occasion an English visitor, boasting about the productivity of his own estate, asked how much wheat an acre in Scotland would yield. Logan named an enormous figure. 'Pooh, pooh!' said the Englishman, 'that's not more than half what is reaped from the very commonest of our lands in the south. And what quantity of beans will an acre of your land produce?' 'No, no!' complained Logan, 'It's my turn to ask first. Turn about for fair play in telling lies!' One other example of his wit occurred when there was a proposal to incur expense in repairing the wall round Cumnock cemetery. Logan declared it unnecessary, for 'It's time enough to repair the dykes when the tenants start complaining'. One who knew Logan of Logan described him as tall, handsome, weighing from eighteen to twenty stones, and always well dressed. He was considered much more moral than his dissipated associates, for he had only one known illegitimate daughter.

A contemporary and acquaintance of Logan was Alexander Fairlie of Fairlie, who was factor who managed the estates of the Earl of Eglinton. Like so many 18th-century notables, he was also a bachelor. Farming seems to have been his whole life, and his Fairlie Rotation was long practised in Ayrshire. He was renowned for the severity with which he imposed his will on his own tenants and those of the Eglinton estates. When one blamed the weather for the failure of a crop, Fairlie took a pinch of snuff and replied sharply, 'If you will only comply to my improved plan of plowing only one fourth of your farm, you will have the *best* of crops *in spite of the weather*'. Among Fairlie's employees was (for a time) William Burnes, father of the poet. Another was Josey Smith, a ditcher who was fond both of versifying and drinking whisky. 'Go and sing ballads and be damned to you,' Fairlie once told him. Josey obliged with the first part of the request and composed a song about his master:

> On the green banks of Irvine lives Fairlie of Fairlie
> Who oft speaks of good things, and does them but rarely.
> Lord Eglinton's tenants they walk very barely,
> Being robbed of their riches by Fairlie of Fairlie
>
> It's in the low regions, oh! how he will fret,
> When there is no farming or farms for to set!
> The devil and him they will scold it right sairly,
> And Hell will resound with the shrieks of auld Fairlie.

Another of the same côterie was William Aiton. Born on Silverwood farm to the east of Kilmarnock, he was 'a Practical Farmer, and performed with my own hands, every operation in husbandry, then known or practised' before becoming a lawyer. It was when practising this profession at Strathaven in Lanarkshire that he was invited by the Board of Agriculture to prepare for publication in 1811 a Report on Ayrshire agriculture. The first *General View of the Agriculture of the County of Ayr* had been published in 1793, prepared by Colonel William Fullarton of Fullarton, soldier, diplomat, politician, and agriculturalist. This fairly brief first report by Fullarton was followed by Aiton's massive volume of 763 pages plus 19 engravings. Not only is the state of farming eloquently described, but Aiton felt entitled to enlarge on every associated topic from coalmining to cottages, from railways to religion. In discussing poor relief he included – as a footnote! – the whole 281 lines of Burns's poem 'The Jolly Beggars'. And as an appendix he includes an account of the dialect of Kyle by Burns's friend William Simpson in which 'Winsome Willie' notes its 'very striking likeness to some of the Greek dialects' and argues that it is less provincial than standard English. Altogether a book worth dipping into, the product of a garrulous but perspicacious personality.

Another native of Kilmarnock parish was the less reputable Tammy Raeburn. He was born in 1769 at Holmhead, east of Kilmarnock on the Grougar road, and this small farm he inherited while still a young man. An old woman kept a few cattle for him, and at first he supplemented his meagre income by working for neighbouring farmers. Then he became involved in a ruinous lawsuit. He objected to a neighbour closing a road, and took him to court, but the case went against him, and he had to pay heavy expenses. He believed himself wronged and vowed never to cut his hair or change his clothes till justice was done. He gave up cultivating his fields, subsisted on vegetables and fruit, and drank only water. He became known as 'the Ayrshire Hermit', his home 'the Ark' was visited by many curious to view him, and a picture of him even appeared in *The Illustrated London News*. Tammy was over six feet high, his matted hair hung over his shoulders, his grizzled beard reached his waist, and his clothes were tattered and patched. He continued to be litigious. When the neighbour who had closed the road trespassed on Raeburn's land a fight ensued in which Tammy was held by the beard and beaten; this was deemed assault, and Tammy for once put on decent clothing for this solitary legal victory. He appeared in court on subsequent occasions to be found guilty – of threatening to shoot a neighbour trimming a boundary hedge; of refusing to pay his rates; of selling spirits to visitors instead of the aerated waters he usually dispensed to those out for a weekend afternoon walk. Tammy Raeburn was a familiar figure in the streets of Kilmarnock; he went to the famous Eglinton Tournament; he often talked of walking to London to present his grievances to Queen Victoria. Shrunken and bent, he died in 1843 in his 74th year. His land was sold by distant relations and his house has long since disappeared.

Much higher in the social scale were other interesting 19th-century characters. Hugh, 12th Earl of Eglinton, built for himself the huge Gothic-style Eglinton Castle, laid out Ardrossan as a new town with harbour, hotels, houses, and baths, and left uncompleted a grandiose Glasgow ship canal. Archibald William who succeeded him founded the Eglinton Hunt, instituted the Scottish Grand National Steeplechase at Bogside racecourse, and spent £40,000 in 1839 bringing the cream of polite society in period costume to view the mock-medieval Eglinton Tournament – a gorgeous spectacle spoiled by torrential rain. But he was able to recoup some of his losses by investing in local coal, iron, and railway undertakings. Less fortunate was the luckless line of Loudoun. A suicide in 1786 left an infant heiress Countess of Loudoun who by marriage would become Marchioness of Hastings. Her last years were blighted by a court scandal involving her daughter Lady Flora Hastings, who was Lady of the Bedchamber to the Duchess of Kent, Queen Victoria's mother. In 1839 she began to suffer from an enlarged liver, which would lead to her death later that year. There were unkind and ugly rumours that she was pregnant, rumours which should have been stifled by court doctors, government ministers, and by the Queen herself whose popularity plummeted. A generation later the 4th Marquess of Hastings was, with justice, called 'the Wicked Marquess'. He was a degenerate and dishonourable rake who lost £120,000 on one gamble, and to pay off all his creditors had to sell off to Lord Bute all his Ayrshire estates – including even the family burial vault at Loudoun.

James Paterson, the Ayrshire historian, deserves special mention. He was born in 1805 at Struthers farm on the banks of the River Irvine by Kilmarnock. The son of an unsuccessful farmer, he was a stable boy at the age of eleven. Two years later he began his apprenticeship as a printer in Kilmarnock and Ayr, then was printer and publisher of the short-lived *Kilmarnock Chronicle*, for a time editor of the *Ayr Observer*, but working for periods in Glasgow and especially Edinburgh, produced over a dozen learned studies in Scottish history and literature. These ranged from *Origin of the Scots and the Scottish Language* to his *History of the County of Ayr* in two volumes, 1847, 1852; a second edition in five volumes, 1863-66, re-issued in

D

two volumes, with addenda, 1871, before his death in Edinburgh in 1876. None of this would seem particularly remarkable. Yet his only formal schooling comprised brief and interrupted spells at Hurlford, Maybole, Kilmaurs, and Kilmarnock. And he taught himself historical research while employed at 25 shillings a week writing the script for *Kay's Edinburgh Portraits* which came out in monthly parts from 1837 to 1839, and went on to decipher medieval texts with the aid of a little Latin he had learned in Kilmarnock.

Among the numerous school teachers who could be designated worthies Kilmarnock contributed John Graham, master of the grammar school from 1763 to 1779, who departed thereafter for London where he was hanged in 1782 for forging banknotes. His near-contemporary as master of Ayr grammar school from 1746 to 1761 was John Mair who taught arithmetic, bookkeeping, geography, navigation, surveying, geometry, algebra, natural philosophy, and Latin. He was author of textbooks on Latin and what is regarded as the pioneer work on modern bookkeeping methods. He was the first to teach science in a Scottish school. He created in Ayr what he called 'a sort of academy' and went on to Perth to take charge of the first Scottish school designated an academy. After Ayr burgh school was converted into an academy in 1796, one of its most remarkable masters was Dr John Memes who served as Rector (headmaster) from 1826 till 1844. He was appointed at the age of 31, having studied Latin, Greek, Divinity, Mathematics, Natural Philosophy, Chemistry, Botany, and Anatomy at Aberdeen, and travelled abroad to acquire fluency in French, Italian, and German. At Ayr he taught a variety of subjects in an innovative manner, not only the senior classes but even the infants 'in the first formation of their letters'. He created a botanical garden, for geography he personally painted maps on the walls and even the ceiling of the school hall, and he had his mathematics pupils making plans of the harbour at five in the morning. This was because his regular classes commenced at 6 a.m. and continued for 12 hours, after which he took evening classes in astronomy, superintended the library, lectured to the Mechanics' Institute, and on Sunday evenings addressed crowded meetings in Wallacetown Chapel on the Evidences of Christianity. During his stay in Ayr he also had published books on sculpture, architecture, poetry, history, and in 1839 one of the first books on photography, entitled *Daguerre's History and Practice of Photogenic Drawing*. From time to time his advice was sought by local doctors, the railway company, the Sheriff (to calculate the trajectory of a bullet), and the town council (to report on the feasibility of a piped water supply); and when Ayr Town Hall was struck by lightning, Memes 'quieted public alarm' by climbing the 225-foot (68m) steeple to check that the structure was safe. Latterly his energies flagged, he had various disappointments, and he removed to Hamilton to spend the rest of his life as a parish minister.

The 19th century saw the creation of the Ayrshire Constabulary in 1830 with the appointment of a Head Constable and policemen stationed at Girvan, Newmilns, and Beith – these places chosen, I guess, not because of a high incidence of crime but because of the dangerous political activities of the weavers campaigning for a vote. By 1858 there were 884 officers in 17 police stations serving the county outwith Ayr and Kilmarnock which had their own burgh forces. At the beginning of the present century the Ayrshire Constabulary was commanded by a colourful character who is still remembered with respect. Captain Hardy McHardy, after retiring early from the Royal Navy because of illness, was appointed Chief Constable by the special committee of elected and nominated persons then responsible for police. McHardy was a strict disciplinarian but a fair man who was immensely popular with the force as well as the public, despite his gruff manner. During the South African War when no soldiers were available to provide a guard of honour for a distinguished visitor he refused to allow policemen to be used. 'It is not a police duty', he insisted. 'Though, if a distinguished criminal comes to Ayrshire, I shall provide a guard with pleasure!' He was always in a hurry, and in the days before motor cars got about by bicycle and train. He was known to ride his bicycle into Ayr Railway Station and across the platform, where he was catapulted into the guard's van, leaving his cycle to be collected later.

A kenspeckle character remembered in Craigie and adjoining parishes for many years after his death in 1924 was

Will Straehorn, who made a living as a cattle dealer. Like all bearing that surname – or its anglified version of Strawhorn – he was descended from Hugh Strathearn or Strahorne who farmed Mossbog in Tarbolton parish in the later 17th century. Will Straehorn was born at Mossbog, but when his father died young the family moved to Muggerslandburn near Craigie where Will (who never married) lived with his widowed mother till her death in 1895, and then moved into Ayr. 'Uncle Wull' as he was known to his nephews and nieces embodied pride and poverty. He rode about the countryside on horseback, wearing an Inverness cape, and followed by his dog. But his socks often needed darning, and he lit up a cigar only when approaching a farm in order to impress his clients. He enrolled in the Ayrshire Yeomanry Cavalry – that select body of part-time soldiers – became the quartermaster sergeant of the Mauchline Troop, and was a member of teams which won the National Rifle-shooting Championships at Wimbledon and Bisley. He went beyond himself by setting his cap at the daughter of a neighbouring laird. He made a habit of attending the church where she worshipped. But when Will made too daring an advance – passing her a peppermint during the sermon – her brother threatened to horsewhip him. Will Straehorn died at the age of 70 after falling off a bicycle in Mill Street in Ayr.

One Ayrshire family which in successive generations produced a series of distinguished soldiers and statesmen was the Fergussons of Kilkerran. In the 20th century this family tradition was continued by two brothers from that south Ayrshire estate. Sir James Fergusson who inherited the baronetcy was journalist, broadcaster, author of a number of books on Scottish history, and latterly occupied the post of Keeper of the Records of Scotland. His brother Bernard Fergusson was a soldier who in kilt and monocle, backed by his Gurkha batman, appears as an impressive and respected figure in many books about the Second World War in South-East Asia. He himself wrote *Beyond the Chindwin* and other books on military topics. Later as Lord Ballantrae he was – as his father had been – Governor General of New Zealand.

Last in this selection of Ayrshire worthies comes a bespoke tailor from Newmilns who was a foundation member of the Communist Party and died on 2 August 1966, aged 80. Willie

Deans was one of a considerable group from the Irvine Valley who followed the local radical tradition by opposing the First World War as conscientious objectors and began his prison sentence in Ayr Gaol looking out at the holiday crowds on the beach. He joined the Communist Party when it was set up in 1920 and continued a member for the rest of his life, though always interpreting the party line in his own individual manner. For though he had the lean and hungry look of a revolutionary, that concealed a humour, a compassion, and a gentleness which endeared him to all who made his acquaintance. When he went round the town on Fridays to collect payments for his tailoring, hard-luck stories affected him so much that he often finished up with less in his pocket then when he started. Latterly he gave up his own business to become an employee with the local Cooperative Society; when he brought home his first pay packet, his wife Lizzie could hardly believe it was all theirs. In his spare time he sometimes with his fiddle joined a few cronies as a concert party entertaining old folk. He himself was always in demand as a speaker at Burns Suppers and Golden Weddings, and could have his audience one moment almost in tears, the next convulsed with happy laughter. One of his stories concerns the folk of Darvel who are alleged to be mean – at least by their neighbours in Newmilns. A beggar from Lanarkshire going round the doors of Darvel was getting little or nothing in the way of alms. When one further housewife refused him anything, he cried out in final exasperation: 'Are there nae Christians in Derval?' She thought for a moment then replied, 'Weel, there are Mortons, and Gebbies, and Clelands, and Boyds – but nae Christians that I've heard of!'

CHAPTER 11
Out and About on Holiday

This chapter is a kind of introduction to those following which provide guided tours round the different corners of Ayrshire. If you wish a general account of some of the attractions Ayrshire has to offer, miss the next seven paragraphs which provide an aside on the development of the local tourist traffic.

Long ago, in that golden age which never existed, the happy and carefree peasantry enjoyed holidays in a calendar which was full of such holy days. That at least was the nostalgic opinion of the 19th-century industrial worker whose life lacked seasonal variation and who was confined indoors for long hours – made possible by gas lighting, an invention welcomed only by employers. Certainly the factory worker who was ruled by the clock enjoyed less freedom than the independent handloom weaver who when the sun was shining could desert the loom to tend his garden and when the ice was bearing would enjoy a day's curling. With increased commercialism in farming, landlords expected from tenants and workers a closer devotion to routine. Thus the Board of Agriculture report on Ayrshire in 1811 complained that 'There are not less than 200 fairs or races in the county of Ayr, every year, and, on an average, there cannot be fewer than 1000 people at every fair or race; supposing the half of these have no necessary business, and that, on the average, their loss of time, and expenses at the fair were not to exceed ten shillings each, the aggregate loss to the public by fairs and races, in Ayrshire alone, must be not less than £50,000 per annum'.

William Aiton who thus criticised the fairs incidentally provides us with interesting details of what were the only holidays most people then had. He regretted that many 'spend the day in tippling at poisonous spirits'. Others purchased 'ginger-bread, fruits, confectionaries, etc., called fairings' which Aiton deemed 'nauseous and unwholesome'. Children wasted their pennies on 'the most loathsome trash'. He noted especially that 'The manner in which the unmarried people, of both sexes, conduct themselves at fairs and races, is far from being decorous'. He tells how each lad at the fair finds a partner, then takes his chosen lass into an alehouse. Aiton describes them there indulging in a practice – which American readers will recognise as similar to the New England custom of 'bundling' – when the lad 'hugs her in his arms, tumbles her into a bed, if one can be found, though many persons be in the room, then with one arm under her head, the other, and one of his legs over her, he enjoys a tete a tete conversation'. Later they 'adjourn to some long-room, mason lodge, or barn, to dance reels, and found their ways home about midnight.

The gentry of course enjoyed holiday trips. In the 18th century the Ayrshire nobility were to be found often in London or Bath. Young gentlemen were taken by tutors to visit France and Italy on the Grand Tour. To one of these, James Boswell of Auchinleck, we can award the title of founder of Ayrshire tourism. In 1769 he organised a visit by his Corsican hero Don Pasquale Paoli, who was granted the freedom of Kilmarnock. In 1773, after a tour of the Highlands, Boswell brought back to Ayrshire the London literary lion Dr Samuel Johnson. A trip round Ayrshire included visiting the ruins of Dundonald Castle. Later literary visitors to Ayrshire included John Keats on a walking tour in 1818 and William Wordsworth in 1833. Each visited the birthplace of Robert Burns and penned an appropriate sonnet. Later in the 19th century Penkill Castle became a holiday home for Pre-Raphaelite artists including William Bell Scott, Dante Gabriel Rossetti, and William Morris.

From the 18th century, however, what attracted most visitors to Ayrshire was the opportunity for sea bathing. This was the fashionable panacea for all ailments – though it did nothing for King George III's insanity and probably hastened Robert Burns's death. In 1791 Saltcoats was attracting from 300 to 500 people during the summer months 'for sea-bathing, from the inland country, especially from the towns of Paisley, Glasgow and Hamilton'. Further up the coast, 'Many of the sickly inhabitants of Glasgow and Paisley have felt sensible advantages from the air of Largs . . . It has been frequented a good deal of late, in the summer months, by many persons and families, for the sake of health or amusement'. Troon was also 'an excellent situation for sea bathing, and is much resorted to by the inhabitants of Kilmarnock'. Indeed once the

Kilmarnock-Troon railway was constructed in 1808, Kilmarnock weavers travelled down to Barassie beach in the horse-drawn coal waggons, on what were probably the world's earliest passenger railway excursions. What really made the Ayrshire coast accessible for holidaymakers was the opening of the Glasgow-Ayr railway in 1840. The railway company was from the beginning wise enough to realise that travel for pleasure could be a profitable sideline. Indeed even before the line was complete, special trains were run from Ayr to Irvine in 1839 to take spectators to the celebrated Eglinton Tournament. And long before the Burns Federation was inaugurated, the Glasgow and South Western Railway Company was advertising the attractions of the Land of Burns. In 1885 a branch line to Largs was opened to cater for passenger traffic to that part of the coast. In 1886 the G & S W Railway Station Hotel was opened at Ayr. In 1891 the company established its own fleet of steamers, designed for pleasure cruises on the Firth of Clyde. In 1906 a scenic coastal line from Ayr to Girvan was provided to serve the new railway hotel at Turnberry. The first British Open Golf Championships were played at Prestwick from 1860 till 1872, made possible by the railway services available; and for many years Glasgow golfers filled regular excursion trains taking them to Bogside, Gailes, and Barassie where stations were provided which were especially convenient for the courses. From the beginning of the present century, extra trains were needed for the increased number of summer trippers, particularly at the Glasgow Fair. Saltcoats, Troon, and Prestwick were especially favoured by Sunday Schools chartering trains for their annual Saturday trips to the shore. In 1938 a peak was reached, when the LMS Railway Company estimated that from 40-50,000 trippers arrived by train one Saturday afternoon at the Ayrshire resorts; cheap 'Evening Breathers' that year carried 397,000 passengers; one evening there were 20 special excursion trains to Largs. And all this despite growing competition from bus companies offering day tours as well as their regular services.

The railways made the Ayrshire coast accessible to day trippers and sportsmen, and in the first half of the 20th century the Ayrshire resorts became busier as more people

A sunny breezy day on the Ailsa golf course at Turnberry with Ayrshire's only mainland lighthouse in the background, standing within the remains of Turnberry Castle where Robert Bruce was probably born in 1274. This course has provided a spectacular setting for the Open Championship twice, and can dent the best golfer's ego – especially when Atlantic gales roar in.

found they could now afford family holidays. The coastal towns also attracted incoming residents who settled in the extensive private housing developments of the '30s and later. There were business and professional persons who could commute daily by train to Glasgow. Also there were retired people who enjoyed the pleasant atmosphere of the coastal towns, their full range of facilities, and the mildness of their winters. There was thus a spectacular expansion of all the Ayrshire coastal towns. In the first half of the 20th century when the inland industrial town of Kilmarnock grew in population from 35,000 to just over 42,000, the coastal county town of Ayr grew from 29,000 to surpass it by a few hundreds. In the same period population nearly doubled at Saltcoats (8 to 14 thousand); more than doubled at Troon (4.8 to 10.1) and

Largs (3.2 to 8.6); and quadrupled at Prestwick (2.8 to 11.4 thousand).

Those coastal towns which happened to be burghs benefited from the efforts of their councils to improve facilities for holidaymakers. Esplanades were constructed along the beaches. Italian ice cream merchants provided kiosks and cafes. Ayr's Gaiety Theatre (1902) and Pavilion (1911) provided variety shows, an example copied by other resorts. Prestwick and Troon after 1931 offered the additional attraction of outdoor bathing lakes. The continuing appeal was noted in the Third Statistical Account of 1951: 'The Ayrshire resorts are equipped with hotels, boarding houses and private lodgings to accommodate those who come whether it be for golf, a family holiday on the beath, a young folk's holiday with bathing, dancing, and entertainments, or the quieter holiday of older folks . . . Since the war an addition has been made by the establishment just south of Ayr of a holiday camp by Messrs Butlin'.

Since that was written, holiday fashions have changed. For a new generation cheap chartered flights and package holidays to sunny Spain offered an irresistible counter-attraction to families in general and young people in particular. The brochures seemed to guarantee eternal sunshine as compared with wet days in Scotland, heated swimming pools as compared with spartan conditions on Ayrshire beaches, lively festivities as compared with dreary evenings experienced at home, luxurious hotels as compared with apartments run by hatchet-faced landladies. But the brochures are not always reliable. Ayrshire continues to exercise an attraction for a wide variety of holidaymakers. For its varied attractions, read on . . .

The Ayrshire coast remains extremely popular with day trippers, now arriving many of them by private car. For families with young children sandy beaches retain their attraction. In addition to the familiar sea shores of Ardrossan South Beach, Saltcoats, Troon, Prestwick, Ayr, and Girvan, places like Maidens are now more accessible, while Irvine has come into its own with the removal of those industrial features which once disfigured the approach to its fine sands. The outdoor bathing lakes are now mostly redundant; there are indoor pools at several coastal and inland centres open all year

round; and when it is hot in summer the safe sandy beaches
are thronged with bathers. They do not seem too concerned
with reports that the Firth of Clyde is polluted with sewage – it
is, but so are the Mediterranean and most other enclosed
waters of Europe.

More visitors are now attracted to the rockier coasts of north
and south Ayrshire. North of Ardrossan there are magnificent
vistas across the Firth towards Arran, scuba diving for the
energetic, picnic places for casual meals, plenty of other eating
places, and a range of attractions in Largs. South of Ayr there
are similar attractions along that other scenic route past the
Heads of Ayr, Dunure fishing village, the curious 'Electric
Brae', Croy Beach, Culzean Castle and Country Park, Maidens,
Turnberry, Girvan, by the rugged Kennedy's Pass to
Ballantrae; with views across the Firth to Ailsa Craig, and
Ireland on clear days. All within a short drive by car.

For those many who come to stay, the coast has other
possibilities. There are opportunities for sailing, boating, and
sea fishing. There are fewer pleasure cruises on the Clyde now,
but each summer the paddle steamer *Waverley* operates
excursions from Ayr, day trips to Arran are possible by the
regular steamer service from Ardrossan, and there is a ferry
from Largs across to the Island of Cumbrae. For those not
hurrying home in the evening from the coast there are summer
shows in the theatres of Ayr and usually elsewhere as well;
cinemas, dancing, discos, cabarets, and extended licensing
hours for leisurely drinking.

Ayrshire has a full range of hotels. Most are of course on the
coast. There are 4-star establishments at Turnberry and Troon.
Ayr has 50 hotels and guest houses, and many more places
offering bed and breakfast, and self-catering accommodation.
But car drivers may find it just as convenient to choose an
inland centre. This is especially true of campers and
caravanners who may find coastal sites rather busy in high
season. In any case more holidaymakers nowadays are finding
the country as attractive as the coast, and prefer activities to
lazing on a beach. The following chapters suggest walks round
various towns and villages, and (for the experienced) longer
hill walks from places like Dalmellington, Straiton, and Barr.

For long enough sportsmen have been attracted to Ayrshire.

Golf holds pride of place, with 28 coastal and 9 inland courses. Enthusiasts for other participatory sports will find facilities for tennis, bowling, squash, swimming, skating, curling, hunting, shooting, fishing, horse-riding, and cycling. Recently there has been a revival of athletics, with numerous half-marathons and fun-runs, as well as track events. The Magnum Leisure Centre at Irvine, opened in 1976, provides for a range of sports and other leisure activities; Kilmarnock has its Galleon Leisure Centre. Spectators are attracted to Scotland's premier race course at Ayr which offers throughout the year 35 days of horse racing, both Flat and National Hunt. Also in season football fans are attracted to Somerset Park in Ayr to watch Ayr United, or to the oddly-named Rugby Park in Kilmarnock, home of Ayrshire's other senior club. Kilmarnock, formed in 1869, is Scotland's second oldest football club; Ayr United was formed by amalgamation in 1910 of two older clubs. There are also 20 junior clubs; a hundred others affiliated to the Ayrshire Amateur Association, and as many juvenile and youth teams playing on Saturdays. Less popular now than in the '30s is greyhound racing, although there are still several local tracks. There has never been more than limited local interest in the few local cricket and rugby clubs. Large crowds of spectators are attracted whenever Ayrshire hosts golf's premier event, the British Open Championship. This was held at Prestwick between 1860 to 1872 and altogether on 20 occasions until 1925; at Troon five times between 1923 and 1982; and at Turnberry in 1977 and 1986.

There is something to be said for avoiding the crowds at such events, and if possible holidaying off-season. Often the weather is just as pleasant, and there may be events which visitors will enjoy. Ayr, for example, has in April the Scottish Grand National and the Ayrshire Agricultural Show; in May the Ayrshire Arts Festival; in June a Burns Festival and a Golf Week; in August Ayr Bowling Tournament and the nationally-renowned Ayr Flower Show; and in September the contest for Ayr Gold Cup at the Western Race Meeting. Throughout the year theatres in Ayr, Kilmarnock, and Irvine provide programmes with professional casts interspersed with amateur productions. Music ranges from orchestral and operatic performances to brass bands and folk groups. There are

For those who prefer to do more than sit on the beach on holiday,
inland Ayrshire has much to offer – though the inexperienced should
not attempt climbing the south face of Loudoun Hill near Darvel.

frequent art exhibitions at Rozelle in Ayr and the Dick Institute in Kilmarnock. The local press carries details of a range of local organisations offering lectures or catering for special interests from archaeology to wine-making.

Subsequent chapters present a series of tours around Ayrshire's towns and countryside. The discerning reader will decide whether to make leisurely trips, inspecting most of the many places mentioned, or to pass quickly along the route and stop only at the principal places of interest.

CHAPTER 12
The County Town

AYR, the county town, is divided unequally into three parts, with the central and most interesting section bounded on the north by the River Ayr, and to the south by the River Doon. The River Ayr and the town hall steeple are easily found features in the town. River Street (339222) on the north side of the river is near both and is a good point from which to explore. Avoid taking a car into the town centre as it can take half an hour to travel the length of High Street at times – and the situation worsens yearly. An inner ring road and an outer by-pass to the east link the north and south sides of the town.

It requires considerable energy and zeal to see all Ayr's attractions at one visit, and space does not allow them all to be listed in one chapter. Two main lineal routes can be followed to the south: on the lines of the New Bridge, Sandgate, and Wellington Square; and Auld Brig, High Street, and Burns Statue Square. These can be linked up along connecting roads by those with extra energy. The River Ayr Walk, in a south-east direction, also requires a separate expedition for the average tourist, but can be linked with the High Street route for the most enthusiastic explorers.

River Street stretches between the Auld Brig and New Bridge. The former is a cobbled medieval bridge (pedestrianised) of four arches with steep approaches. Robert Burns wrote 'The Brigs of Ayr' forecasting correctly that the old would outlast the new, and in 1878 a new New Bridge had to be constructed, and stands today with five spans carrying a heavy burden of vehicular traffic funnelling into and out of the town centre. The Auld Brig was endangered itself soon afterwards and would probably have disappeared by now had Burns not written his poem about it. It was substantially repaired between 1907-10 and is still of great use to the town as well as being a very attractive antiquity.

The Newton Cross stands at the north end of the New Bridge, having been moved from the middle of the Main Street of the burgh of Newton-on-Ayr which was annexed by Ayr in

1873. From the cross you can look northwards past the district library to the former Orient Cinema. The Georgian Newton Steeple opposite the cinema was retained as a compromise when the adjoining council chambers and church were demolished in the 1960s to make way for road expansion. The district library's headquarters are housed in a Carnegie building opened in 1893. As well as lending and reference stocks and exhibitions, the building houses an extensive local collection of books, maps, newspapers, and illustrations. A staircase window by Stephen Adam and Co. commemorates Andrew Carnegie and his gift to Ayr.

The town steeple is seen well from the north end of the New Bridge. It was designed as part of the Assembly Rooms by Thomas Hamilton and erected between 1827-32. The slim 70m-high octagonal clock spire, garlanded with gryphons, columns, urns, and other classical features, is a breathtaking monument to a simpler but ingenious age.

The pleasant approach to the town centre could have been lost had conservationists not fought for the retention of the double bow-fronted building adjoining the New Bridge. With the bow-fronted building across the street, it provides an elegant gateway to the main part of the town and blends with the steeple in a splendid townscape.

Ayr has managed to retain considerable quality in its architecture despite the brazen incomers who would subvert its eight centuries of development for their own quick profit. Loudoun Hall is the oldest building surviving in the town and is found within a small garden to the west of the traffic lights (where the site of the Malt Cross is marked on the road) between the New Bridge and the Town Buildings. Loudoun Hall dates from about the start of the 16th century and was restored from a derelict state in the 20th century – leaving the top floor out of use, but bringing the vaulted ground floor and first-floor hall back to a fit state for use by numerous local organisations and others.

The west gate from the garden leads to the South Harbour at the foot of Fort Street – which has a double bow-fronted Custom House of old on the left and Ayr Academy on the right. Three heads on the wall of the Academy are modelled on Sir David Wilkie, Robert Burns, and James Watt, as

Newton upon Ayr was a separate burgh till it amalgamated with the burgh of Ayr to the south in 1873. Newton's redundant council chambers and the adjoining parish church were demolished in the 1960s for a new road system. As a compromise, the steeple of the town house was retained as a traffic island.

inducements to pupils to emulate their achievements. The early 19th-century church beyond the Academy was transformed into a dance studio and cafeteria in 1984, preserving a fine building by finding an alternative use for it.

Continue along the South Harbour, where the piers of a former railway bridge can be seen in the river. This brought a spur line to the quayside on the south bank from Ayr's first station (whose site is now occupied by the housing development on the north bank). Farther west on the North Harbour, the red and white 19th-century lighthouse and keeper's house beneath are being restored by the Scottish Maritime Museum.

As you head seawards along the South Harbour notice the high ground and high masonry walls on the left. The site of Ayr Castle (1197) is thought to be in this area, while the walls belong to a citadel built here in the 17th century by Cromwell's forces. The hexagonal plan of the citadel shows up well from the air in the present street pattern. The corbelled turret facing the harbour has been dubbed 'Miller's Folly' after the eccentric who bought the 'fort' area in the 19th century and remodelled parts of it to his taste.

The fish market at the South Harbour is a congested and animated area when boats are unloading in the late afternoon. The paddle steamer *Waverley* has operated from the South Harbour and hopefully will continue to do so.

Go between Ayr Baths (1972, designed by Cowie, Torry, and Partners) and the Citadel walls, following a half-hexagon (and bastions) round to Cromwell Road (331221) and turn in towards St John's Tower, which juts above trees and roof line.

The tower is all that remains of a large church which stretched to the east. Robert Bruce held a parliament here in 1315 and Cromwell requisitioned the building for part of his Citadel in 1654. The partly-infilled arched entrance to the Citadel can be seen in a lane north of Citadel Place (33452210).

Go south from St John's Tower by Cassillis Street to the early-19th century porticoed Sheriff Court at the west end of Wellington Square. Regional Council departments occupy the former County Buildings behind, opened in 1931 on the site of the jail. On the sea side of these buildings there is a memorial to the Royal Scots Fusiliers – who occupied the now-demolished barracks to the north; and a fountain (1892) recently renovated in honour of Ayr's twin town, St Germain-en-Laye. The Pavilion, to the south on the edge of the Low Green, dates from 1911 (architect, J.K. Hunter).

Wellington Square was developed at the start of the 19th century as the burgh expanded southwards. It has a formal layout with buildings surrounding a garden area containing a cenotaph designed by J.K. Hunter, a bronze memorial to John Loudon McAdam, and statues of the 13th Earl of Eglinton, Sir James Fergusson, and General Neill. The 19th-century new town stretched east from Wellington Square along Barns Street and southwards along Alloway Place. Barns House (336215) is now the oldest inhabited dwelling in the town.

Turn north-east from Wellington Square past the Baptist Church (built about 1812 as a hall and theatre), into the Sandgate with the Western S.M.T. bus station, the Norman-style former Free Church (1845), the Post Office and its more elegant red sandstone predecessor beyond, at the site of an entrance to the medieval town.

The Sandgate widens here, due to a former Tolbooth once standing in the middle of the street, and contains a fine array of 18th to 20th-century dwellings, banks, and commercial properties, including an elegant shopping precinct at the restored Queen's Court. These blend well – despite some blemishes – and present an attractive townscape looking down the slope to the majestic town steeple.

Weary travellers can return to their starting point from here. Others keen to see more can turn right along the dog-legged Newmarket Street. This pedestrianised thoroughfare joins the High Street under a statue of William Wallace, which stands on a building near the site of the Laigh Tolbooth, where Wallace is thought to have been imprisoned once.

Turn right at the High Street and very soon go left up the Kirkport to the Auld Kirk, which sits beyond a stone lych gate. A pair of mortsafes for protecting graves from body snatchers lie within this arched entrance. The church was built in 1654 to replace the Church of St John the Baptist commandeered by Cromwell for part of his Citadel. Compensation of a thousand marks was paid to the town towards the cost of the new church, as promised in a letter displayed within what is now the Auld Kirk. The tower is all that remains of St John's, but the Auld Kirk continues in use, with an interesting and well-maintained interior.

Among the sculptured headstones in the churchyard, one shows a tradesman at work seated on a stool, another shows a two-masted sailing ship, a third shows a figure apparently on his deathbed, while a fourth has two heads worked on the edge of the stone which features, within a circle, a lion-like animal, a fish, and a hand holding a cross crosslet. A finely-renewed stone shows a writer at a table, while a looker-on rests on his elbow below a figure with sword and scales, and angels

overhead awaiting the outcome. The finest of all is a massive
and corpulent image of this church's first minister, William
Adair, kneeling in prayer on a cushion, within an ornate
classical memorial: a crowned and robed skeleton leers over his
shoulder, while Father Time in the opposite corner balances
his foot on what must be the world but looks like a football! A
headstone to seven Covenanters states:

> Boots thumbkins gibbets were in fashion then
> LORD let us never see such Days again.

Return to the High Street, which shows much good character
yet, despite some deplorable modern developments. The street
funnels to a bottleneck at the Gothic-style Wallace Tower
(1834, architect Thomas Hamilton) which carries another
statue of the patriot Wallace. The southern and newer part of
High Street is more nondescript, but contains the Tam
O'Shanter Museum – a former inn with a thatched roof which
now contains exhibits commemorating Robert Burns.

At the Y-junction follow Alloway Street towards Burns Statue
Square. Much-altered red sandstone buildings (designed by
James A. Morris, a noted local architect) curl round the corners
as Alloway Street widens into the Square. The statue of Burns
(by George A. Lawson) stands in the centre of this square, and
is overlooked by an ugly office block called Burns House,
rented by Kyle and Carrick District Council as its headquarters
– lacking the civic dignity of the Town Buildings. The former
Station Hotel (1886) and the Odeon Cinema (1938), on either
side, do their best to retrieve the honour of the area.

Dalblair Road and Miller Road at the west end of the Square
both lead back to the Georgian expansion of the town south of
the Sandgate. Other roads lead north to the river. A catwalk on
the west side of the rail bridge can be crossed to the north
bank. River Street is a short journey downriver.

The walk upriver from the Auld Brig by either bank can be
recommended. The north bank has been developed with
council offices and housing, including the district's only multi-
storey blocks, constructed by Bison in the 1960s. Two massive
stores on the south bank are oversize for the townscape,
dwarfing the Auld Brig and Auld Kirk and blocking the view
to the town steeple.

The main entry to the town centre of Ayr from the north crosses the River Ayr by the New Bridge. The double bow-fronted building on the left was threatened with demolition in the 1960s but was saved by conservationists. The town steeple designed by Thomas Hamilton soars above the roofline and appears to outstretch the much higher Carrick Hills beyond.

The walk up the south bank is interrupted by the County Hospital, but is soon regained by following a road between the hospital and the well-restored large yellow stone Holmston House, once a poorhouse now the social work headquarters. The walk continues through trees to the Craigholm Bridge (pedestrian) and on past a three-draw limekiln to the stepping stones at the site of the Overmills nearly three miles from the river mouth. Some of the stones are frequently under water, but the road bridge on the Ayr by-pass just to the west guarantees a walk back on the opposite bank.

The 18th-century Craigie House on the north bank, opposite Craigholm Bridge, is used by several departments of the nearby Craigie College of Education. There are formal gardens on the south side of the house, with a great border of pansies stretching several hundred metres along the river.

On the south side of the town are the better-known parks of Belleisle and Rozelle. The A719 passes the entrance to Belleisle while the B7024 runs between the two. Belleisle House is now a hotel while Rozelle House (1750) is a district council museum and art gallery along with the Maclaurin Gallery in former outbuildings attached to the east. The gallery houses visiting exhibitions and has a permanent collection of fine arts, which includes a bronze 'Reclining Figure' by Henry Moore in the courtyard and a number of granite sculptures by Ronald Rae in the grounds.

ALLOWAY to the south is the birthplace of Robert Burns, where multitudes of tourists stop to see the thatched cottage and museum commemorating him. The museum features attractive murals by Ted and Elizabeth Odling and numerous relics of the poet. The village hall opposite was restored by Sir Robert Lorimer in 1929 and was the last commission completed by this famous architect before his death. Half a mile farther south on the B7024 the Land of Burns Centre has an audio-visual theatre and presents a Burns interpretation. It is built at the site of Alloway railway station, near the ruins of Alloway kirk. Burns's father is buried, and his mother commemorated, in front of the two-light window gable of the auld kirk.

The Gothic-style church opposite was opened in 1858 (architect Campbell Douglas) and contains windows by Stephen Adam, C.W. Whall, Clayton and Bell, W. & J.J. Kier, Guthrie

This shelter for dustbins was once the entry to the Cromwellian citadel. Four centuries ago soldiers on horseback may have ridden through this archway, but since the abandonment of 'the fort' the ditch has been filled in and the surface of the lane built up. One of Ayr's lesser known monuments, it may be seen behind Ayr Academy, with access off Citadel Place.

and Wells, and Douglas McLundie. The last artist has designed a fine memorial to D.F. McIntyre who took part in the first flight over Everest in 1933. The window shows the mountain and one of the successful biplanes.

A square-section tunnel curving under this area used to take trains to the Doon Viaduct. The road bridge gives a view downriver to the viaduct and in the other direction to the Auld Brig O' Doon, made famous in Burns's poem 'Tam O'Shanter'. The eastern approach to the old bridge passes between the tea gardens and the Burns Monument – a classical open temple designed by Thomas Hamilton and erected in 1820. It contains good sculptures of Tam O'Shanter and Souter Johnnie and other Burns relics.

The Sandgate displays an impressive facade of shops and dwellings under the soaring steeple fronting the town hall. The width of this street is due to a tolbooth which once sat in the middle of the road.

CHAPTER 13
The Carrick Coast

Carrick lies south and west of the River Doon. Take the A719 through Ayr's expanding suburb of Doonfoot, for splendid coastal scenery.

Greenan Castle is conspicuous on its now undercut cliff-top site and stands inside a bailey protected by a ditch on the landward side. The door carries the date 1603, commemorating the marriage of John Kennedy of Baltersan, whose initials are decipherable, though not those of his spouse. This ruinous tower is a stark and imposing sight from the shore below, a reminder of times when the Kennedys dominated Carrick.

Greenan farm to the south shows a lime kiln with an access ramp to the side. The Deil's Dyke to the west of the castle is a rocky rib formed by volcanic intrusion projecting above the shoreline and running into the sea.

A bay curves between the dyke and the Heads of Ayr with Butlin's Holiday World occupying the hill slope to the south. A chairlift transports campers up the slope to the A719 while outsiders can walk the right of way alongside the western perimeter fence. A memorial stone inside the camp commemorates H.M.S. *Scotia,* the naval training station established here in 1942 and converted to a holiday camp in 1947. It was served by special trains from England until 1968.

The Heads of Ayr can be inspected from below if tides allow. The impressive volcanic cliffs are unsound to climb. A promontory fort (285187) sits above the cliffs where the coast turns into Bracken Bay. A right of way leads down to the bay. To the west, the cliff line advances and steepens up again, making shoreline walking subject to the tides.

The A719 has been taking a higher route – looking to the sea and inland to the good farms under the Carrick Hills. Perryston was designed as a model farm by Ninian Johnston in 1939. You can take your car up Brown Carrick Hill by a narrow road at Genoch farm. An indicator by the road gives wide views to Arran, Ayr Bay, and Highland hills such as Ben

Lomond, Stobinian – and even Ben More (Mull) at 88 miles. The road continues down to join the B7024.

The A719 contours round the western slopes of the Carrick Hills paralleled by the line of the railway which once linked Ayr with Girvan along the coast. After Fisherton Church look out for the ruined Dunduff Castle (272164) on the hill above. South-west of Dunduff farm there are remains of the medieval parish church of Kirkbride, on the line of the 18th-century coast road.

DUNURE is a fishing village reached by a minor road looping off the A719. Go past the harbour to park at the playing fields beside Dunure Castle. The Castle was a cliff-top tower of the 14th century, extended considerably with the addition of ranges stretching inland. It is notorious for an event in 1570 when the 4th Earl of Cassillis roasted the Commendator of Crossraguel before a fire to force him to sign away the lands belonging to the abbey. The ruinous tower, having defied the elements for centuries, faced its greatest threat in 1973 when Ayr County Council debated its future. One councillor argued that the ruin was only of local interest, while another saw it as a relic of the feudal system, which deserved to be removed from the fair county of Ayr. But Dunure Castle has outlived Ayr County Council, to remind us not only of the greed and cruelty of usurpers, but also of the folly of some of our elected representatives. A 16th-century dovecot of beehive shape stands to the east of the castle, and nearby are two single-draw lime kilns.

The harbour was built about 1811 and has a small tapering light tower above the basin, with weird shapes carved into the stone by erosion. Few fishing boats are seen in the harbour now but pleasure craft find it a haven. An L-shaped layout of buildings formed the original settlement. Note the arched rock on the beach at the end of Seaview, the single-storey terrace facing the sea. Harbourview is the terrace facing north, starting as a single-storey cottage at the top of the hill and finishing as a two-storey shop at the harbour. Dunure House to the north dates from the early 19th century.

The loop to Dunure rejoins the A719 at Dunure Mains. Those who have followed the high road have enjoyed good views of Dunure below and Ailsa Craig, Kintyre, and even

Greenan Castle is a 17th-century tower house sitting on a cliff and defended by earthworks on the inland side. Elderly locals can recall from their youth when it was possible to walk around the tower above the cliffs. Erosion is steadily wearing away the cliff-face and will one day bring about the fall of the tower.

Ireland. Dunure Mains was the home of 'The Baron of Buchlyvie', a champion Clydesdale stallion which sold in 1911 for a record sum of £9,500. Dunure Mill is an 18th-century secular building, despite its crosses and twin and triple-windowed ecclesiastical style.

As the A719 turns round the south-west flanks of the Carrick Hills the road appears to descend Croy Brae. In reality it is ascending for this is the famous Electric Brae where there is an optical illusion caused by conflicting ingredients in the landscape. Visitors may test the hill for themselves and see if they can roll 'up' the slope – but beware of other traffic! The 25-inch O.S. map shows a rise of 13 feet between the west and east ends of the hill despite what appears to be a descent. A side road runs down to a bathing beach on Croy shore.

There are views down the coast to Culzean Castle and Turnberry lighthouse, before the road turns inland to Pennyglen, where at the T-junction the A719 is joined by the B7023 from Maybole. Mochrum Hill (270m) is a volcanic intrusion rising south of the road junction. It gives a good view over the coast line and a distant inland view of Crossraguel Abbey over Mochrum Loch. From the road, looking back to the skyline of the Carrick Hills, a circular fort (277118) can be seen. A quarry in that same area near the lonely ruin of Howmoor cottage is of geological interest for its exposures of conchoidal fracturing. On a road near Cargilston there is an obelisk to Covenanting martyrs (295110). On the A719 at Pennyglen Lodge (264109) a narrow road to the shore passes an overgrown dun at Balchriston (257111) and drops to an end at Goats Green on Culzean Bay. A 19th-century cottage here has been converted into a fine modern house.

Culzean Castle is a property of the National Trust for Scotland, which also runs the Culzean Country Park on behalf of the local authorities. On the drive in from the A719, the Country Park Centre is reached first, then the Castle. Both have car parks, and there are others at the Walled Garden and the Swan Lake, which last is handy for the shore at Port Carrick. The park centre was created from the Home Farm and won a European Architectural Heritage Year Award in 1975. This restored Adam complex now incorporates an information and exhibition wing, restaurant, and other facilities. The exhibition area portrays the story of Culzean and those who have lived and worked in the area since the 18th century when the 10th Earl of Cassillis engaged Robert Adam to design a stately home for him. The resulting castellated mansion built round an ancient tower house is famous for its magnificent cantilevered oval staircase surmounted by two floors ringed with classical columns, and the round drawing room which forms a great drum tower above the cliffs. An Eisenhower Room explains the U.S. general and president's connection with Culzean, where

Culzean Castle was designed by Robert Adam for David Kennedy the 10th Earl of Cassillis and built on the site of an older keep. In 1945 the castle was presented to the nation and it is now cared for by the National Trust for Scotland who also look after the estate as a country park in association with local authorities. The Victorian West Wing is divided into flats and is just seen above the Orangery.

he enjoyed the tenancy of a flat as a gift from the people of Scotland for his wartime services.

The cliffs below the Castle are pierced with caves, which probably hid smuggled cargoes at times and have at some time in the past been enclosed by masonry and doors. A boat shed, launching ramp and little harbour recall the yachting enthusiasm of the 3rd Marquis of Ailsa, which encouraged the development of shipbuilding at Ayr and Troon.

Back on the A719, Thomaston Castle (240095) adjoins the Marquis of Ailsa's Kennels at a back entry to Culzean. It is a 16th-century L-plan tower with two re-entering angles, in one

of which is a high pended doorway. As the road drops to the
coast it passes below the line of the old railway, just to the south
of which is a mound, visible from the road and known as
Shanter Knowe, which may have been a motte (219074).

MAIDENS is a popular holiday village with layers of houses,
caravans, and chalets behind a sandy beach. The harbour has a
breakwater zig-zagging out to the Maidenhead Rocks, but the
entrance is narrow and suitable only for small craft. Notice
above the shore the tall chimneyed brick-built chambers
holding cast-iron pots – in the past preserving brews were
boiled up in these for treating nets. A small tower stands on a
hill south-west of the harbour, with a standing stone one field
beyond it. The Bruce Hotel at the sea front exploits a local
hero with a fine wall sculpture by Bruce Weir. It shows Robert
the Bruce in the famous incident when the dispirited king was
encouraged to try again by a spider's refusal to accept defeat in
spinning its web.

Turnberry Castle (197072) was the home of a widowed
Countess of Carrick who is reputed to have kidnapped the son
of the lord of Annandale before marrying him in 1271. Their
son, Robert Bruce, was born in 1274, probably at Turnberry.
The future victor at Bannockburn returned from exile to land
near Turnberry in 1307 when, reputedly taking heart from the
spider, he began a long fight back for his throne. There is little
left of this castle. The lighthouse was built at the heart of the
site and lit in 1873. Turnberry is the land base for helicopters
serving the light on Ailsa Craig twelve miles off to sea.

The airfield inland from the golf course, still used by small
planes, was a base in two world wars. There is a memorial on
the golf course east of the lighthouse to British, Australian, and
American airmen.

Turnberry Hotel is conspicuous with its long red tile roof
and cream-painted walls. The hotel was constructed by the
Glasgow and South Western Railway Company (architect,
James Miller) and opened in 1906 to coincide with the
inauguration of their new railway from Ayr to Girvan along the
coast. Rail passenger services between Alloway and Turnberry
closed in 1930 and Girvan to Turnberry services in 1942.
Turnberry's Ailsa golf course has been the venue for the Open
Championship on several occasions since, and congestion on

Girvan is the largest town in Carrick and has a harbour in which fishing boats are becoming scarcer and pleasure craft more numerous. The port has been formed at the mouth of the River Girvan which rises in the Southern Uplands to the south of the boundary fault marked by the hills in the distance.

the roads would have been less if the railway had been retained! And a train service on this picturesque line serving Butlins and Culzean could now be a moneymaker – but alas the line is dismantled.

The A77 from Maybole joins the A719 at Turnberry. Along its route it passes the L-plan 16th-century castle ruin of Baltersan. Then there is Crossraguel Abbey, founded by the Cluniac order in the 13th century and now an Ancient Monument. Most of the remains are from later periods including a fairly intact gatehouse and a considerable part of the abbey church, the Abbot's Tower, chapter house, refectory, dovecote, and other work.

Farther west on the A77 is the village of KIRKOSWALD. The National Trust for Scotland looks after Souter Johnnie's Cottage which was built in 1785 and occupied by John Davidson, the souter (or shoemaker). Robert Burns took the real man and transformed him into an immortal supporting character of fiction in his poem 'Tam O'Shanter'. Life-size stone figures of Tam, the Souter, the innkeeper and his wife –

sculptured by James Thom — are to be seen in the restored ale house in the garden behind the thatched cottage museum. Across the road the old parish church is a roofless ruin surrounded by headstones. John Davidson is here, along with Douglas Graham — who was the model for Tam O' Shanter — and a number of others associated with Burns. A new church was opened in 1777 on the hill to the south. It contains a Culzean loft for the Earl of Cassillis and shows the style of Robert Adam who was working for the 10th Earl at the time. The former Free Church (1851) to the north has been converted into a dwelling. The attractive Richmond Hall at the east end of the village was opened in 1924, and was named after Sir John Richmond whose fine house at Blanefield (1914) can be seen across the fields to the east. Both buildings were designed by James Miller.

The A77 continues south of Turnberry, running along the edge of a raised beach under the ancient coast line. Dowhill (203029) has an earthwork fortification commanding a clear view of the area. A seaweed processing factory across the road produces derivatives for a wide range of industrial uses. A chapel once stood at Chapeldonan (195005) where ground to the west is now reserved by the South of Scotland Electricity Board for a possible nuclear power station. Nearer Girvan there is the Grangeston Industrial Estate, where the whisky distillery is open to visitors by appointment. Road re-alignment near Girvan Mains recently revealed remains of a Roman marching camp. A former early 19th-century mill stands between the B741 and the River Girvan.

A stone by the roundabout north of Girvan is a memorial to Constable Alexander Ross. In April 1831 a procession through the town for parliamentary reform was attacked by Orangemen. In retaliation, on 12th July as Orangemen arrived for their traditional parade, they were met at the Dailly road-end by townspeople determined to prevent them from proceeding. In the ensuing riot Ross was shot and fatally wounded.

The A77 enters GIRVAN, passing the attractive railway station. The railway from Ayr in 1860 was laid to the harbour, with a terminus which later became the goods yard. Extension of the railway to Stranraer in 1877 required this new station to serve the line which here begins its ascent to conquer the 1 in 60 gradient to the south.

There is a convenient car park beside the information centre just before the town-centre traffic lights. Cross the A77 to the old churchyard with its pyramid and baluster decorated walls, and enter by the triumphal arch. These were erected in 1907-08 as a memorial to his parents by Alexander Johnston. The massive entrance was designed by James A. Morris and contains a bronze tablet by Robert Bryden. Among the varied memorials here is one to Alexander Ross, the constable shot at the Dailly road end. There are a number of interesting pictorial carvings including a figure standing within what appears to be a cruck-frame arch. Several slabs are thought to be medieval, with incised crosses or swords. One is dated 1681.

Face back along Old Street towards the station but turn right, opposite the Ailsa Arms Hotel, into Montgomerie Street. The North Parish Church in Early English Gothic style has a spire 46 metres high rising above its competitors in the town. It was opened in 1884 to the design of J. McKissock and W.G. Rowan. Internally a frieze and ceiling decoration are of note, depicting the elements in Creation.

Beyond the attractive police station turn up the Avenue, with its substantial dwellings. Past the public gardens is the Davidson Hospital – a neo-Georgian building with bowed ends, designed by Watson, Salmond, and Gray and opened in 1921. Its light-coloured stonework and grey-green patinated slates blend admirably.

Return to Church Square with its fountain. St Andrew's Church built in 1870 is no longer used for worship. Hamilton Street has some good 19th-century commerical buildings – particularly the round-arched premises of the rival building societies. The Italianate former bank building at the traffic lights was designed by Peddie and Kinnear in 1856.

The McMaster Hall at the traffic lights was burned down and the 18th-century townhouse tower and steeple known as Stumpy have been left isolated on a rather self-conscious gap site. Go south along Dalrymple Street which has some good buildings including a bank building of 1863 by David McGibbon, a dignified 19th-century post office, and the McKechnie Institute in Scots Baronial style designed by

E

McKissock and Rowan. This library and reading room was opened in 1888. The library has moved to Montgomerie Street and 'The McKechnie' now houses regular exhibitions. Behind it in Ailsa Street West there is a walled garden, open during museum hours, featuring scented plants and shrub roses, and a relief mural is under construction.

Continue along Dalrymple Street to the Methodist Church on the corner of Wesley Road. This is a fine Arts and Crafts style building by Watson and Salmond dating from 1903. The adjoining hall was added in 1926, and was a 'do-it-yourself' but very sympathetic design by the church's own minister, Rev. Arthur B. Cannon. Would that more ministers and congregations had some architectural training!

Also at the south end of the town, off Dalrymple Street in Piedmont Road is St John's Scottish Episcopal Church (186971). This was built in 1857, but the planned transepts and tower have never been completed. The church contains a notable 16th-century oak chancel screen of Italian workmanship brought from Brougham Hall, Penrith. The east window is by Gordon Webster.

From Dalrymple Street turn west into Duff Street and cross Wilson Street (in which the first Methodist Church of 1823 is situated at the north end). Notice the narrower streets in this area and the single-storey rows – a pattern established by the handloom weavers who once lived and worked here.

Duff Street leads to Henrietta Street and Stair Park on the sea front. A tall granite memorial dominates the park, while a pavilion on the south side has attractive cast-iron work. The local cricket club uses the pavilion and uneven park. The South Parish Church on the corner of the park dates from 1842.

Go north along the promenade, where a memorial fountain (1927), and a now somewhat amended willow-pattern design boating pond by James Wright, are to be found. There is a good sandy beach, and other attractions for visitors. The harbour has some commercial fishing and opportunities for sea angling and pleasure sailing, including trips to Ailsa Craig.

From the harbour turn inland along Knockcushan Street. There is a public garden with an aviary behind Knockcushan House. The house is used for council offices. A memorial in the garden commemorates the holding of a court here in 1328

The rugged granite isle of Ailsa Craig rears out of the Firth of Clyde ten miles off Girvan and can be reached from there in summer when some boatmen allow several hours ashore – enough time for the fit to reach the summit or walk around the shoreline if the tide is out. For an hour or two at low tide the doorstep to the Water Cave is uncovered and the slippery rocks can be crossed with caution.

by King Robert I. Notice a 19th-century two-storey Italianate range bearing a central pediment above an arched entrance. You are now back at the traffic lights near the start of the walk.

Opposite the information centre the road past a former cinema leads to a bridge across the River Girvan and the north side of the harbour, where there is a boat-building yard. Notice where the railway crossed the river at one time. Grass-grown ridges and depressions show where wagons were trundled to and from the loading bays above the harbour. You may continue on a walk along the shore to the north, and round half of the golf course, returning over Knock-a-Vaillie, which gives a fine view of the town.

AILSA CRAIG is one of Ayrshire's most spectacular but least visited attractions. A number of boatmen make the ten-mile crossing from Girvan in summer and will land you on the Craig for a few hours if tides allow. The lighthouse, occupying a boulder beach on the east coast, has operated since 1886. Remains can be seen of the former gas preparation plant, and the old foghorns on north and south shores; also the buildings and tram lines required when the fine-grained micro-granite was once quarried for curling stones, kerbstones, and setts.

A ruinous castle perched high on a shoulder of the island is reached by an airy path which continues past a small loch to the summit. The castle had three storeys and carries the Hamilton coat of arms – Thomas Hamilton being entrusted to defend it in 1597 after an unsuccessful attempt by Hew Barclay of Ladyland to seize it for Philip of Spain.

Ailsa Craig has one of the largest colonies of gannets in the British Isles and these can be seen from the Ayrshire coast diving headlong into the firth in pursuit of fish. It is possible to walk around the base of the Craig at low tide passing under the columnar cliffs where they breed. The Water Cave at the south-west corner of the island is passable only at low tide.

Leaving Girvan, the A77 and A714 go their separate ways from a roundabout at the south end of Girvan. A track goes up into the hills from the road behind the roundabout. It climbs over the railway and passes north of Dow Hill (158m), an ancient fort and good viewpoint. This old route continues past the Laggan Loch, drops down to Tormitchell and the Water of Assel valley, then climbs from Dupin over Auchensoul Hill to Barr. A much shorter hill walk, with fine sea views, begins by climbing the prominent Byne Hill (214m), from whose summit a ridge continues past Grey Hill (297m) to Pinbain Hill (224m) before a steep descent to the coast. En route there is a monument to Lord Ardmillan, a Scottish judge who died in 1876, looking down to his burnt-out mansion and the caravans around it.

The A77 follows the coast and at Kennedy's Pass goes between the cliff and a large upstanding rock. A short way to the south where the cliff ends you can see (looking north) a profile of Queen Victoria in the rock formations just inland of the road. Near Lendalfoot a memorial stone by the road (133903) commemorates the master and crew of a ship from Arran drowned in a shipwreck of 1711. There is another monument on a knowe (134899) in memory of Charles Berry, a local naturalist.

Lendalfoot is a popular holiday area with a well-screened caravan park, an outdoor centre in the former school, and timber-built chalets in varied styles of the last fifty years. On the minor road inland to Colmonell, the ruined tower of Carleton Castle (133896) stands beside a farm, with a motte across the road. Balsalloch Hill (187m) is a steep little hill which gives an uninterrupted view along this splendid coast line.

Not far south is Games Loup (103880) where the False Sir John of Carleton had the reprehensible habit of throwing his wives to their deaths into the sea until the eighth threw him instead. An even more celebrated and grisly legend tells of Sawney Bean and his family of cannibals preying on travellers passing Bennane Head (091866). From the big lay-by at the summit a steep path drops in a Z-bend to the cove below. It is not signposted, for the local authority was afraid of tourists falling on to the rocks. In fact it is an easy enough descent for the careful well-shod visitor. A gully gives access from the shore over a fallen rock to 'Sawney Bean's Cave', which is wide, high, and well-lit at the entrance, though it narrows and lowers as it runs in 30 metres. A more likeable cave dweller was 'Snib' Torbet whose memorial is at the Bennane Lea (091860) where he died in 1983 after many years as a recluse.

The A77 coast road now crosses cultivated fields on the raised beach as it heads south for Ballantrae. The former cliff line lies well back from the sea, and on the skyline one notices a ruinous windmill tower (090833). It is cylindrical in shape with arched stonework internally.

BALLANTRAE lies north of the mouth of the River Stinchar. The church, built in 1819, has a small red-sandstone clock tower and grey spire added in 1891. There are memorials inside the church to David MacGibbon, the architect; a postman who died in a blizzard at the top of Glenapp; and a gamekeeper who died in another blizzard on Beneraird. The churchyard to the south has the Kennedy Aisle, which formed part of the old church built about 1604. The Aisle contains a grand memorial to Gilbert Kennedy of Bargany who was slain at Maybole in 1601 by the Earl of Cassillis in a mafia-style family feud. There are some interesting old headstones in the yard outside.

A road between church and churchyard passes the old manse

and turns along the shore front to the harbour with its stone-flagged quay. Ballantrae was once a calling point for the Stranraer to Glasgow steamer but all ships pass well out to sea now and only small fishing boats and pleasure craft frequent the haven. The harbour is more than a mile north of the river mouth. The Stinchar is diverted south by a spit formed by the shingle, which juts southwards from the edge of the village to form a nature reserve where the oyster plant grows; and arctic, common, and little terns breed. Access is restricted in the summer.

Ardstinchar Castle commands the river crossing. Once an imposing tower on rocky ground at the south end of a ridge, it has been plundered of its stone for other uses, but the south end remains, seemingly defying gravity. An attractive 18th-century bridge below, with two main arches and one approach arch, has been superseded by a plain bridge to the west. The new bridge speeds the traffic but cannot attract the photographers as the old one did, with its curved refuges, mortise and tenon jointed parapet, and toll house at the north end. There are standing stones at Garleffin to the south (087817).

The B7044 runs inland along the north bank of the River Stinchar to Colmonell. Knockdolian (265m) was designated by sailors as 'the False Craig' since navigators could confuse it with Ailsa. An ascent of this spectacular little hill is a most cost-effective expedition for the rewards it offers for energy expended. The north and south faces are steep, so take it by the SW or NE ridges. The winding Stinchar is laid out below, threading its way from the Galloway hills by way of Colmonell to its estuary, and the seascape extends to Ireland. Over the north-east side of the hill you can look down on a small boss of rock jutting up from the fields of Bougang farm. It is crowned with a fort called Duniewick. There are two single-draw lime kilns to the west of Bougang (115856).

Foliage may make it difficult to observe the small tower called Knockdolian Castle (123854); or Kirkhill Castle (145859) at the west end of COLMONELL. This is a linear settlement with some attractive one and two-storey buildings along the Main Street and Manse Road. The parish church was built in 1772, with 19th-century alterations, some by Robert Lorimer.

The Bargany Aisle in the kirkyard at Ballantrae is a memorial to Gilbert Kennedy of Bargany and Ardstinchar who was killed in a fight with his near relative the Earl of Cassillis in 1601. The aisle was part of a church erected in 1604 which has been replaced by the church seen in the background.

It has good interior work with linenfold decoration on the oak pulpit and reredos, and an organ by Norman and Beard. The three-light west window behind the pulpit by Louis Davis is outstanding. A nativity window by the same artist flanks it on the north, beside another fine example by Douglas Strachan. The south side has works by Ballantine and Gardiner; and Powell and Sons.

A memorial above the vestry door commemorates John Snell, founder of the Snell Exhibition bursary. Snell was born in the parish at Almont – where there is a memorial to him on the 'motte' (188873). He became an eminent lawyer and Seal Bearer to Charles II. In his will he conveyed the revenues of his estate at Ufton in Warwickshire to be applied in perpetuity for the promotion of learning. The ablest graduate at Glasgow University is sent to Balliol College, Oxford, under the terms.

The churchyard contains a recumbent slab memorial to Snell's parents; a headstone to Matthew McIlwraith, Covenanting martyr; some old pictorial stones, including one showing a plough team of four horses; and the McConnel Mausoleum. This is dated 1663 or 1665 and carries the builder's name – John Masoune of Ayr – probably the John Masonn whose grave is in the old kirkyard at Ayr, where he built the kirk in 1655.

Across the Stinchar, Craigneil Castle sits on a rocky site. Once it was a halfway house for the Kennedys journeying between Cassillis and Castle Kennedy. It survives, badly cracked, despite quarrying operations and a mysterious explosion one night in 1968.

Bardrochat, on a higher vantage point, was designed by George M. Watson, and altered by Robert Lorimer in 1906. The hill road passing it reaches the Water of Tig where there is a mound known as Peden's Pulpit (173832), and downriver a ruinous settlement of close-standing rubble-built dwellings (159824). At Kirkholm may be seen the ruins of Kirkcudbright Innertig church (117838) which was the parish church until one was built at Ballantrae in 1604.

The A77 heading south from Ballantrae towards Stranraer deserts the coast after it crosses the Stinchar. To the west there are some farm roads which split and degenerate into tracks, reaching towards the rocky coves which punctuate this remote and seldom-visited coastal stretch. To the east of the A77, intrepid walkers or cyclists may take a narrow road to Kilwhannel, which continues as a hill track past the summit of Beneraird (439m) to drop down by Lagafater Lodge to the Main Water of Luce and ultimately New Luce or Craigcaffie on Loch Ryan in Wigtownshire. It is worth pushing a bicycle up the hill for the big advantage it offers on the return journey.

The A77 on its climb to the south passes Glenapp Castle (094808), a baronial mansion designed by David Bryce and built in 1870. A monument west of the summit of the road commemorates Robert Cunningham, the postman who died here in 1908 during a snowstorm. Although the climate of south-west Scotland is temperate, this area can suffer very disturbed spells, as testified by the ragged snow fences which line the road here. Carlock Hill (319m) gives a good view over Kilantringan Loch to Ballantrae.

The A77 makes a curving descent to Glen App from heather moors through a dark plantation to flatten out in a green valley. Glenapp Church is an attractive little building, with a porch and bellcote. Dating from 1849, it was altered in 1910, and again in 1928 when the chancel arch was raised to accommodate a memorial window to Miss Elsie Mackay who was killed attempting a transatlantic flight. The three-light window by Kelley and Co. carries the likeness of this remarkable lady in the panel on the right. Her father, Lord Inchcape, is commemorated by the fine west window opposite by Douglas Strachan, by another window on the south, and by a tomb behind the church.

The A77 rejoins the coast at Finnart's Bay and turns along Loch Ryan to cross the Galloway Burn into Wigtownshire.

CHAPTER 14

Maybole and Inland Carrick

The A77 and the railway use the valley of the River Doon as they run south from Ayr. The railway crosses to the valley of the River Girvan but the road takes a more northerly but parallel course to the river as they run towards the sea. The road crosses the Doon by a modern bridge beside the now redundant Monkwood Bridge of 1798.

The Coats Memorial church at the entrance to Minishant was designed in Early French Gothic style by Thomson and Turnbull of Glasgow and opened in 1878 with a library and reading room behind. The church was non-sectarian with different ministers conducting services alternately. It has now been sold for conversion to a dwelling.

The B7024 from Ayr passes the 16th-century Newark Castle and runs parallel to the A77 at a higher level. 'Wallace's Stone' at Blairstone Mains is a large boulder on which is the outline of a sword or cross (332165). The road bends through Culroy past the smithy, where an old roundel gives the interesting if not entirely relevant mileage to Ayr 5, Maybole 3, and London 398.

MAYBOLE developed as a route centre on the south-east side of the Carrick Hills. Ten roads converge on the town from all directions. Only two of these are normally busy, funnelling heavy traffic through the narrow High Street which has to serve as a section of the A77. The town slopes steeply down a hill with the A77 contouring across its middle. Narrow streets, high buildings, and traffic prevent a proper appreciation of the town from a vehicle, so park if you have one, in the town hall car park by the A77 and take a short walk.

The town hall dates from 1887 and has been grafted on to a higher 17th-century tolbooth tower, once part of the town residence of the lairds of Blairquhan. There are some good 19th-century buildings to the south-west where the main road becomes Whitehall. The Royal Bank of Scotland dates from 1857 and was designed by Peddie and Kinnear. Go along Carrick Street from the start of Whitehall and turn right into

Ladyland Road to the Town Green. Some of the buildings grouped around the edge of the square were built in the first half of the 19th century, and the red sandstone railway station dates from 1880. The footbridge and the roadbridge to the west give access to the upper part of the town. Culzean Road and Cargill Road running just above the railway contain a good variety of the larger houses in town and the tiny St Oswald's Scottish Episcopal Church dating from the end of the 19th century.

Go east from the station along the lower part of Culzean Road. The former Free Church on the left is ruinous and its future appears bleak. While it lasts, look for a stone on the outer wall commemorating a conventicle held by the Covenanters. Return towards the station and turn left down Castle Street to the High Street. Many of the properties here date from the 19th century with some good 20th-century infills – and some bad. Look for the metal cross lying flush in the middle of the road above the traffic lights, on the site of the town cross. The white bust of Robert Burns on a shop stands above the traditional meeting place for the first time of his parents.

The Castle stands high above the A77 at the junction of six streets. At one time it almost blocked off this end of the town and the High Street was a cul-de-sac. The building is 4½ storeys high, dates from about the 16th or 17th century and is a powerful symbol of Kennedy power in the capital of Carrick. The castle features in the ballad of Johnnie Faa, who, as King of the Gypsies, persuaded a Countess of Cassillis to run off with him, but was overtaken and hanged with his band. The little oriel window facing up High Street is reputedly the Countess's room where she was imprisoned for the rest of her life. The window is decorated with sculptured heads, which tends to confirm the story, while there are more heads above the crow steps – but similar versions of the tale appear elsewhere.

The post office (1913) across from the Castle is an elegant building – it had to be to please the neighbours! Next to it stands a Carnegie Library of 1906. A complex of industrial buildings occupied the sloping ground between the diverging St Cuthbert's Street and St Cuthbert's Road. One of the town's boot and shoe factories was here – an industry which made Maybole famous but has now almost died out in the district. Go north-east along Cassillis Street where there are attractive 19th-century two-storey dwellings with pleasing detailing. The Old Parish Church has an astonishing lumpen steeple which looks as though it has been designed by a beginner. It was opened in 1809 and has windows by J. & W. Guthrie Ltd and Stephen Adam and Son. The 19th-century engineering works to the east made agricultural implements but has been much altered and reduced in size.

Cross the main road opposite it and turn back along Kirkland Street passing the R.C. and Cairn Primary Schools. The latter dates from 1890 and was designed by Morris and Hunter. Continuing parallel to the High Street you come to the old graveyard where there are some interesting monuments as well as the Collegiate Church. A chapel, founded here in 1371, was made Collegiate by 1382. A 14th-century lancet window faces south here but the early-looking doorway was built later.

Leave the oldest building in town and ascend the very steep John Knox Street back to your starting point. A plaque on the last house on the left marks the site where the Abbot of Crossraguel and John Knox argued over the doctrine of the Mass for three days in 1562. The result was described as a draw by Rev. Roderick Lawson, author of a number of books on the area.

The West Church (296096) built in 1842 was Lawson's charge from 1863-97 and he is commemorated there, along with Sir James Fergusson of Kilkerran, in bronzes by Robert Bryden. A tall war memorial stands above this church and looks over the golf course to the Girvan valley. The R.C. Church to the south-east was opened in 1878 and has interesting decoration. The interior shows Corinthian columns of Peterhead granite and sixteen sculptured heads of saints. Numerous heads of individual form decorate the sandstone exterior as well.

From Maybole take the B7023. You can continue by Crosshill and Dailly (as later described) or branch off for Kirkmichael and Straiton.

KIRKMICHAEL is grouped about a triangle of roads with the Patna road turning awkwardly round the church at the east

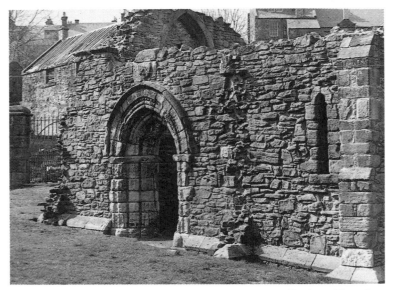

In 1373 the Kennedys of Dunure established a Collegiate Church at Maybole. The ruins date from the 15th century and can be found in Abbot Street.

end of the village. The church was opened in 1787 and is entered through a round-arched lych gate. Many of the houses in the village were built as weaving cottages, and terraces of these good-quality 18th and 19th-century dwellings look set to last for centuries yet. Some of the houses show snecked stonework patterns in which a layer of small squared stones alternates with larger blocks. The northern part of the village is the oldest and most interesting.

There are two lime kilns at Troquhain (377098) and a roofless 18th-century dovecot at Drumfad (360080).

Cloncaird Castle (358075) dates from the 16th century but was substantially rebuilt in the 19th century with a drum tower in the castle style. The interior was subsequently and splendidly reconstructed in the Edwardian era.

Blairquhan (366054) is a Regency-style mansion of 1824 designed by William Burn. It is open to the public in summer and contains a good collection of paintings and furniture and a museum.

STRAITON nearby is a charming village with a short Main Street of great character. East of the village shop and the Black Bull Hotel (which is dated 1766 over a window) two rows of stone cottages face each other across the street in harmony. The south-facing row is greatly enhanced whenever possible by colourful floral displays in the ground available at the edge of the street, while the north-facing neighbours do their bit with pots and boxes of plants to brighten the shade. The War Memorial and the 18th-century former manse close off the east end of the street and your eyes are drawn upwards over the trees to the monument on Craigengower commemorating Colonel Blair of Blairquhan who died at the Battle of Inkerman in 1854.

The church dates mainly from 1758 and was restored in 1901, when a pre-Reformation wing subsequently used as a burial aisle for the lairds of Blairquhan was incorporated with the main building. The churchyard contains some interesting stones. Two stones commemorate Thomas MacHaffie (a Covenanting martyr) beside a very poignant family memorial bearing the chiselled figures of six sons and three daughters who died early in life. There are other pictorial representations including a plough team of four horses; Adam and Eve; and the cogged wheels of a miller (?).

A short distance along the B741 towards Dalmellington a scenic walk (385052) goes uphill on to Sclenteuch Moor. The track to Patna by Loch Spallander reservoir is still present among the firebreaks of recent afforestation but is for experienced walkers only. The best views are to Straiton and the Girvan valley in the first mile. A mile farther up the B741 there is a parking place and walk in honour of Lady Hunter Blair provided by Blairquhan estate. The walk goes upstream through woodland by the Lamdoughty Burn which tumbles over a succession of waterfalls in its glen. The greatest fall is called the Black Linn or Rossetti's Linn from an incident in which D.G. Rossetti, the melancholic poet, is reported to have almost thrown himself over.

A hilly road to Newton Stewart runs south from Straiton up the Girvan valley, becoming wilder and lonelier as it climbs.

A side road to Tairlaw passes within sound but not sight of Tairlaw Linn (408010). The ruins of an old farmstead (426004) with a grain kiln, turf dykes, and rig and furrow cultivation face Knockdon from slopes west of the river. In 1913 a water supply works was opened at Loch Bradan. A low masonry dam at the north end made it and Loch Lure one sheet of water. A 30 metres high mass concrete gravity dam was completed in 1972 north of the original and now submerged dam, with a subsidiary dam at the west end of Loch Lure. Doon of Waterhead (437988) gives a good view of the reservoir as well as Derclach Loch and Loch Finlas.

Back on the hill road to the south, the rest of the county lies within the Galloway Forest Park. Plantings of the 1940s and '50s are now being cut down and views long enclosed are opening up again. Stinchar Bridge is an attractive picnic spot with forest walks to the west to a fine waterfall and high viewpoint of the river valley, and to the east to a rocky hill top, a lonely loch, and exciting hill and river scenery. A side road goes east from Stinchar Bridge to Ballochbeatties where a hill path may be followed to Loch Brecbowie (432960) or a forest road can be walked to Loch Doon.

A large sign marks the summit of the Straiton-Newton Stewart road at 1407 feet (429m) and it is a convenient place to start from for an ascent of Ayrshire's highest hill – Shalloch on Minnoch (769m). Apart from a short drop from a lesser northern top, the ascent is straightforward for experienced walkers in good weather. It can be featureless, confusing, and dangerous for anyone in bad weather.

The road now drops into the valley of the Water of Minnoch, a major tributary of the River Cree. A road from Barr and Crosshill comes through the impressive Nick of the Balloch to meet the Straiton road at Rowantree Toll. Just north of the junction there is a car park, picnic site, and a cairn with a bronze relief map of the Galloway Hills and an inscription commemorating David Bell who wrote weekly cycling articles for 30 years in the *Ayrshire Post* under the name of 'The Highwayman'.

The cairn is a good point for viewing the Galloway Forest Park. The high range of hills to the east is known as The Awful Hand. Five long fingers lead back to the high summits of Shalloch on Minnoch, Tarfessock, Kirriereoch Hill, Merrick, and Benyellary.

Shalloch on Minnoch (769m), Kirriereoch Hill (784m) and Merrick (843m) are collected by climbers as 'Corbetts' – being included in J. Rooke Corbett's list of Scottish hills between 2,500 – 2,999 feet, in the style of Munro's Tables of those of 3,000 feet and over.

A ruined dyke runs up the ridge of Kirriereoch Hill on the county and regional boundary. At its highest point the dyke is about 10 metres higher than Shalloch on Minnoch, but as the summit of the hill is on the Kirkcudbright side of the dyke, Ayrshire cannot claim this hill.

Merrick is the highest hill in the Southern Uplands and the highest mainland hill in Scotland south of Ben Lomond. Vast forests spread up the western slopes of these hills making an approach difficult for ill-prepared walkers, but a number of forest roads and rides give relatively quick access to those who know them. A few dwellings are still inhabited in the area though most farms have lost out to forestry developments. A wigwam-shaped bothy was placed by the Cross Burn (391879) by the Forestry Commission for the use of walkers. Shalloch on Minnoch farm (369896), and Kirriemore (373852) in Galloway have been centres for large military exercises, and astute observers are worried about the Ministry of Defence's plans for the area.

Ayrshire ends at Suie Toll. The toll house is now just a pile of stones. Just to the north, a gated road goes off to the west into another extensive area of forest. This area is little used by the public as it is generally low-lying and contains few features of interest, but the forest roads offer long through routes. The forest road from near Suie passes the ruin of Fardin, the still-used dwellings of Ferter, White Clauchrie, Shalloch Well, and Mark to Pinwherry. A branch from White Clauchrie leads north-west past Loch Scalloch to continue as a track then a road to Barr. Another branch from north-west of Fardin (325868) becomes a rough track for a mile before winning through to Black Clauchrie and the road out to Barrhill.

From Suie Toll the motorist may continue to the A714 and return to Ayrshire via Barrhill, which can be reached by the route from Maybole now described.

The B7023 from Maybole turns sharply at CROSSHILL to follow the Girvan valley. The oldest and most interesting part

The church at Straiton was founded in the 13th century but dates
mainly from the 18th century. It was much restored in 1901 and has a
neo-Norman tower and a 15th or 16th-century south transept. There
are a number of interesting memorials in the churchyard.

of the village extends along the Maybole road and continues
from the crossroads and war memorial along a minor road
which is heading south to the hills. This line through the village
along King Street and Dalhowan Street features for the most
part one and two-storey dwellings stepping straight on to the
pavement, where cast-iron stand pipes linger from the past.
Dalhowan Street is remarkable for its nearly-continuous terrace
of mainly single-storey dwellings, with a slight bend in the
street adding a subtle charm to the scene. Although a few of
the properties have been dormered, the street retains much of

its integrity and is unusual in the county for its expanse of dwellings surviving in this traditional style. The church on the north-east side of the village was built in 1838.

There are lime kilns at Balgreggan (348052), and at Lannielane (313018) where an impressive quarry face is supported by stoops or pillars of unquarried rock, but the workings are flooded.

The B7023 from Crosshill joins the B741 to New Dailly. A minor road from Maybole passes the restored Kilhenzie castle (308082), swings under the railway beneath Kildoon Hill and turns west down the Girvan valley on the north bank. A fort guarded by a vitrified wall and ramparts to the west occupied the east end of Kildoon Hill. In 1853 a granite obelisk was erected within the fort to Sir Charles D. Fergusson of Kilkerran.

Kilkerran House (304030) developed from an old tower incorporated in re-building at the end of the 17th century, while James Gillespie was called in as architect for additions in 1814-15 and David Bryce in 1855. The old walled garden is now a Camping and Caravan Club site. The Fergussons of Kilkerran have been improvers and the well-wooded valley is a result of their efforts. Aviation is a recent interest, and there is a narrow landing strip running parallel to the river. James Gillespie designed a number of lodges on the estate. Aird Bridge (293034) and Drumgirnan Bridge (305042) were built between 1779 and 1817 and feature up-curved parapets, vermiculated arches, quatrefoils, and merry and sad-faced monarchs' heads.

The ruinous Kilkerran Castle (293005) was abandoned in the 17th century when the name was taken to the present house. Dalquharran Castle (273019) is a three-storey ruin standing by the River Girvan near Dailly. It has a fairly straightforward facade to the south save for a buttress on one corner and a circular tower on the other; but the north elevation is very complicated with additions and alterations from later dates.

The castle was abandoned for a great castellated mansion which is conspicuous on higher ground to the north-west. It was built about 1786 to the design of Robert Adam with a splendid spiral staircase in the centre of the house behind the large round tower. Wings were added to left and right of the house in 1880. In 1936 it opened its doors as Scotland's grandest youth hostel, but the war intervened and Dalquaharran never recovered. It was unroofed later and the opportunity was lost to put it on the tourist trail along with its now-much visited neighbour by Adam at Culzean.

DAILLY grew as a coalmining village. The carboniferous rocks overlying the Old Red Sandstone have been exploited in several areas in the past but nature has been quick to cover most of the dereliction.

Dailly Church was built in 1766 as a T-shaped Renaissance building with a bell tower at the north-west end standing above the Main Street. The windows include works by Guthrie and Wells Ltd; and Heaton, Butler, and Bayne. A massive pedimented slab-roofed mausoleum of the Bargany family in the churchyard stands nearly as high as the church. A headstone near the highest point of the yard is in memory of John Brown, a 66-year-old collier who was trapped underground by a roof-fall in Kilgrammie pit in 1835 and was brought out alive 'Having been 23 days in utter seclusion from the world and without a particle of food'. Sadly he survived only three days after release.

The most interesting part of the village is around the church, where a small square is overlooked by a white granite war memorial. In Greenhead Street a little museum opens on Wednesday afternoons in summer. Little survives of Brunston Castle (261012) or Camregan Castle (215988). Hadyard Hill forms a steep southern boundary to the valley along the Southern Uplands edge with a fort on the summit ridge.

Bargany House (244002) was built in 1681 and extended over the centuries. An application for demolition was refused and the decision upheld by a public inquiry in 1980. A splendid balustraded bridge spans the river in front of the house. The grounds are open to the public for much of the year and are particularly attractive at daffodil and azalea time.

Old Dailly, three miles west of Dailly, is a hamlet with an attractive but ruinous church from about the 17th century. There is a belfry on both gables and burial vaults have been added within and behind the church. Two hefty boulders on the north side are known as the Charter Stones and were used in trials of strength to see who could lift them. The churchyard

contains memorials to a number of Covenanters. The Boyds of
Penkill are buried in an enclosure at the west end of the
church. The artist William Bell Scott also lies here with a
bronze and granite roundel on the wall to commemorate his
close association with Penkill.

Penkill Castle, three-quarters of a mile to the south-east, is
open to groups by appointment (Tel. Old Dailly 261). It was
restored and added to in the 18th and 19th centuries after the
original tower had become ruinous. Numerous members of the
Pre-Raphaelite Brotherhood stayed here in the 19th century.
William Bell Scott has left a splendid mural, adorning the spiral
staircase, based on King James I's poem 'The King's Quhair'.
He also designed the wrought-iron gates by the lodge and
other work. The castle also contains tapestries by Aubusson
and William Morris.

Killochan Castle (227003) on the north side of the Girvan
Water is a noble five-storey tower house which impresses with
its strong walls, its pepper pot turrets, and its sheer verticality.
A carved inscription over the door commemorates John
Cathcart of Carlton and Helen Wallace his spouse, 1586. The
Baron's Stone near the river is a huge boulder weighing about
37 tons, transported from the Galloway Hills by the ancient
glaciers.

Trochrague (213004) dates from the 17th century and is now
run by the Sisters of St Joseph of Cluny as a guest house.

Craighead Quarry (233013) formerly supplied ground
limestone to farmers and colliers and all grades of stone for
road materials. It has also supplied numerous fossils to
geologists, who were horrified when the district council
proposed (but later rejected) using it as a rubbish dump.

An extensive area of upland farms stretches north of the
forested slopes of the Girvan valley to Kirkoswald. The summit
of Kirk Hill (265044) is surrounded by a ditch and low
rampart. It is reported that about 1795 a stone coffin was
found on the summit. Hallowshean (2444061) is a hill fort
defended by several lines of earthworks to the east.

The B734 from Old Dailly runs south-east past the
Penwhapple reservoir and drops down 'The Screws' to Barr.
Auchensoul Hill (314m) is easily climbed from the top of this
twisting road and gives a fine view of the village.

A pastoral farming scene at North Balloch in the Stinchar valley east of Barr with dense coniferous forests occupying higher slopes beyond the farms at South Balloch and Pinvalley. A narrow and quite exciting road climbs to the Nick of the Balloch, left of centre on the skyline, where the view opens out to the higher hills of Galloway.

BARR is a very attractive village, with the Water of Gregg flowing through its centre to join the River Stinchar near the latter's 1787 bridge. The church stands nearby at the smaller 19th-century Gregg bridge and was designed by Alan Stevenson and opened about 1878 to replace one that stood near the centre of the village where there is now just a graveyard. The yard contains headstones to two Covenanters and there are some richly-sculptured stones including one showing Rev John Campbell (died 1743) in his pulpit, and another with a figure standing on a skull holding an hour glass and the ring of eternity. The former Free Church (1891) at a high point of the village is now a dwelling. The village can be explored easily without a lot of walking, and on Sundays and midweek in the summer months afternoon teas are served in the Village Hall.

A road east of Barr ends after a mile at a picnic site in the Changue forest. Walkers can continue on forest roads past High Changue or through the Howe of Laggan to the Stinchar valley. A memorial cairn (311922) stands at the west end of the Howe of Laggan to Christopher McTaggart, a shepherd who died in a snowstorm in 1913.

Another forest road leads west of the Water of Gregg to Dinmurchie Loch and a track leads on past the ruins of Darley to the Nick of Darley under an ancient cairn on Cairn Hill. Armstrong's Map of 1775 shows this as a route to Galloway and states: 'the Road leads on the side of a very steep Hill, its not above two feet broad and if you stumble you must fall almost Perpendicular six or seven Hundred Feet'. Ayrshire does not have that sort of scenery, but the slope is steep and the pass is worth a visit. A through route can be made from Barr to join forest roads south-east of the pass leading to the hill road between Straiton and Bargrennan – provided an up-to-date map of the forests is used.

Some of the hills in this area give good views to the big Galloway hills to the east. Haggis Hill (325925) appears just like a haggis when seen from the north! Pinbreck Hill (348937) has an ancient cairn for a summit. A huge granite erratic sits to the south-east near the fence – miles west of its granite homeland.

The B734 runs south-west from Barr along the south bank of the River Stinchar. Kirkdominae (254928) was an ancient church which gained notoriety for the secular nature of the festivities at the annual hiring fair. The Struil Well (252929) issues from the hillside above the site but the arch above this holy well was destroyed by a fallen tree.

The B734 joins the A714 at an attractive stone arched bridge (1802) over the Stinchar at Pinmore. The main road and railway have struggled over the hills from Girvan, rising to 147 metres at the 496 metre-long summit railway tunnel. Dinvin Motte (200932) above the tunnel is one of Ayrshire's most impressive ancient earthworks. Its central mound is defended by two very well defined circular ramparts and ditches.

Road and railway leapfrog each other down the valley of the Stinchar with the road taking a U-bend under the eleven-arch Pinmore Viaduct built in 1876. There is a tiny Scottish Episcopal Church between the road and railway (202896). Daljarrock (196882) derived from a tower house.

PINWHERRY is a route centre with the Duisk Water from the south joining the westward-turning Stinchar, the A765 from Ballantrae meeting the A714, and a passing loop and signal box to split up the rail section between Girvan and Barrhill.

Pinwherry Castle is a five-storey ivy-hidden 16th-century ruin near the road bridge over the Duisk water. The Glaik Stone in the hills to the north-east (217878) is a slab-shaped pointed monolith with a curious bowl-shaped depression on both broad upright faces. Those who like to practise their mathematics at the solstice may be interested to test the good sight-lines to Knockdolian Hill in the south-west, and to nicks in the hills at Cairn Hill ridge to the north-east, and the Kirriereoch Hill-Merrick gap to the south-east.

As the railway climbs south-east to Barrhill it looks across to Kildonan House then turns away from the valley. Kildonan is a large and splendid Cotswold-style mansion designed by James Miller, completed about 1920. The house was used as a convent for a time and is to become a hotel. The original owner was married to a daughter of Sir Edwin Lutyens, the distinguished architect who influenced Miller's style. Miller was also chosen to design the War Memorial Hall in Barrhill (1924) with financial help from Kildonan.

The village of BARRHILL is the meeting point for three lonely roads from the south with one busier one from the north. Most of the houses are spread along the Main Street with traditional one or 1½ storey terraces towards the south end and two-storey detached buildings to the north. The street bends slightly as it bridges the Cross Water. The parish church was designed by Robert Ingram. The letters BBC on a pavilion signify Barrhill Bowling Club and not an outpost of broadcasting. Just before the once-important livestock market on the climb to the station, a path goes left and crosses the

Kildonan House at Barrhill was designed by James Miller and built in 1917. The Cotswold-style mansion house became a convent for a time and plans have been made to convert it into a hotel. The building is hidden from the public road by a fine mixture of trees but can be seen clearly from the railway which crosses the open slope above.

burn to a memorial for two Covenanting martyrs. High up, at the juncture of the moorlands with the wooded glen, the Linn Dhu tumbles over a sill into a deep pool. The station opposite plays an important part in the detective story *The Five Red Herrings* by Dorothy L. Sayers.

The scenery becomes bleak to the south. Wide views feature the Galloway hills to the east, but the immediate surroundings are desolate. As the distance signal for the up-line is left behind, the single-track road climbs through rough moorland pastures and vast ranks of spruce towards the summit where Chirmorie shelters in an oasis of hardy sycamores near the county boundary. The railway crosses the 210-metre high summit in a twisting course known as the Swan's Neck to reach the Cross Water of Luce and the descent out of the county. A train was snowed up for two days in 1947 in this section and another was trapped for eight days in 1908 farther down the line.

The B7027 and A714 take lower routes to the east heading for Newton Stewart. The first leaves the county between Lochs Maberry and Dornal. The main road crosses the River Cree at the county boundary and joins with the hill road from Straiton after four miles at Bargrennan.

CHAPTER 15

The Doon Valley

The A713 climbs steeply from Ayr with a good view back over the town to the sea and Arran. Off to the right Mount Oliphant (356172) was farmed by Robert Burns's father. Off to the left, Martnaham Loch by the B742 has castle remains on an island. West of the A713, the B742 passes within sight of the former Purclewan Mill (380159) and under the 16-arch Burnton railway viaduct before reaching Dalrymple.

The most attractive part of DALRYMPLE forms a T-shape about the Kirkton Inn, with 19th-century 1½ storey rows of cottages along the pavements avoiding the common Ayrshire failing of discordant dormers. One cottage shows Aberdeen bond masonry, but most walls are painted. The smithy is dated 1868. Near the Doon bridge (1849) is the parish church, opened in 1850. It has two windows by Stephen Adam and Son. A headstone in the churchyard shows a plough team of four horses. The river flows on past Cassillis House (341128) where a possibly 15th-century tower is masked by turrets, chimney heads, and other 19th-century additions. Dunree (348124) is an ancient hill fortification which looks down on Cassillis. A motte by the River Doon (338139) can be seen from the Ayr-Maybole train.

East from Dalrymple an attractive walk follows the north bank of the river towards the policies of Skeldon, where there are splendid trees around the garden. Skeldon House is an impressive Georgian mansion. The old castle ruins to the east have been rebuilt into a dwelling. Skeldon Mills were rebuilt in 1961 but the old weir and a long lade survive. Notice the return channel to the lade near the downstream buildings.

Balgreen farm (385146) was famed for its Clydesdale horses and still keeps a few. It has high arched entries to its courtyard (1882) and a brick factory-type chimney. Hollybush on the A713 is a minor route centre which once had its own railway station. The Elizabethan-style Hollybush House became a hotel and is now a home for ex-servicemen and women.

The Craigs of Kyle (430156) form a whinstone ridge which

144

Steam locomotives hauled coal wagons at Waterside in the Doon valley up till the late 1970s. Only the derelict coal preparation plant remains now in this view but a few miles away at the Scottish Industrial Railway Centre at Minnivey engines can still be seen in steam on 'open days' and plans are being laid to restore the railway to Waterside where plans have also been made to restore the former Iron Works.

gives a wide view of Ayrshire. South-east of the summit is the Boarstone – an erratic in the shape of a boar's head. From here you can look eastwards to Littlemill, which had a colliery till 1974, and the line of council houses forming Rankinston. Beyond to the south are numerous forestry tracks and relics of former mining activity. The B730 from Littlemill joins the A713 near Polnessan. North of the junction at Smithston a branch from the railway ran towards Old Smithston and continued by a rope-worked incline (422127) to the Summerlee Iron Company's mines in the hills. The Houldsworth Colliery is worked privately on the hill east of Polnessan.

PATNA has collected many of the former mining communities from the hills and has expanded monotonously with council housing. The oldest part of the village starts at Patna Bridge over the Doon and rises past two churches to Patna Cross (411107). The war memorial on Patna Hill is a good viewpoint for the valley. Notice the abutments down by the river (413114) where a viaduct led to mines on the west bank. Across the valley, a road runs up to the former mining villages of Lethanhill and Burnfoothill. Only a few piles of stones and a war memorial mark the sites now, along with a TV transmitter. An inclined plane slants down the hill from Burnfoothill to Drumgrange (434099).

At WATERSIDE in 1847 Messrs Houldsworth erected blast furnaces to exploit the local ore and abundant coal. David L. Smith's *The Dalmellington Iron Company*, 1967, tells the fascinating story. Iron making declined at the start of the 20th century and the furnaces were demolished, but coal mining and brick making continued at the site and a washing plant was provided for coal from the surrounding area. Now industry has vanished, but people remain, and efforts are being made to preserve the unique heritage of the area. The Dalmellington and District Conservation Trust is working with local councils, statutory bodies, and other parties to give the Doon Valley new life through tourism and recreation. An initial task is to safeguard the most important buildings at Waterside. The company offices are at the west end of the complex (440083). Beyond the weighbridge is the impressive Italianate Blast Engine House, part of which dates from 1847. Brick kilns and two tall chimneys are grouped around and behind it as the slope rises to the furnace bank. On the opposite side of the A713 a slag bing was reached by bridge, but that colossal landmark has been reduced and landscaped recently. Among the buildings to the north of the bing and the company offices are the Institute, the railway station, the company store (still selling drinks at reputedly the longest bar in Ayrshire), Waterside Church (now a dwelling) and a roadside row of workmen's cottages. Two white-painted stones by the roadside (430090) commemorate the unemployed. East of the bing is another cottage row, and the R.C. chapel which is still in use. South of the Doon a grassy mound behind a dwelling is all that remains of Keirs castle (430080).

Dunaskin glen (450085) is a remarkable area. The bed of a tramway runs into it from the west and over the burn by a ruinous bridge which still carries an aqueduct to Waterside. The sides of the glen have been eroded to reveal on its

Pine trees frame the northern end of Loch Doon where the River Doon spills from the dam to the wooded Ness Glen. The loch has a smaller dam at its north-east corner and a tunnel through the hills which diverts water to the east and south for hydro-electric power purposes.

precipitous sides bands of ironstone, shales, and clays. Laight Castle (450089) occupies a promontory on the east bank, defended by steep slopes and a deep ditch. Notice the turf dyke north of the burn from here. Above the crags on the Burnhead burn sit the remains of Corbie Craigs (457089), another of the ghost villages. A wagonway loops across the Dunaskin Burn to follow a shelf towards Waterside. Higher still was Benwhat (461097) where little remains besides a war memorial high on the Hill.

The former colliery at Minnivey (475073) is now the Scottish Industrial Railway Centre. Open days with locomotives in steam are held regularly and a long-term plan envisages re-laying a track to Waterside. The Chalmerston incline rises above the site to an interesting group of mining ruins and a superb view of Dalmellington colonising the morainic ridges which spill across the Southern Uplands boundary fault. The peak-shaped bing of the former Pennyvenie Colliery and Bogton Loch are conspicuous, and there are plans for open-cast coal mining north of the A713. The moss between Bogton Loch and the A713 was the surprising site chosen for an aerodrome. Between 1916 and 1918 Dalmellington became the centre for an extraordinary scheme to create a School of Aerial Gunnery at Loch Doon. The platform near Craigengillan Lodge (474059) and route of a light railway to Dalfarson can still be seen. Loch Doon proved too hostile for development, but the area north-east of Bogton Loch became a landing strip with hangars for a brief spell.

In the centre of DALMELLINGTON, just off the Square is the Cathcartson Interpretation Centre in a line of weavers' cottages dated 1744. The centre contains a display on weaving, mining, railways, and other aspects of the area. Some interesting buildings lead off from the Square along the High Street, notably the Dalmellington Inn; the Doon Tavern; 'Ye old Castle House'; the Black Bull Hotel, and the hall next to it with a '1747' skewputt showing initials and mason's mark; then a dwelling house with block and sneck masonry opposite the former Cross Keys Inn; and a house surmounted by a bust of its former owner, Dr Jamieson, dated 1861. Off High Street, the old Cemetery contains a classical mausoleum of the Macadam Cathcart family of Craigengillan and a Covenanters' memorial cross. The modern public library at the foot of Townhead is an attractive split-level building containing a useful local collection. Above it there is the umbrella-shaped St Barbara's R.C. Chapel built in 1961. Above both is the Motte Hill, constructed probably about the 13th century from morainic debris, and worth a climb for the good view. North-east of the Square is Knowehead with the parish church built in 1846, replacing the older church of 1766 which was restored in 1887 to become the Cathcart Hall. The present church has windows by Ballantine and Gardiner; and Gordon Webster. Running uphill from the cemetery is the Pickan's Dyke – a mysterious turf boundary and ditch.

Through the former Camlarg estate a northern path is lined by rock specimens including the Spider's Web Stone (486065). The southern track was the old Cumnock road and crosses an ancient bridge. Farther out the B741 track goes off near

Clawfin to Benbain and for the conspicuous and craggy Benbeoch (464m). The cliffs are composed of reclining columns of basalt. A boulder field below was used to form a dry-stone sheep pen of massive proportions, with overhangs facing outwards to deter foxes. An old wagonway crosses the track below and forms a ride through the forest.

West of Dalmellington the B741 crosses the Doon by an attractive hump-backed bridge near the river's exit from Bogton Loch. The loch is a winter haunt for whooper swans, goosander and other ducks. A minor road down the west side of the loch leads to the farm of Dalcairnie. A track leads on uphill to a bridge over the Dalcairnie Linn – which falls into a capacious vertical-sided 'pot'. The track continues over the moor past Little Shalloch ruins and three lochs, to Knockdon in the upper Girvan valley. Traces of a number of settlements with turf banks and rig and furrow cultivation may be seen on this walk, and there is a remarkably rocky summit on the Wee Hill of Glenmount. Looking back towards the Doon valley, notice the crag and tail formations near Berbeth where the glaciers overrode the narrow valley and planed across the landscape on their journey northwards.

From Dalmellington the A713 goes southwards, entering the impressive glen of the Muck Water, with steep crags fringing the narrow valley. Then the road rises to the watershed and the county boundary at Loch Muck, with distant scenic views of Loch Doon and the Galloway Hills. A track goes north-west between Loch Muck and Cairnannock and meets the Loch Doon road at Gaw Glen.

The Loch Doon road leaves the A713 at Mossdale and offers good views down the Doon valley, across to Craigengillan estate, and south across the loch to the Galloway hills. The road passes across a dam at the north end of the loch. This was constructed in the 1930s as part of the Galloway hydro-electric scheme which raised the level of the loch, and discharges eastwards through a tunnel to generate power on its way to the Solway Firth. From the dam looking north can be glimpsed the River Doon escaping through the Ness Glen. This is a spectacular gorge, but shrouded in trees and difficult of access. The path hewn many years ago along the west bank is now ruinous.

Opposite the dam on the east shore of the loch can be seen the concrete blocks which carried the monorail target for the aerial gunnery school of the First World War. A concreted area and foundations of demolished buildings occupy the west bank of the loch near the Garpel Burn. After the ill-conceived scheme was abandoned, a Government Select Committee took a very critical look at its planning and expense.

Loch Doon Castle, dating from the 13th century, was originally on an island site, but when the water level of the loch was raised in the 1930s it was rebuilt on the west bank. The curtain wall has eleven irregular sides, with skilled ashlar work. The original island site appears and vanishes as the water level fluctuates. Above the castle is the Wee Hill of Craigmulloch (421m) which gives a magnificent view of Loch Doon, a number of other lochs, and the surrounding hills. The public road peters out at the south end of the loch, but forest roads continue into the enormous sitka spruce plantations.

Another 'Loch Doon Scandal' arose in 1978 when the nuclear industry submitted a planning application to drill 32 bore holes into Mullwharchar (692m) in the search for a repository for highly radioactive nuclear waste. The locals responded with great determination and fought off the threat in a prolonged campaign. This was a famous victory for common people against the sneers, misrepresentations, and double-dealing of certain academics, scientists, politicians, and journalists who were often deplorably ignorant of the issues.

This is fine territory for hill walkers: but it is difficult and unsuitable for unprepared or solitary walkers. A fine ridge walk leads over Hoodens Hill (455893) and above the cliffs of the Slock, the Yellow Tomach, and the Tauchers to Mullwharchar. Granite pavements, striated rocks, moraines, and perched boulders make this ice-sculptured location the wildest place in Ayrshire. Another very tough but rewarding expedition goes up the water course called Eglin Lane, following the county boundary to Loch Enoch, around Mullwharchar, and down the Gala Lane past the dykes and ruins of Starr (marked as a hunting lodge in Armstrong's map of 1775). Macaterick Hill (499m) above Loch Macaterick is another savage corner of this district, with an unlocked bothy at Tunskeen (424905) available as shelter. Details of routes

Sheep being clipped at Beoch farm on the west bank of Loch Doon in early summer. Few sheep farms remain in this area now as forestry has taken over much of the grazing lands. Those farms which survive are much more likely to use electric clippers today.

among the hills beyond Loch Doon will be found in *The Southern Uplands* by K.M. Andrew and A.A. Thrippleton (Scottish Mountaineering Club). *The Merrick and the Neighbouring Hills* by J. McBain is a classic book on the area, written before the forests returned.

CHAPTER 16

The River Ayr

The A70, B743, and B758 roads run along the north side of the River Ayr's valley between Glenbuck and Ayr. It is a direct route by road, but the river writhes like a snake as though struggling to escape from its east-west course. Because of this characteristic, the River Ayr is relatively unknown for much of its length.

The B758 leaves Ayr at the Whitletts roundabout, passing the red-tile roofed Hannah Dairy Research Institute's buildings, grouped upon a hillock, and the West of Scotland Agricultural College at Auchincruive. The Auchincruive estate dates back to the 13th century. In 1764 it was purchased by Richard Oswald, who saw his mansion – known today as Oswald Hall – completed in 1767.

Hanging gardens fall from Oswald Hall to the River Ayr. Robert Adam designed the small drum-towered tea house in 1778, which is seen from the B758 between the west and east lodges. The Gibbsyard buildings, which have a clocktower over the entrance arch, date from the same time. A 15KW aerogenerator sits on high ground to the west of the College. In 1985, the first plantings were made in an arboretum east of the tea house. A woodland walk is planned to link the arboretum to the gardens by the river.

Oswald's Bridge crosses the River Ayr, carrying a minor road from St Quivox to the B744. It was built as an estate bridge in 1862 with three arches high above the river springing from battered hexagonal cutwaters. Although narrow by today's standards, it was spacious for the days of horse transport, yet has eight ample-sized refuges as well as pallstones to protect the masonry from carriages.

A cairn in the Leglen wood on the east bank was erected by the Burns Federation in 1929 to William Wallace and Robert Burns. Just to the south-east (388229) the road crosses a skewed bridge over an old wagonway which is heading for the river. Coal was transported to Ayr Harbour this way until a dispute between the coalmaster and the Oswalds in 1870.

There are pleasant walks along the river from Oswald's Bridge, but beware of giant hogweed, which is spreading rapidly along much of the River Ayr. This can burn your skin if you come in contact with it. The walks upstream pass a small waterfall and remains of a mill dam opposite the gardens of Auchincruive. The piers of another bridge of the wagonway to Ayr stand in the river near the end of Auchincruive woods (400234).

ST QUIVOX, north west of Auchincruive, is an attractive hamlet. The bow-fronted Mount Hamilton was formerly the factor's house for Auchincruive. The former manse across the road from it dates from 1823. St Evox, north of the church, has hood-moulded windows, and overhung chimney-heads set at an angle to the gables.

The possibly pre-Reformation church is a T-shaped building with outside stairs to two of the three lofts. A badly-decayed armorial stone on the east wall dates from 1595 and commemorates Lord Alan Cathcart. There is a splendid 'Adam and Eve' stone beside it, and a number of other richly-carved 18th-century stones. The Campbells of Craigie and Bardarroch have a massive classical mausoleum and there is an oval-shaped chest tomb. Highfield farm (371243), across the Ayr by-pass, has a horse engine house.

ANNBANK developed in the second half of the 19th century as a street of miners' rows extending along a ridge. A memorial near the centre of the village commemorates James Brown, a local miners' agent who became an M.P., Lord High Commissioner of the Church of Scotland, a Privy Councillor, and was honoured by Glasgow University.

The B744 approaches Annbank from the south-west, crossing the River Ayr by a concrete balustraded bridge at Tarholm and passing over an old wagonway bridge at Colvinston (402225).

Mossblown and Drumley are neighbouring communities forming an extended village with Annbank. Neilshill House and Lodge (409262) are Moorish in character and were reputedly built by North African workers specially engaged for the task.

The B742 runs through Mossblown past the red and yellow brick R.C. Chapel of St Ann (1898) and Annbank Church

(1903) which has a window by W. Meikle and Sons. A footpath
starts from the car park opposite the latter and goes south to
the River Ayr at Auchincruive. The chimney and remains of
Annbank Brickworks stand to the south-east of the church with
the former baths of Enterkine 9/10 Colliery beyond.
The road to Coylton from Annbank crosses the River Ayr at
Gadgirth Bridge. Gadgirth House was demolished but
Gadgirth with its lancet windows and archway (411225) and
Gadgirth Holm (1906) are attractive survivors. There are traces
of an ancient hall stronghold downstream (406219). Privick
Mill (407223) on the opposite bank is now a store. The river
bank can be walked some way in both directions from Gadgirth
Bridge.

An impressive railway viaduct on high stone piers crosses the
River Ayr at Enterkine (417230). It was built for double track
between 1868-71 by Charles Brand & Son (as four oval
contractor's name stones testify) and carries platforms along
the upstream edge for signal and telegraph lines. Enterkine
Wood (425241) is a Scottish Wildlife Trust Reserve with a
mixture of beech, oak, and other trees about an artificial pond.

TARBOLTON is dominated by its tall parish church. The
church was opened in 1821 and is a squarish two-storey
building with chimneys at the corners under a hipped roof. A
three-stage clock tower ending in a spire springs from a
projecting three door entrance. The churchyard contains a
Covenanter's memorial and a number of interesting heavily-
carved stones.

The Bachelors' Club, a short distance east from the church
gate, is a 17th-century thatched building in the care of the
National Trust for Scotland. Robert Burns and a few friends
formed a debating club here in 1780 when it was an ale house.

The Town House (1832) is a humble structure to the north-
east of the church with a plaque beyond it on the site of
Manson's Inn which stood at the time of Burns. Another
plaque (433275) marks the poetical encounter invented by
Burns between 'Death and Dr Hornbook'. Between the two
plaques stands a much more substantial motte and bailey castle
site, which looks north to Tongue farm behind its horse engine
house and north-east to Willie's Mill which featured in the life
and poems of Burns.

This round castellated building is a source of speculation to travellers passing Auchincruive. It was designed as a tea house for the Oswald family in 1778 by Robert Adam. Mining in the area has damaged the structure and it is closed up at present.

The interests of two great rival Ayrshire families met at Tarbolton and are reflected in the street names along the main street traversing the village. Above the low pend known as Parliament Close – where the locals could gossip and shelter from the weather – the sign says 'Cunningham Street'. A few yards along the straight, suitably buffered by the Lorimer Library (now a district council branch), a plate marks the start of 'Montgomerie Street'. The Erskine Hall, west of Montgomerie Street, has an 1850 date stone.

Going east along the minor road from the Black Bull Inn and the war memorial at the south end of the village, you get a good view of Daisybank, an early 19th century dwelling, and come to the entrance to the Montgomerie estate. Montgomerie House was one of the most distinctive mansions in Ayrshire but was destroyed by fire and demolition. Some remarkable earthworks are to be found under scrub woodland above the Fail Water at the second entrance (443269). They are known locally as 'the Roman trenches'.

Montgomerie House was also known as Coilsfield, and the tumulus at Coilsfield Mains (447262) is by tradition the grave of King Coil or the old King Cole of the nursery rhyme. The district of Kyle may take its name from this link.

FAILFORD on the A758 has a monument (458262) commemorating the last meeting between Robert Burns and Highland Mary. The Fail Water joins the River Ayr here after flowing under a high rail viaduct of nine arches. To the west, the railway crosses the A758 on a handsome elliptical arched bridge.

A path follows the north bank of the River Ayr from Failford towards Stair, passing, near the start, the Montgomerie sandstone quarry. Red sandstone is conspicuous at the Burns Monument and the bridges but is particularly vivid in the natural setting along the River Ayr here. The path goes through the Ayr Gorge Woodlands Wildlife Reserve of the Scottish Wildlife Trust, and climbs across a cliff face on an airy staircase of steps cut into the rock, before emerging from the oakwoods to the fields near Stair.

Stair Bridge (438234) is a narrow three-arch 18th-century structure with mortise and tenon jointing, at a bend in the river and a bend in the road. A lade on the west bank at a dam upstream from the bridge leads to the Tam O' Shanter and Water of Ayr Hone Works downstream from the bridge. Another lade starts on the opposite bank, downstream from the bridge at another dam curving across the river. The works are situated on both banks of the river and are linked by a suspension footbridge. Honestones have been manufactured here for about two centuries from natural stone quarried or mined in the vicinity. The mill on the south bank shows remains of its wheel and 'W. Heron 1821' under a carving of a wheat sheaf on a west wall. There is another mill and a quarry to the south-west.

On the south side of Stair Bridge there are crossroads at Stair Inn, with the northern route leading a short distance to the church (1864) and the 17th-century Stair House. The latter is a three-storey tower house with a circular stair tower jutting above the eaves, and can be seen from across the river.

The B758 from Failford to Mauchline passes north of the secluded estates of Stairaird and Barskimming and passes under two rail bridges where the line from Mossblown and Ayr converged with the Glasgow-Dumfries line. A footpath (489268) leads north to Bogwood and under a wider split in the lines where the minor track turned west to cross the six-arch Redcraig Viaduct (477274). The footpath climbs towards Laurieland and a north-west entry into Mauchline.

The B744 from Tarbolton has taken a higher route with much wider views, curving round towards Mauchline past the road to Lochlea, and Ladyyard, Skeoch, and Mossgiel farms. Lochlea (455301) was rented by William Burnes and his family from 1777-84. After his death, the family moved to Mossgiel, the poet Robert dropped the 'e' from his surname and began to head south-east rather than west as the girls of Mauchline supplanted those of Tarbolton in his affections. There is an unusual spiral-shaped sheep buchty or gathering fank near Ladyyard (471288). Skeoch has a grand doorway for a farmhouse with two Ionic columns at the porch. Between Skeoch and Mossgiel the road passes an air-shaft from the 625-metre long Mossgiel railway tunnel below.

MAUCHLINE, an important centre for Burns enthusiasts, has winding lanes and ever-changing streetscapes. There is a convenient central car park north of the B758 and west of the church and crossroads. A lane at the north-east corner of the car park leads alongside the burn to Mauchline Castle, also known as Abbot Hunter's Tower. This 15th-century tower is a relic of a priory established by the Cistercian monks of Melrose. The east wall shows twin lancets along with squared windows from the secularisation of the building. The large garderobe chutes on the north wall that once discharged into the Mauchline Burn, that is so near the path, are fortunately now inactive! The harled and crowstepped house adjoining the castle was once occupied by Gavin Hamilton who was friendly with Robert Burns.

The parish church was built in 1829 on the site of an older church. The pinnacled tower dominates the town centre. Two stone tablets near the front gate from the former North Church show the dates 1796 and 1885. The churchyard contains the graves of a number of people associated with Burns; a Covenanting martyr; and William and Andrew Smith who manufactured the beautiful souvenirs of the 19th century

that are prized today as 'Mauchline Ware'. At the back gate
there is a small mortuary used for cholera victims.

A display of Mauchline snuff boxes and other ware can be
seen in the Burns House Museum in Castle Street opposite the
back gate to the churchyard. Robert Burns lived here with Jean
Armour, and the house is now a museum commemorating
Burns and his works along with Mauchline's curling stone
industry and other aspects of local history. There is a bronze
memorial by G.H. Paulin between this and the neighbouring
house to C.R. Cowie who gifted them to the Glasgow and
District Burns Association. The house across from them
(c.1712) was once Nanse Tinnock's Tavern.

Mauchline Cross is a busy route centre controlled by traffic
lights, and the modern post office is an eyesore. The south side
of Loudoun Street has a range of 18th and early 19th-century
buildings. The High Street squeezes past an unroofed Gothic-
style summer house to the Loan, where outside the primary
school an obelisk commemorates five Covenanters. A stone
from the original memorial is set into the school wall.

Going south-west from the Cross along Loudoun Street you
pass the modernised Poosie Nansie's Inn which was the setting
for 'The Jolly Beggars'. The Cowgate opposite the church has
poetical lines inscribed on a tablet referring to the Whitefoord
Arms which Burns frequented. Further west, a well spouts its
water into a drain in Loudoun Street and has been doing so
since anyone can recall. Netherplace House was demolished
beyond the gate next to it, but attractive lodges survive farther
out the Ayr and Kilmarnock roads.

Opposite the spout Barskimming Road leads past the yard of
Andrew Kay and Co., where curling stones are smoothed and
polished for worldwide export, and past the cemetery where
there is an elaborate memorial to Marcus Bain, a quarrymaster.

Barskimming Mill (492253) is a three-storey brick building
on the south side of the River Ayr and was built at the end of
the 19th century after a fire destroyed its predecessor. The
road to Stair crosses the river to the west of it, with a cave cut
into the sandstone cliff at the north end of a single-arch bridge.
A footpath goes east between the sewage treatment plant and
Mauchline Creamery on the north bank and past the Swiss-
style works, where spectacles were made, to the Haugh and

Additions in the 18th, 19th, and 20th centuries have added greatly to the 15th-century tower on the right of Sorn Castle. James VI spent a few days here in 1598.

another road bridge over the river.

The Haugh road from Mauchline passes the former Ballochmyle quarries to reach this point. It was at the Haugh in the mid-19th century that Andrew Kay established the first curling stone works in the world. The building (498253), north of a lade, is now used by a farm. A walk to the west on the south bank leads to the confluence with the Lugar Water. The north bank leads east to the A76.

The National Burns Memorial and Cottage Homes at the north end of Mauchline on the A76 were designed by William Fraser of Glasgow and opened in 1898. The tower is now an information centre.

The Welton road, south-east of Mauchline Cross, offers a walk by West and East Welton farms and on by a track to join the B743 Sorn road near Grassyards. East Welton has an oval window facing the courtyard and a splendid boundary dyke of red sandstone slabs north of the track. Mauchline Hill on the B743 gives a good view of the town and far beyond, with Sanda prominent in the sea south of Arran.

The A76 runs south-east from Mauchline past the tall classical column of the War memorial at the B705 junction. The River Ayr is crossed on the reinforced concrete Howford Bridge – a single span of 90 metres opened in 1962. The old two-arch bridge below shows mortise and tenon jointing and is still in use if you wish to take the long winding drop and ascent. It is worth doing this to reach the start of a splendid walk and to see a remarkable display of prehistoric cup and ring markings on a vertical sandstone face (511255). As well as the normal cup and rings there are tadpole, S-shaped, and other markings on the face. A path to them starts at a stile on the most westerly bend of this old loop road near the high piers of a former footbridge over the road. The path can be followed down to the River Ayr along the rim of the Ballochmyle Gorge and under the railway viaduct. Both are recommended as the area is one of Ayrshire's greatest splendours, and one of Scotland's most spectacular river scenes.

Great bosses of bright red sandstone display their tilted bedding planes along the way as the path rises and falls amidst lovely woodlands, leading to lofty vistas of the river far below. Great care needs to be taken above the drops such as that from Table Rock (512254) – yet an easy path leads to the waterside for a dizzy view of the rail viaduct far above.

The bridging of this gorge was a great engineering feat as it is the highest railway bridge in Britain (51½ metres), and the main span is the longest masonry arch railway bridge in Britain (55 metres). The bridge was completed in 18 months between 1846-48 with John Miller as chief engineer, using sandstone from Ballochmyle, Auchinleck, and Dundee. Three smaller arches on each side of the gorge lead to the great semi-circular span across the chasm. The path on the north cliff of the river can be followed westwards to the Haugh, passing near the ruins of the L-shaped Kingencleugh Castle (503256) and meeting the lade which carried water to the mills at the Haugh.

The B705 from Mauchline to Catrine passes north of Ayrshire and Arran Health Board's hutted hospital at

Ballochmyle. Ballochmyle House, in the grounds to the east, is a B-listed red sandstone building, but is in a sorry state with dry rot and brick infills to deter intruders, and gaping holes in the roof which will not deter the weather. The house was designed by the Adam brothers in the 18th century and enlarged in Jacobean style by Hew Wardrop about 1890.

CATRINE was founded in 1787 when Claud Alexander of Ballochmyle and David Dale erected a cotton spinning works village beside the River Ayr. Dale was heavily committed in setting up New Lanark at the time, where the Clyde – unlike the Ayr – tumbles over spectacular falls. New Lanark has been restored as a fascinating tourist attraction today. Part of Catrine survives and some good restoration work has taken place, but the mills have been demolished, leaving great gaps in the village plan. This is an interesting place nevertheless, with significant traces of its industrial past.

The original five-storey mill stood in the middle of Mill Square until it was gutted by fire in 1963. A pair of gigantic wheels (15 metres diameter) were installed in 1827 to work power looms and operated for 120 years. A new mill was built to the west and worked from 1950-68. The road passes through the Square today – where four mature lime trees survive – but formerly had to go round the mills and alongside an open lade.

Go west along Mill Street and Ballochmyle Street to the bend leading to Mauchline. The former Catrine West U.F. Church designed by James Ingram (1836) is now the church hall. Retrace your steps past the R.C. Church (1962) and the Congregational Church (opened 1845 as the Free Church), noticing the attractive Ayr Bank House across the street with its fake windows. Ascend the Chapel Brae to Catrine Parish Church (1792). This is a fine building blending classical detailing with Gothic arched windows. The imposing pedimented frontage to the south is set off with a cupola bell tower. The church demands a strenuous climb from the faithful but rewards with a bird's eye view of the village.

Continue along the Sorn road to a tall grey granite obelisk commemorating the dead of two world wars. A footpath from the memorial brings you back down to Catrine, or you can continue a short way along the Sorn road, take the first turning right and come down the Radical Brae. Both routes converge on Laigh Road on the north bank of the River Ayr, where turn uphill again to St Cuthbert's Street. Here a row of millworkers' houses looks into the mill lade and voes which controlled the flow of water to the wheelhouse powering the mill. Water hens enjoy the cover of bulrushes on the voes directly in front of the dwellings.

St Cuthbert's Street leads to the bowling green on the site of a medieval chapel, where a private suspension bridge crosses the River Ayr to Daldorch House which was built for the works manager at the start of the 19th century and later extended. From the river bank there is a good view upriver to the weir and start of the mill lade.

Return by a path between the voes to Laigh Road and cross the river past the power house and bleach works (now a bonded whisky warehouse). Turn west for the centre of the village past Avonlea and take the left fork along Newton Street past Catrine House. This dates from 1682 and has one of three urns left on the pediment. In 1786 Robert Burns dined here with Professor Dugald Stewart and Lord Daer a few months before the professor's rural retreat was invaded by the mill complex and workers needing to be housed. In 1903 the Glasgow and South Western Railway Company made a branch line to Catrine with its terminus just outside the front door.

Continue south-east along Newton Street and turn right to the A.M. Brown Institute (1898, architect R.S. Ingram), a Ballochmyle sandstone building with a squat octagonal clock tower above a columned entrance. Brown was a director of Finlay and Company which operated the mills from 1801 till closure in 1968. Notice the two-storey row with backyard outhouses just off Institute Avenue. Cross the River Ayr by the footbridge near the door of the Institute and go along Bridge Street, which has been restored. This leads into Mill Square again where more restoration work is in progress.

The B743 from Mauchline to Sorn passes the entrance to Sorn Castle which dates from the 15th century, was enlarged in 1793, restored in 1865 by David Bryce, and enlarged again in 1907. A museum of vintage cars is planned in the grounds. An early 19th-century iron footbridge crosses the river beside a lade and turbine house which, aided by the Grid, supplied

The route of an old wagonway crosses the Garpel Water by Tibbie's Brig near Muirkirk. The monument on the right stands on the site of Tibbie Pagan's house, who, some claim, composed the song 'Ca' the yowes to the knowes'. The large cairn on Cairn Table in the distance was raised as a war memorial.

power to the castle. The surrounding district was extensively planted in the 18th century by the Countess of Loudoun.

SORN is a pleasant village lying in a hollow by the River Ayr. All roads drop down to its main street which runs parallel to the river. The church at the west end was built in 1658 and repaired in 1826. It has three outside stairs, and jougs hanging by the door. There are two memorials on the east wall to a Covenanting martyr. A stone by the gate shows what looks like a shepherd and lamb, with a skull suspended menacingly above. The former manse sits next the church and has several sundials in the garden.

sandstone bridge stands upstream with restrained segmental arches and a stone inscribed 'Built 1871 G. Reid, Catrine'. Sorn has won British and European awards for its tidy environment and floral displays. High standards are maintained in domestic gardens, and public areas such as the the bowling green, pleasance, and picnic area by the river. The school (1850) has Venetian windows, red snecked walls, and a wooden cupola bell tower. A former woollen mill sits by the river towards the east end of the village. Further east still at Dalgain at the foot of the big hill on the road out to Muirkirk there is an indistinct inscription on the bridge which looks like 'Jean Smith Mahon 1778'.

A circular walk from Dalgain follows the road on the north bank of the Ayr to Glenlogan Bridge, then by a track on the south bank to cross the 1871 bridge back to the starting point. Alternatively stay on the north bank and continue east to South Limmerhaugh on the Muirkirk road. This walk passes two pairs of limekilns (566264, 573263) west and east of Glenlogan House. This is a fine 2½ storey house above the south bank. The house was once occupied by J.G. Stephen of the Linthouse shipbuilding family. A ship testing tank was constructed at the farm to the north of Glenlogan House and now holds slurry.

The road south from the 18th-century bridge at Sorn passes Smiddyshaw farm with the ruin of a possible windmill tower (547264). Gilmilnscroft originated as a 17th-century tower house.

The big hill climb east from Sorn on the B743 takes you quickly into moorland. Blacksidend is a prominent ridge north of the road, with a Bronze Age cairn on its summit. Glen Garr at the north-east end of the ridge has another. A circular walk can be made over both from Sorn, descending through an area of coal and lime working hollows (573310) by the Burn O'Need to Meadowhead and the B7037.

The Pennel Burn rises on the east side of the ridge and drops over a waterfall into a gorge where more mounds and hollows tell of former haematite mining (601300). A public road leaves the Ayr valley near Garpel (624272) and runs up the Whitehaugh Water to Heath Cottage where the Pennel

Burn comes down. It is a scenic road, running along the top of a terrace for much of the way, with good views down the river. The remains of a chapel set up by the monks of Melrose stand on the west bank of the Greenock Water (635280). South of Townhead of Greenock are the remains of the 18th-century iron foundry of Terreoch on the south bank of the Ayr (643270). Haematite from the area was shipped to Bonawe in Argyll to be converted into pig iron and was then shipped back to Ayr and transported by pony to Terreoch forge. The ruins of the forge, the lade cut across a loop of the river to power the forge, the ruins of an arched bridge over the lade, and a number of man-made mounds remain. A cairn on the north bank (645269) commemorates William Lapraik, a friend of Robert Burns.

Memorials to Richard Cameron and eight other Covenanting martyrs stand at Airds Moss (643259) where they lost a skirmish with the dragoons in 1680. Another martyr gravestone stands by a burn west of Upper Wellwood (672256). Upper Wellwood has a triangular 1606 marriage stone on its walls. There is a burial cairn on a hillock (665262) in a wood to the south of the B743-A70 road junction.

MUIRKIRK advertises itself, appropriately, with wrought-iron signs. This was a coal and iron working settlement in the past which now lacks industry for its sizeable population. A war memorial gateway with an interrupted pediment stands near the crossroads at the entrance to the park (695273). A stone by its side is the Glenbuck war memorial and was shifted here when the bulk of Glenbuck's population was re-housed in Muirkirk.

The church near the east end of the village, is a rather austere fortress-like building, but distinctive and unusual. It was built in 1812-13 and was the work of William Stark who designed St George's Church near Glasgow's Queen Street Station. The chancel window by Stephen Adam and Son came from the church at Kaimes to the south-west. The churchyard contains interesting stones, including the 'Cat Stone' commemorating two children reputedly killed by a wild cat, and showing the children and a fierce animal head. There is a Covenanting martyr, and Isobel Pagan who was (arguably) the composer of the song 'Ca' the Yowes to the Knowes'. The red sandstone R.C. Church of St Thomas (1906) stands to the west. The new cemetery at the north end of the village contains an obelisk commemorating Covenanting martyrs and was erected in 1887.

Kaimes, where the iron works used to be, south of Muirkirk, has a few residents left in what a nameplate identifies as 'Ironworks Cotts'. The Institute beside them is now an outdoor centre. To its west, the tiled mosaic floor of the demolished Kaimes Mission Church faces the sky. The former railway yards are now a motor sports area.

A track goes off beyond Kaimes to an attractive old bridge on the Garpel Water (689258) with a memorial stone beside it. The stone is on the site of the house of Isobel ('Tibbie') Pagan. 'Tibbie's Brig' was a wagonway for the mining industry. The old Sanquhar road is a track through the hills to Kirkconnel from Kaimes. It passes a cairn (695257) to John Loudon McAdam on the site of Lord Dundonald's tar kilns (1786-1827).

The old road rises to a col at 410 metres between Cairn Table and Wardlaw Hill, passing a light-coloured boulder known as the White Horse (705234). Both hills have very large conspicuous cairns at their summits – modern cairns superseding ancient ones. The western cairn on Cairn Table was constructed to those who died in World War I. The Wardlaw Hill cairn commemorates Col. J.G.A. Baird of Wellwood who was killed in 1917.

Just beyond the Muirkirk cemetery on the A723 to Strathaven a road to the left leads into a forest to the Long Stone of Convention (686279) on the top of a forested hill. The stone was set up in 1686 but was later broken and repaired. Farther north on the A723 (698300) a farm road goes east to Priesthill to another Covenanting site – John Brown's grave and memorial stone (730315) where he was shot in 1685.

Wetherhill Cairn (722304) is a Bronze Age cairn south-east of Priesthill on the top of the ridge. A rocky scree-strewn gap at the end of the ridge (718306) is the lip of a dry valley perched above the Ponesk Burn. The burn may have flowed through here in the past before taking a new route farther north, then cutting a new valley to the south-east well below the gap of its former channel. Middlefield Law (466m) is easily

The boundary between Ayrshire and Lanarkshire crosses Glenbuck Loch which was formed in the 19th century to secure water supplies for the mills at Catrine. The former railway route from Muirkirk can be seen crossing a causeway and heading left towards Douglas.

climbed from the A723 and bears a cairn commemorating the marriage in 1928 of R.L. Angus of Ladykirk, a leading iron and steel master in the Baird empire.

The A70, River Ayr, and former Muirkirk to Lanark railway occupy the valley east of Muirkirk, with a loop road going off to the north to Glenbuck, and a former railway from Muirkirk to Coalburn traversing the hillside farther north. A standing stone stands north of the A70 at Lightshaw on the edge of an area of opencast coal mining.

Glenbuck has few buildings or inhabitants today. The school and church are ruinous and little remains of the ironworks founded about 1795 save parts of what looks like the furnace built into the hillside (751294). Only the piers stand of the railway viaduct on the route to Coalburn — a line which never carried a train since a viaduct near Muirkirk was found to be unsafe due to mining subsidence.

167

The county boundary runs across Glenbuck Loch which was formed early in the 19th century as a reservoir for the Catrine mills. The youthful River Ayr spills out of the west end and under the A70 at the Glenbuck road-end. Glenbuck has little to show but its fame lingers from the days of the 'Cherrypickers' – the local football team – for a remarkable number of local boys rose through the junior ranks to play for professional and national teams. The loch has drowned the narrow pass, forcing the A70 to wriggle around the edge while the railway took a more direct route with the aid of a causeway into Lanarkshire.

CHAPTER 17
Cumnock and Around

The A70 follows an easy course from Ayr to Cumnock. As it leaves Ayr it is paralleled to the south by a straighter road which gives a good view over Ayr to Arran as it climbs from Masonhill and Crofthead. Masonhill Crematorium (362203) was completed in 1966 and won a Civic Trust commendation. Wee Macnairston (383191) has an observatory.

Following the A70, Sundrum (411212) is an ancient tower house disguised by later additions including a crenellated parapet linking three and four storeys under a roof pinnacled with chimney pots and conical caps. Secret passages exist within the massively thick walls and there is a fine cantilevered staircase. A service wing extends to a pavilion which has a Venetian window at first-floor level and an unusual bell and clock tower erected to celebrate the marriage of Claude and Marion Hamilton in 1877. The house has functioned as a hotel in recent years and looks over a cliff to the Water of Coyle. A waterfall – 'the Ness' – drove a turbine to provide electricity for the house.

On the opposite side of the A70, Carbieston Byres (395201) is an attractive farm with an unusual plan and arched cart bays at its entrance.

The A70 sweeps up a hill from the west into COYLTON. At the east end of the long village is a Gothic-style church, T-shaped with three galleries, a square tower, and crocketed pinnacles. It was designed by David Bryce and dates from 1832. It contains a bronze plaque in the Sundrum gallery by Robert Bryden of John Claude Campbell Hamilton. The Claude Hamilton Memorial Hall sits to the west of the church. The war memorial at the road junction east of the church was another design by Bryden, who was a local man.

Old Coylton, on the Drongan road, had an ancient church (421192). Only a bellcoted gable, an arch, a burial aisle, and a fragment of wall remain on the site, which is grass-covered and surrounded by headstones. Drongan is an unimaginatively designed scheme of council houses.

169

Trabboch (439219) has lost most of its population to Drongan. Two lochs separate a derelict miners' row and its wash houses from the former railway station and the bing of Drumdow pit. The lochs are a relic of mining subsidence, stocked and fished by an angling club. Schaw Church (446207), opened in 1844, is now redundant.

Trabboch Mains (456221) has a long shed with the arched entry in the gable end. Just to the east and visible from the road, part of two walls remain of Trabboch Castle. Muirston (474238) has an octagonal horse engine house; to its east there are attractive estate houses associated with Barskimming.

Killoch Colliery (480205) was opened in 1953 to be the showpiece of the county. Production started in 1960 but was plagued with geological faults, and after 25 years manpower was withdrawn and concentrated at Barony Colliery on the other side of Ochiltree.

OCHILTREE is a lineal settlement sloping down to the east towards the junction of the Burnock and Lugar Waters. Five roads meet at the mercat cross, a good point to explore from, but beware of the traffic. The buildings around the cross are distinctive – including a bow-fronted post office on the corner between the A70 and Mill Street, the Head Inn Hotel across the trunk road, and the Commercial Inn at the top of Mill Street next to a two-storey house with a pend dated 1789.

Along the terrace on the A70 beyond the post office, one door is surmounted by the Glencairn coat of arms with its 'Over Fork Over' motto, while farther on there is an old sundial on the wall. From the Burnock bridge you see the older bridge upstream. Its ruinous arch stops at the boundary of Burnock Holm house. A small public garden to the north-west gives a good view of this old bridge and the attractive three-storey and timpan (centre-gabled) house.

Return to the post office and follow Mill Street to the new bridge over the Lugar Water. The confluence of the Burnock and Lugar Waters is seen to the south, and in the other direction downstream are a weir, lade, picnic site and older two-span bridge. An old cemetery lies between the two bridges on the west. A path starts at the old bridge and goes downstream on the west bank to the early 19th-century Ochiltree Mill, and a smaller mill uses the same lade slightly

The British Legion occupy this 'House with the Green Shutters' in Ochiltree but the tablet on the wall commemorates George Douglas Brown who was born here in 1869. His novel *The House with the Green Shutters*, first published in 1901, is an astonishingly powerful drama centred in a small village which stretches down a long hill – just like Ochiltree.

downstream. A track leads back from the mills to the old cemetery and the cross.

Main Street rises steeply from the cross, widening after a bend and giving a good view eastwards over farmland to Barony Colliery and hills at Muirkirk. One- and two-storey dwellings range up the hill, some with doorways stepping down across the wide pavement. The church (1789) on the north side contains two stained-glass windows by Stephen Adam. Traditional styles of housing have been adapted, modernised, or bulldozed in places, but sufficient quality remains to give this thoroughfare a unique place in Ayrshire village-scapes – due to the unusually steep gradient and the feeling for the past expressed by many of the buildings.

Near the top of the street is the 'House with the Green Shutters' named after the novel by George Douglas Brown. Brown was born here in 1869 and is commemorated by a bronze wall plaque by Robert Bryden. The birthplace is now occupied by the British Legion. *The House with the Green Shutters* is a powerful tragedy which cannot have pleased the inhabitants of Ochiltree at the time as the characters in the story are not very likeable. There has been much discussion about the fictitious village of Barbie. Few who have walked Ochiltree's steep Main Street will have any doubt that this was the stage for the story – with Gourlay, the successful carter, exalting in his eminent position – both in business life and in the situation of his big house – as he looked down the slope, at the foot of which the inferior bodies gossiped at the cross.

Auchinleck House (507230) to the north of Ochiltree is currently being restored by the Scottish Historic Buildings Trust, which purchased the house and part of the estate from the Boswell family in 1986, and eventually should be open to the public by appointment. The house was built about 1760 by Lord Auchinleck and later received a visit from James Boswell (his son) and Dr Johnson on their Scottish tour. The house is one of the most elegant mansions in Ayrshire though the architect's name is not known. The building is fairly modest in size and has a richly-decorated pediment standing above Ionic pilasters. Four pavilions of red sandstone flank the honey-coloured rectangular-plan house.

The ruins of a 16th-century house stand to the west (502232) and the more sparse remains of a 14th-century castle beyond (500232) on a rocky height where the Dippol Burn joins the Lugar Water. The farm buildings to the south-west of the 18th-century mansion include a detached brick dovecot with an open lower stage (506228). There is an ice house, and a summerhouse cut from the sandstone rock beside the Dippol Burn (508232), and three bridges of note lower down the Dippol Burn. The first is just below the ice house, the second has a tall Gothic arch, and the third crosses a very deep gorge and is pierced by a footway on the south bank.

West of the Dippol's meeting with the Lugar Water, Wallace's Cave has been artificially cut into the cliff, but is very difficult to reach by a badly-eroded path.

The B7036 is a tree-lined avenue laid out by the Boswells from their house to Auchinleck Kirk. From this road Dumfries House can be seen to the south of the Lugar Water. Covered conveyors cross the road at Barony Colliery, the only British Coal pit left in Ayrshire. In 1962 a shaft collapsed at the colliery and a winding frame partly disappeared into the hole. A 330 MW power station built to the west in the late 1950s to burn slurry was demolished in 1983. Highhouse Colliery (549217) was worked from 1894 to 1983, and the head gear at one shaft has been retained as the focus for an industrial estate of small workshops.

Within AUCHINLECK the Boswell Museum occupies the old parish church (551215) which has a bellcote on the east gable and the date 1683 on the west wall. The adjoining mausoleum was built by Lord Auchinleck in 1753 and carries a splendid coat of arms of the Boswells. The Barony Church, the present church, was built nearby in 1839. It is a cross-shaped structure of pink sandstone with a bell tower added on an outside corner around 1898. The chancel windows commemorate the Boswell family. Moses is shown on one of the side windows carrying the Ten Commandments – two of which are numbered 'VI'! The churchyard contains a stone to Matthew Tait which states that he was born in the reign of Charles II, served as a soldier at the taking of Gibraltar in 1704, and died in Auchinleck in 1797, aged 123 years! An obelisk by the gate commemorates martyrs and locals of note.

Auchinleck's Main Street, with its derelict castellated Barony Church Hall, long-closed Picture House with Doric pilasters, and former Co-op with Art Deco arch, has seen better days. At the north end of the street the Auchinleck Arms Hotel has a worn mounting stone for horse riders, while the Market Inn's wall retains its tethering ring.

The railway station on the Glasgow-Dumfries line was re-opened to passenger traffic in 1984 after being closed for 20 years. Two red corrugated metal roofed shelters and a flat roofed signal box are modern faces of the railway, but the two-storey former station building of pink and red coursed and pinned masonry is an interesting survivor.

The A70 from Ochiltree to Cumnock passes Dumfries House, built 1754-59 to the design of the Adam brothers. It may be glimpsed through the trees, but privacy is preserved by the steep grassy banks of a ha ha (or artificial view blocker). The estate contains features of architectural importance including a splendid river bridge of three arches with tall pylons.

The A76 and A70 meet at CUMNOCK and chase each other round the outside of the Square on a one-way road system. The bus station and adjacent car park make good starting points for exploration on foot.

Follow the Auchinleck road over the Lugar Water and past the Congregational Church (1883) where James Keir Hardie worshipped. Regarded as father of the Labour Party, in 1891 he built for himself Lochnorris, the two-storey crowstepped house with a date stone on the south side of the A76 at the bend west of the Congregational Church. Beyond this house a path goes off downstream past Cumnock Rugby Club for a view of the ruins of the 15th-century Terrinzean Castle on the opposite bank of the Lugar.

The road between the Congregational Church and the Lugar Water leads to Woodroad Park, with an open-air heated swimming pool (1936), camping and caravan site, and several footpaths. The railway crosses the Lugar Water on the high 13-arch Bank Viaduct (1850, John Miller) which is best seen by crossing a footbridge (572205) and following a path on the south bank leading east under the viaduct to a U-bend in the river. Follow the path back to the arches and take the left fork to the houses on Keir Hardie Hill. All roads here lead to the A70 running downhill past the old cemetery.

An obelisk at the cemetery commemorates Alexander Peden. A thorn tree marks the graves of Peden and other Covenanting martyrs. Among the headstones are those of James Taylor, pioneer of steam navigation; and John Smith author of *Prehistoric Man in Ayrshire*. Continue downhill to the Square and parish church.

Cumnock Old Church is a Gothic-style building rebuilt in 1863-67 to plans by James Maitland Wardrop. Six main gables project in four directions from the church – vying in height with an angle-buttressed clock and bell tower at the south-east corner. A splendid bell in the porch was cast by Quirinus de Vesscher of Rotterdam in 1697. One window is signed by A.L. Moore of London, and a Bute vault stands at the north end of the church. The area round the church was a graveyard till the 18th century, when it was converted into thoroughfares. By the

Auchinleck House is a fine classical mansion built for the Boswell family in the 18th century. It fell into disrepair recently but has been purchased and is being restored by the Scottish Historic Buildings Trust. The pavilion on the left is one of four flanking the house.

1960s these had become congested with traffic. Two sides of the Square have been pedestrianised now.

Near the church stands the market cross, inscribed '1703 repaired 1778'. It was moved here from Townhead Street. The shaft stands on five steps and ends in a sundial and ball finial. Two sides of the sundial show the arms of the Crichtons. A plaque on a boulder nearby tells the story of the redevelopment of the Square, which is bounded by some good 18th and 19th-century buildings.

Bank Lane, just round the north-west corner of the Square, holds the Baird Institute (1891), designed by Robert Ingram, now run by the district council as a small museum.

To the south, the Crichton West Church on the A70 is a prominent landmark. Built in 1896 of local sandstone (architect, D. Menzies, Edinburgh), it has a pinnacled and spired tower 45m high, a five-sided apse, and a rose window. Several Gothic-fronted shops beside the church were also designed by Menzies.

Glaisnock Street takes the A76 towards New Cumnock. The Dumfries Arms accommodated Sir Walter Scott in 1817. Above it the Picture House survives on bingo. Then comes the Town Hall of 1884 designed by R. Ingram. A bust of Keir Hardie by Benno Schotz sits outside it, upstaged by a bus shelter. St John's Church at the top of the street was built in 1882 with financial help from the Marquess of Bute. It is a remarkable building with a rounded apse, a buttressed section of tower jutting from the side of the chancel with a louvred ventilator replacing the intended spire, and slated pitched roofs over the aisles and nave, which rises in king posts to a narrow barrel vault. Richly-painted boards by J.F. Bentley decorate the ceiling. In 1885 St John's became the first church in the country to install electricity.

To the south, off the A76, steps climb to the top of the 13-arch Glaisnock Viaduct. After closure of the Ayr to Muirkirk railway the viaduct became a footpath from the town to Barshare. That housing scheme won for Sir Robert Matthew and Cumnock Town Council in 1962 a Saltire Society award. You can cross the viaduct and return to the town centre by Townhead Street.

LUGAR, to the north-east of Cumnock, was an ironworks village from 1845 till 1928 though coal continued to be mined till the 1960s. Some well-maintained miners' rows have been retained along the A70 and at Craigston Square beside the Institute designed by R.S. Ingram (1892). The church behind is on the site of the original foundry. An inclined plane ran to the plateau above, where new works were established in 1866, and a century later the National Coal Board established regional offices. These are now Cumnock and Doon Valley District Council headquarters. The early 19th-century Craigston House once an ironmaster's house, sits by the road connecting the lower and upper works sites.

The Lugar Well is by the A70 (595214). Bello Mill house (597216) has been rebuilt on the site of the birthplace of William Murdoch, who produced gas lighting from coal gas among other discoveries and achievements. A bronze tablet commemorates this remarkable man who lived from 1754 to 1839. Stiles east and west of the house lead to the Lugar Water and a rock-cut cave where Murdoch carried out some of his experiments.

Just downstream is the roofless Bello Mill (where Murdoch's father was miller) with lade, mill wheel, and drive mechanism still in place. The Bellow and Glenmuir Waters meet above the cave. A tall seven-arch rail viaduct on the former Cumnock-Muirkirk route crosses the Glenmuir Water just above the confluence. It can be seen from the mill but looks even more impressive from underneath, where a dark cliff comes into view upstream on the north bank.

Two public roads meet to run up Glenmuir Water to Dalblair. The Glenmuir limeworks (630208) beyond High Glenmuir are of unusual construction. Near Dornal there is a possible motte hill (632194). Nether Guelt to the south-east has a three-bay cart shed. Little is left of Kyle Castle (647192) where the Guelt and Glenmuir Waters meet. A fine waterfall plunges into an impressive and remote gorge at Connor Craigs (713195). Near Logan there is a Covenanting memorial (593194).

The A70 climbing from Lugar towards Muirkirk looks north across the plateau of Airds Moss. Mining communities have vanished from the area, leaving behind trapezium-shaped vegetated pit bings, a few families living on in six traditional two-up two-down county council blocks at Cronberry, and open-cast mining. Trackbeds of G. & S.W. lines from Auchinleck and Cumnock to Muirkirk are still apparent, and a three-span railway bridge crosses the Bellow Water just east of an unusual brick signal box at a colliery junction (600225). A monument at Birnieknowe (577223) commemorates a nun killed by a train in 1888.

South of the A70, an old barytes mine above the Gass Water (655219) is of considerable interest and is worth visiting by those who can take care and look after themselves. For others it is a dangerous longitudinal gulch with deep fenced-off mine shafts.

From Cumnock the A76 heads south-east towards New Cumnock past Glaisnock House (575179) designed by James Ingram and now an educational centre. At Borland (583172) there is a former corn mill. The Black Loch, Creoch Loch, and Loch o' the Lowes lie at the watershed. The last two feed south through the River Nith to the Solway Firth. The Black Loch flows north for the Firth of Clyde – though after heavy rain it is reputed to spill to the Nith also. Ruined limekilns can be seen at Benston (580159), where minor roads cross. One heads north-west to join the B7046 which runs towards Skares and Sinclairston past open-cast coal workings.

The road south-east from Benston to Connel Park gives a good view over the River Nith to Glen Afton where the Nith has eroded a great scar fringing the road. A Covenanting martyr's grave (548147) sits in a hollow surrounded by plantations south-west of the summit of Carsgailoch Hill, and can be reached from Dalgig. A wagonway from the New Cumnock Iron Works (closed 1854) to workings at Beoch near Dalmellington can be traced along the Nith valley. A road from Benston crosses it at the Lane Burn (573112) before it rises by an inclined plane east of Sunnyside to descend to Waterhead; there it runs south of the prominent Castle Hill to a bridge point at the Nith, where ashlar work remains; another inclined plane takes it up the edge of the forest to a col and the vicinity of present open-cast coal workings at Benbain.

South of the B741, in the spruce forests south-west of Enoch Hill, the River Nith has its source, reached by a forest road from east of Clawfin (516080). The infant Nith is heading towards central Ayrshire, but soon turns east and eventually south to the Solway Firth – though it may in a past age have gone to the Firth of Clyde.

The A76 takes a Z-bend through NEW CUMNOCK between Pathhead and Afton Bridgend. The middle of the town, known as the Castle, is the most interesting part. A short road to the west up Castlehill brings you to the old church, but no castle. The hill is a natural site for a castle at the juncture of four valleys. Perhaps the stones from the castle were used to build the church, which is a T-shaped ruin now, showing Gothic and round-headed window spaces, and walls of ashlar.

A slim-spired church of 1912 to the north is no longer used. The parish church to the south was opened in 1833 (architect James Ingram) to replace the church on the Castle Hill. It is built of grey stone and has a tower whose design is reminiscent of that on Mauchline Church. The original high pulpit is still in place with curving stairs and a lofty sounding board.

A southbound class '3' locomotive is pictured in the 1960s hauling its wagons round the curve at Cumnock station after crossing Bank Viaduct. The station was closed in 1965 and, along with the Barony Power station on the horizon, has disappeared from the scene, while diesel power has ousted steam.

Opposite Castle Hill a memorial commemorates 'New Cumnock Mineworkers who lost their lives in the course of Duty'. It is in the form of a safety lamp on a plinth and is made from ebony and grey granite, and stainless steel rods, within a circular fence composed of black-painted chains, coal drills, and other tools of the mining industry.

At the north end of the town, part of the former railway station, closed in 1965, survives in the industrial estate. The railway line runs parallel to the River Nith and to a minor road running east from Pathhead towards Corsencon Hill. Between Mounthope and Mansfield Hall there is a triple draw 'improved' limekiln developed by Sir Charles Stuart-Menteath (639150).

The former Craigdullyeart Lime Works (663154) are by the roadside north-west of Corsencon Hill. Various openings in a crag face dip down into 'room and pillar' workings which are

Murdoch's Cave on the banks of the Lugar Water acted as a natural and secluded laboratory for William Murdoch when he carried out experiments with coal gas lighting in the 18th century. The cave is reached from the nearby ruin of Bello Mill at Lugar where his father was once miller.

linked by a remarkable paved roadway. The Guelt Lime Works to the north have high-arched double-draw kilns looking down on a water-filled quarry. These are interesting workings but require care and prudence and are not for the inexperienced.

Corsencon Hill is shapely, easily climbed, and offers good views of road, railway, and river in the valley which snakes its way out of Ayrshire through the pass to Kirkconnel. Thames-Clyde expresses no longer use the route, and it is being steadily downgraded in importance but it can be busy on Sundays when traffic is sometimes diverted from the main line over Beattock. Across the valley two Covenanting martyrs are commemorated by a memorial above the A76 (663130).

South of New Cumnock there is an attractive road up Glen Afton to the waterworks near the reservoir (1935). The cemetery near the start of the road contains many victims of mining accidents, including the Knockshinnoch Disaster of

1950 when 'the moss' to the west caved in, flooding the workings and entombing 129 miners; 116 were eventually brought out alive. The explosives house for Knockshinnoch Castle Colliery stands in a field opposite the last houses of New Cumnock, while the baths and other pithead buildings are across from the cemetery north of the moss. The screening plant to the west for open-cast developments is linked by rail to the main line west of New Cumnock. Farther up the Glen Afton road there is a cairn to Robert Burns celebrating the poet's verses, 'Flow Gently sweet Afton'.

The steep slopes of Blackcraig hill (700m) are impressive near the head of the glen. What looks like a cave on this face is only a gully with a waterfall splashing down it. The lower Craigbraneoch Rig (575m) is more majestic and gives a better viewpoint. The slopes look along the Afton Reservoir for some of the district's best views. Castle William across the river is a conspicuous rocky boss but is shown on Armstrong's 18th-century map as a building.

A good ridge walk goes round the reservoir over Windy Standard, Alhang, Alwhat, Meikledodd, Blacklorg, and Blackcraig. From Alhang you can look the length of the Afton Reservoir or south out of the county to the Holm Burn where a remarkable valley is pimpled with a multitude of drumlins.

CHAPTER 18

The Kyle Coast

PRESTWICK is the only coastal town in Ayrshire which does not have a harbour or jetty. In compensation, Prestwick has the airport. It is in an ideal location for weather and safe approaches and often handles diversions from other airports shut by fog and snow. The airport developed from a grass field in the 1930s to become Britain's main transatlantic base during World War II. After the war it was designated by the government as 'the second major international airport of the United Kingdom'. Vested interests in other parts of the country have seriously eroded its position.

The airport terminal (352271) was designed by J.L. Gleave and opened in 1964. Its spectators' gallery gives a good view of the apron and any planes present. Across the runway, below Monkton, British Aerospace Civil Aircraft Division occupy the former Palace of Engineering building which was brought from the Empire Exhibition site of 1938 in Glasgow by Scottish Aviation Limited. This factory has produced a number of notable aircraft including the Prestwick Pioneer, the Twin Pioneer, the Bulldog, and currently the Jetstream 31.

Behind the 'Palace' can be seen, on hill tops, a windmill/doocot (362280) and Macrae's Monument (366283). James Macrae became Governor of Madras in 1725 and returned to Ayrshire with a fortune in 1731. He purchased Orangefield estate and his mansion eventually became the airport terminal at the time of World War II but was demolished after the opening of the present terminal. 'Westburn', east of the airport apron, is a fine house in half-timbered style.

The terminal building contains a memorial plaque to David F. McIntyre who played a leading role in pioneering the development of Prestwick Airport and aircraft production here. He is also known for his exploit with the Marquess of Clydesdale in 1933 of piloting the first planes tȯ fly over Mount Everest. Beside the plaque hangs a large tapestry worked by the Women's Rural Institute celebrating the jubilee of the airport in 1985.

Prestwick celebrated 1,000 years of existence in 1983 on more precarious evidence. To see most of the town's attractions, start from the railway station car park and walk east to the Mercat Cross, rebuilt 1777 and resited 1963 in the town centre. The Town Hall and War Memorial were designed by James A. Morris in 1899 and 1921. John Keppie, the Glasgow architect and artist (1862-1945), lived with his sisters at Haddington Park West on the west side of the post office. Jessie Keppie was a distinguished artist, and fiancée for a time of Charles Rennie Mackintosh after he joined the firm of Honeyman and Keppie. John, Jessie, and other members of the Keppie family are buried in Prestwick cemetery (362263). The church-like Freemen's Hall to the north-east was built in 1844. The spire, added later, overlooks the original site of the mercat cross. The church beyond was built in 1874 as the Free Church. John Keppie designed the grey tower which was added in 1896. Two windows in the church are by James Benson. The arcaded hall to the side dates from 1932.

Turn down Kirk Street from the Freemen's Hall to the roofless pre-Reformation church of St Nicholas which stands on a hill surrounded by gravestones. Some of the older stones are intricately carved with winged souls, symbols of mortality, and trade emblems. One shows a cogged (mill?) wheel, and two stones carry similar teams of four horses pulling a plough.

The Prestwick Airport Club at the bend of the street was formerly a golf club house (1908, J. Gibb Morton). Beyond are the fin-shaped gables of a sewage pumping station and transformer and the airport terminal, which have taken over fairways of the golf course. Continue to the end of the street, pass under the railway, and cross the Old Prestwick Golf Course to the shore – there is a right-of-way, but beware golf balls! A cairn can be seen by the boundary fence on Links Road (348261) commemorating the first twelve British Open Championships which were held here from 1860.

The sand dunes above the shore make a good viewpoint. The sewage pumping station at the north end of the promenade won a Civic Trust Award in 1986. Walk the prom southwards, past the site of the Bathing Lake, noting the Links Hotel (1901, James A Morris) and the Cotswold-style 'Stonegarth' (1908, J.K. Hunter). A Polish War Memorial stands in the garden of the latter. It is dated 1945 and was moved from the vicinity of the former Monkton Station where a Polish unit occupied an army camp at the time of World War II. At the far end of the prom beyond the sailing club are two venerable buildings associated with the salt pans where salt was once produced from sea water.

Turn inland at the south end of the prom and follow Maryborough Road over the railway to the ruins of St Ninian's Chapel at the site of Kingcase Hospital, beside Bruce's Well. Robert Bruce is reputed to have derived benefit from the water and endowed a lazar house here. St Ninian's Episcopal Church nearby was built in 1926 as a smaller replica of St Margaret's in Newlands, Glasgow.

Follow the A79 northwards past St Nicholas Church, the dominant landmark of the town. It was built in 1908 in Romanesque style as designed by Peter MacGregor Chalmers. Notice the oblique jointing in the Ballochmyle sandstone of both church and manse. The church contains windows by G. Maile and Gordon Webster. Continue north by the Main Street. A short way up St Quivox Road is the R.C. Church designed in 1933 by James A. Carrick. Further along Main Street is the former Broadway Cinema, opened in 1935 to the design of Alister G. MacDonald. Just beyond, a baker occupies 'moderne' premises.

The South Church beyond the cross roads was designed in Gothic style by James A. Morris and opened in 1884. One window is signed W. Meikle and Sons. The dressed grey freestone church hides its cramped predecessor behind, designed by John Mercer only four years before. Across the road to the north-east a restaurant at No 61 Main Street displays good Art Deco design despite alterations. The Main Street leads back to the cross and station.

On the outskirts of the town is the 19th-century Shaw Tower (367261) reputedly built as an observation point for hawking. The former St Cuthbert's Church (357267) was designed by David Bryce, 1837; to its east on the Pow Burn are traces of Pow Mill.

The village of MONKTON was once a busier place, but the westward extension of the airport runway required a re-alignment of roads and Monkton is now by-passed. The Cross

Waves lash across the almost deserted promenade at Troon in a January gale. In midsummer the scene can be busy with holiday makers and day trippers enjoying the shoreline while farther inland golfers crowd the links created on the raised beach. This view is from the Ballast Bank which was built up with excavations from the harbour and ballast brought from Northern Ireland by returning coal boats.

is the centre of the village. It is surrounded by the older part of the school; the Carvick Webster Memorial Hall gifted to the village in 1929; the Wheatsheaf Inn; and a two-storey dwelling which was once the Crown Inn (see north-east gable). The bellcote on the hall is a relic of the building's original role as a Free Church. The village retains some vernacular buildings in the terraced rows facing the principal streets but most have been modernised.

The old St Cuthbert's Church at the south end of Main Street was de-roofed after the opening of Bryce's church in 1837. A half-round arched doorway in the south wall of the old church has 13th-century mouldings. The churchyard contains a large classical-style memorial to William Weir of Kildonan and Adamton, and a variety of older stones. Notice the ingenious hinging of the churchyard gates which open

outwards to lie against the walls. The old manse to the east
dates from 1822 and its stables back on to the churchyard.
The Hare Stane (358282) sits in a field north of the village.
Fairfield Lodge (357283) and cemetery (353284) are survivors
of Fairfield House estate. There is a conical capped
wheelhouse to the south of the A78/A79 roundabout, and a
small doocote to the east.

The now-ruinous church at Crosbie (344295) and its small
graveyard were sufficient for the needs of Troon till the 19th
century. Fullarton House stood to the north (345302) but was
cleared away, leaving only two classical pedestals on the wings.
The re-developed courtyard to the south is private, but most of
the estate is now a public park and some items of estate
'furniture' can still be seen.

TROON shares the same sandy bay as Ayr and Prestwick. All
three have suffered from the tourists' new preference for
foreign beaches. Troon has turned the inner harbour of its
declining port into a yachting marina.

It was the construction of this harbour which led to the
development of Troon in the early 19th century when the 4th
Duke of Portland needed an outlet for coal from his lands at
Kilmarnock. The nose of land jutting into the Firth at Troon
provided the harbour, and a plateway railway was opened
about 1812 with horses pulling wagons of coal, and later
passengers. In 1816 the Duke introduced a Stephenson
locomotive to the line. So, was it the first steam passenger
railway in the world? The *Guiness Book of Rail Facts and Feats*
accepts it as 'the first 'proper' railway in Scotland'. A silver
model of the locomotive, *The Duke*, was made for the silver
wedding of the 6th Duke and Duchess of Portland, and can be
seen in Troon Town Hall. *The Duke* also features in the town
coat of arms on the lamps outside, and on the nearby war
memorial at the sea front.

The neo-Georgian Town Hall was designed by James Miller
and opened in 1932. It is a good starting point for a walk
round the town as there is a car park beside it (322307). The
Portland Church to the east was built about 1914 and has a
hammerbeam truss roof.

Go north-east along St Meddans Street where, on the next
corner, is St Meddan's Church (1888, architect J.B. Wilson).

This has a soaring broach spire, and windows by W. Smith; John Blyth; and Norman M. Macdonald. Both these churches have Church of Scotland congregations, but continuing along the street under the railway bridge we come to the Catholic Church of Our Lady of the Assumption and St Meddan (1911). This was designed by Reginald Fairlie who based some of the detailing on the 15th-century Church of the Holy Rood in Stirling. The Troon church features an unusually broad tower, from which juts a smaller stair tower bearing an open timber crocketed spire.

Retrace your steps to the railway where the station is another of James Miller's designs (1892). Unusually there are four approach roads to the elevated station, which gives a good view over the level town. The two St Meddan's churches are important landmarks, and to the east the copper-domed Marr College opened in 1935.

Return along St Meddan's Street and go along Church Street into Academy Street. The former St Patrick's Church was the first Catholic church in Troon. They had a long wait for it. The 5th Duke of Portland refused them a site, so he became a feature of the prayers of the itinerant congregation as they intoned the 'Bona Mors'. These prayers for a happy death to the Duke were answered in 1879 and the church was opened in 1883.

Turn right from Academy Street into Ayr Street. The two churches standing side by side belong unusually to one congregation – Troon Old Parish Church. The grey stone classical church was opened in 1838 with the steeple and clock being added later. It was soon found to be too small for the growing congregation. In 1895 its red sandstone neo-Gothic successor was opened (architect, Hippolyte Jean Blanc) and the older church was retained as a church hall. The newer church contains windows by Gordon Webster and Gordon McWhirter Webster.

Beyond the Cross is the curving Templehill, named after a folly that once stood on it. The buildings at the far end, overlooking the harbour, date from the beginning of the 19th century, including the Anchorage Hotel (which displays two large anchors) and the Bank House at the corner of Bank Street.

Follow Harbour Road past the marina and shipyard where a covered berth allows all-weather shipbuilding and repairs. Take a look at the harbour, then go west at the row of 19th-century cottages and offices at the entrance gate, to a picnic area beside a large anchor.

If the weather is favourable, the walk south-east along the Ballast Bank can be very enjoyable. The bank was built up over many years, partly by ballast unloaded from coal boats returning from Ireland. The views are good from here and a view indicator identifies important landmarks. Lady Isle two miles offshore is an uninhabited bird sanctuary. Descend to Titchfield Road and follow it, then Portland Terrace, round the bay past the site of the swimming pool. At the junction, West Portland Street leads back to Ayr Street past the Bethany Hall (c.1847), while the Esplanade leads past the Concert Hall, Walker Hall, and war memorial to your starting point. The bronze figure of Britannia on the war memorial was sculpted by G. Walter Gilbert.

If you continue along the Esplanade you can see a stone (324304) marking 'The Northern Boundary of the Port of Ayr' – the southern boundary being at Carleton Bay between Girvan and Ballantrae. South Beach and Bentinck Drive run parallel to the Esplanade and contain buildings from about mid-19th century in a wide variety of styles. The Welbeck Hotel in Bentinck Drive is in the Arts and Crafts manner. St Ninian's Episcopal Church to its south was designed by James A. Morris and features oak doors and furniture by Robert Thompson of Kilburn, bearing his distinctive carved mouse trade mark. Piersland Lodge (331298) in Craigend Road was designed by William Leiper in black and white timbered style. Also beside the golf courses are the Marine Hotel (329296) and the Sun Court Hotel (332292) which has a court for Real Tennis.

The A759 runs from Troon to Loans and continues east as a minor road to cross the Dundonald Hills, which carry important navigation and communication equipment for Prestwick Airport. Because of the isolated nature of this rocky intrusion on the coastal plain, the views from these hills are extensive and can be spectacular at sunset. A ring fort (360325) above Harpercroft has two widely separated and ruinous defensive walls. The remains of another fort lie a short distance

Ponies scrape snow from their grazing below the royal castle of Dundonald. The impressive keep dates from the 14th century but the site was used long before that and has recently yielded important archaeological evidence.

to the north-west. A walk goes through Dundonald Glen, leaving the road near the entrance to Hallyards quarry (361336) and past Collennan reservoir on the east before joining the road between Barassie and Loans.

DUNDONALD has developed beside a royal castle which sits on an elevated site with good prospects in all directions, save to the west where the wooded hills rise above it. The site has been in use since ancient times, and archaeological work is proving its importance prior to the days when Robert II lay dying here. The castle has developed over several periods and should be open to the public once present repair work is concluded. Its true status as an ancient monument and as a piece of scenery may then be recognised, and people may well wonder why Ayrshire's tourist industry has so neglected it.

The main street of Dundonald lies beneath the castle and is the most interesting part of the village. The houses come right up to the street and traditional 'long riggs' stretch well behind to the west to give those on that side of the street very narrow but long back gardens. A terraced row of one and two-storey buildings occupies much of the west side of the street, while a shorter range on the east turns single-chimney, double-windowed gables to the street. The local whinstone is in evidence as a building material, though roughcast and paint frequently try to hold their secrets. Sometimes the whin is coursed in sett-like blocks as the local quarry produced paving setts for Glasgow and elsewhere.

The street undulates upwards to the narrow steepled church at the south end, built in 1804, with a chancel added later. It contains a window by Gordon Webster and two portraits by J. Kelso Hunter. The churchyard has a number of decorated symbol stones including an Adam and Eve stone and a stone of 1734 showing horses pulling a plough. Beyond the village hall to the north, a driveway leads past a lodge built for the beadle, to the former 18th-century manse. Auchans (355346) is a ruined 17th-century or earlier fortified house which has been much extended. Johnson and Boswell visited the Countess of Eglinton here in 1773.

DRYBRIDGE is a hamlet with a standing stone (358365) and a pharmaceutical factory. It gets its name from the road bridge passing over the railway, which was said to be the first bridge built in Ayrshire which did not cross water; 1½ miles to the east is the 'Wet Bridge' which was even more special – it was the first railway bridge built over water in Scotland. Both were constructed for the plateway railway from Kilmarnock noted under Troon. That old four-arch river bridge still stands (383369) half a mile downriver of the modern five-arch railway bridge. The route can also be traced to the site of a timber bridge between them – the second in chronological order – built when standard gauge replaced the 4-foot wide Glenbuck cast-iron plates. The oldest bridge can be seen from the road at Laigh Milton Mill (384373).

SYMINGTON has a notable church built in Norman times, altered in the 18th century unfortunately, but restored by Peter McGregor Chalmers in 1919 – retaining the north gallery but removing others from the extensions. The church features several Norman windows and a collar-beamed roof showing

The church of Symington dates from Norman times but was clumsily altered in the 18th century when the central window in the chancel was destroyed to give access to a new gallery. In 1919 the church was restored by Peter McGregor Chalmers who removed two of the three galleries, stripped off the ceiling to reveal the original oak timbers and restored the central window.

original oak timbers. Some splendid stained glass has been added in this century by Douglas Strachan and Gordon Webster.

The road to the south of the church, and the Main Street which it joins, are part of a conservation area which has a number of attractive buildings. There are interesting streetscapes at the gateways to the church and by the war memorial. Narrow streets bend round corners and out of sight in a manner which has been largely destroyed elsewhere in the interests of traffic.

Coodham (396327) is a Georgian mansion with an interesting stable block and lodges in wooded grounds which contain a sizeable lake. In 1874 a magnificent private chapel was built adjoining the house, featuring splendid craftsmanship in marble, oak, and stained glass. This Anglican chapel was converted later to a Roman Catholic chapel when the Passionists bought the estate as a retreat. A recent proposal plans to convert the estate into a time-share complex. The hill at Barnweill is crowned with a Gothic-style tower (406295) built in 1855 in memory of William Wallace, the Scottish patriot. An earthwork fort (407301) and the ruins of an ancient church (405299) can be found to the north, with farther north yet the ruins of Craigie Castle (408317). Craigie is a quiet village set in the hills with a church, an inn, a few dwellings, and an ancient dun (427327). Farther off to the east is Carnell (467322), a grey three-storey tower, possibly 16th century, from which a more modern two-storey house extends, beside fine gardens which are open to the public from time to time.

CHAPTER 19
Kilmarnock and Around

You need to search hard to find Kilmarnock's attractions represented on calendars, post cards, or in the tourist press. It is Ayrshire's biggest town and most other places of this size in Scotland are much better known. Kilmarnock has done little for its image. The town made the great mistake of turning its back on its river during successive redevelopments. Much of the town centre has been reconstructed with buildings of nondescript and anonymous character. Yet Kilmarnock is well worth visiting, for it has many fine buildings, attractive open spaces, and interesting features of historical note.

A one-way traffic system circulates around the town centre, with the main car parking at the north end between the railway and the bus stations. This is a good starting area for a tour of the town. The multi-storey car park and the adjacent Clydesdale Bank with its offset drum tower are two of the better modern buildings in the town. The upper deck of the car park makes a good viewpoint.

Walk north under the 23-arch railway viaduct built in 1848 and still carrying a main line south from Glasgow via Dumfries. Beyond is the Old High Kirk, a plain classical building with a conspicuous steeple, built between 1731 and 1740. The churchyard contains the graves of Thomas Morton, telescope maker and inventor; Thomas Kennedy, water meter manufacturer; John Wilson, who printed the first edition of Robert Burns's poems; and the Tannock brothers who were artists. A fluted column and tablet in the outer wall and a plate on the road commemorate Lord Soulis, an English nobleman said to have been slain in a skirmish in the 14th or 15th centuries.

Cross Wellington Street to the west, between the Gothic-style West High Church and the former Kilmarnock Infirmary. Go along Garden Street behind the church and turn right up Hill Street to the pinnacled St Joseph's R.C. Church (1847) and the red sandstone Nazareth House. Across the road is the massive blending and bottling plant for Johnnie Walker Whisky, completed in 1955.

Retrace your steps down Hill Street and enter the railway station by the underpass. This extensive station has seen busier days when this was the centre of a network of branch lines. As you walk down the approach road from the booking hall the original station building is at the entrance to the Freight Depot – three storeys of paler sandstone (1843) contrasting with the redder two-storeys of the later building (1878).

Turn right uphill at the traffic lights and go along West Langlands Street to see the Caledonia Works of Andrew Barclay Sons & Co. Ltd. The firm was established in 1840 and has built up an international reputation in engineering with its 'pug' locomotives and colliery machinery. Barclays were pioneers in the production of fireless locomotives in this country and are still producing locomotives today. A venerable grey stone range beyond of two storeys and two lines of attic windows has an odd dormer at the north-west corner – said to have been used by Andrew Barclay as an observatory.

Turn left into North Hamilton Street, noticing the pyramid-shaped modern housing farther to the west. Turn left again around the Barclay Works into Park Street opposite a white-glazed brick tenement row, dated 1883, designed by Robert Ingram.

Descend the hill towards the town centre and turn right along Grange Street past the birthplace in 1784 of James Tannock, identified by a bas relief panel showing a reclining figure in front of an artist's easel. Tannock studied under Alexander Nasmyth and became a notable artist in London. His brother William stayed at home and erected a picture gallery at the end of the house with a venetian window.

The Renaissance building at the south end of the street on the same side was altered for use as a store, but has a fine elevation round the corner. Notice the variety of heads decorating the sandstone facade. The former 'Kilmarnock Standard Printing Office' advertises itself on the wedge-shaped building opposite. Johann Gutenberg and William Caxton's heads are identified by their initials. The Grange Church towers above these buildings. It was built in Early English style 1877-79, to the design of R.S. Ingram.

An impressive array of banks can be seen in the opposite

Kilmarnock railway station from the north-west with the line from the Ayrshire coast at Barassie curving round in the foreground alongside the main line from Glasgow to Dumfries. The station has lost much of its former importance now and the platform on the left is seldom used. The Johnnie Walker whisky blending plant developed over several decades as the original plan was interrupted by World War II.

direction where Grange Place joins John Finnie Street. The T.S.B. in red sandstone has a rather ponderous classical style with Corinthian pilasters. To the east, in Bank Street, the Bank of Scotland shines with simpler creamy virtue. Between the two intrudes the brash new Royal Bank of Scotland building, with its glazed walls reflecting the street scene, and further eroding the street tradition of building in red sandstone.

Go south along John Finnie Street to the traffic lights at the end. To the east in St Marnock Street is the modest and classical former Sheriff Court (1852). Across from it is the Gothic St Marnock's Church (1836, James Ingram) between the Police headquarters and the massive new Sheriff Court (1987). The contrasts in court buildings must say something significant regarding the advance of crime or of lawyers between Victorian times and today. To the west from the traffic lights a short distance along Portland Road is the Howard St Andrew's Church, where fluted concrete panels and rounded corners have produced an attractive modern building. Three older panels of stained glass have been preserved opposite the main door. Cross the road to the Holy Trinity Episcopal Church, built in Early English Decorated style in 1857 to the plans of James Wallace. The chancel, by Sir Gilbert Scott, was added in 1876, and is decorated with roof panels of the twelve Apostles and twelve Prophets, as well as wall murals. Windows include the work of Powell and Sons; Clayton and Bell; and William Aikman.

Go south from the traffic lights along Dundonald Road past the Winton Place E.U. Congregational Church (1860, James Ingram). This side of the street has a Victorian Gothic character due to the church and two houses beyond. Enter Howard Park on the corner. This area once formed part of the grounds of Kilmarnock House and a terminus for the Duke of Portland's early railway to Troon. Keep along the right-hand edge of the park to find a memorial to the cholera victims of 1832 who were buried here.

Leave the park at its south end, past the monument to a local physician. Cross the Kilmarnock Water by the West Shaw Street Bridge, decoratively panelled in cast iron. Notice the 'B' listed Walker Buildings in Hood Street across the green to the right of the B.M.K. offices. These three tenement buildings were built in 1904 in the Arts and Crafts manner.

Continue past the carpet factory to the traffic lights in Glencairn Square, which was laid out in 1765. Turn left along High Glencairn Street and Titchfield Street past the fire station, sports complex, and the town's only remaining cinema housed in an early 20th-century theatre.

The pedestrianised King Street beyond the traffic lights, the main shopping centre, can be very crowded during the daytime but becomes a lonely place to window-shop in the evening. Several premises still retain their character among the transient fashions and box-like architecture. Take the first turning to the right through the car parks to cross the busy three-lane one-way Sturrock Street at a pedestrian crossing.

To the south may be seen the Baptist Church (1870) and the Original Seceders Church (1857). Closer at hand in Sturrock

Street is the Conservative Club in a Renaissance-style building (1887, R.S. Ingram). Climb the hill by the flight of steps to the clock-fronted Kilmarnock Academy (1898). Go round it to the south, past St Columba's Primary School. At the far end of the Academy is an annexe which was once Kilmarnock Technical School (1909). We are back in the land of red sandstone and the annexe is particularly rich in decorative work. Loanhead Primary School to the south was designed by Robert Ingram c.1903.

The neo-classical Dick Institute sits east of the Academy and contains Kilmarnock's main library with a museum and an art collection which includes work by Constable, Corot, Turner, and the Glasgow School. The building was designed by R.S. Ingram and opened in 1901. Above the pediment of the portico entrance sits the figure of Minerva representing Wisdom. Across the street is an impressive war memorial designed by James Miller and dedicated in 1927. Built of grey stone in the form of a temple, it contains a statue of sorrowing 'Victor' sculptured by David McGill. Nearby is a marble statue by James Fillans of Sir James Shaw who was born at Riccarton in 1764 and became Lord Mayor of London in 1805.

Cross London Road at the traffic lights, take the side road past Kilmarnock College, under the railway bridge, and enter Kay Park.

Within the park, on the highest ground is the Burns Monument designed by James Ingram and erected in 1879. It is a Scots baronial tower of Ballochmyle sandstone approached by a staircase past a statue of the poet by W.G. Stevenson. Nearby is a splendid cast-iron fountain by McDowall Steven and Co Ltd erected in celebration of the coronation of 1902. A tall Corinthian column stands to the north in honour of Kilmarnock pioneers of parliamentary reform, some of whom were imprisoned for sedition in 1817. This Monument (1885) has lost its statue of Liberty in a storm. Notice the fine Scots baronial gateway and west lodge to Kilmarnock cemetery on the east over the boating pond.

Leave Kay Park by going down beside Kilmarnock Water, under the railway viaduct, past pollarded willows, and rejoin London Road at Henderson Church (1907). A tablet can be seen to the south-east, on an upper road, marking the site of

Tam Samson's House where Robert Burns was a frequent
visitor.

Go west past the impressive range incorporating the Grand
Hall and the Palace Theatre – built as a Corn Exchange (1862-
63, James Ingram). Take the underpass to the town-centre
shopping mall. A plaque marks the site of John Wilson's shop
where the first edition of Burns's poems was printed in 1786.
At the west exit a memorial commemorates a Covenanter's
execution. The domed bank, a splendid grocer's premises in
Portland Street and a few other buildings of character survive.

Leave the Cross by Cheapside Street, where a bridge on the
left crosses Kilmarnock Water, and walk around the Laigh Kirk
and its elevated graveyard which has stones to Covenanting
martyrs and Burns associates. The tower is older but the kirk
dates from 1802 and shows seven exits to prevent a repeat of a
stampede which killed 30 people in the previous building. The
present building contains windows by William Meikle and Sons;
A.C. Whalen; and Norman M. MacDougall. Opposite the kirk
in John Dickie Street are the Civic Centre and headquarters of
Kilmarnock and Loudoun District Council; and to their right a
remarkable range of three-storey 19th-century warehouses
which you can follow round a U-bend to return to Portland
Street and your starting point.

On the south side of Kilmarnock, Riccarton has a tall church
dated 1823 (429364) and a ruinous tower (418353) standing at
the junction of old wagonways, which probably housed a beam
engine but is reputed to have served as a signal box also.
Caprington Castle (408362) is an early 19th-century Gothic
remodelling of an older castle.

West of Kilmarnock, off the A71, Annanhill (413379) is a
Palladian mansion, now part of a golf course. Farther west,
Crosshouse has a striking red-sandstone church (1882, Bruce
Sturrock & Co.) with good windows by Meikle and Son; and
others. At the junction of the A71 and B751 nearby there is a
memorial to a local miner, Andrew Fisher, who became prime
minister of Australia.

At the north end of Kilmarnock, east of the A77, Dean
Castle is a 14th or 15th-century tower with a newer detached
house and tower all contained within a curtain wall, at the heart
of a District Council-run country park. The old tower contains

Dean Castle at Kilmarnock is now the centrepiece of a country park administered by the local district council. The tower on the left dates from the 14th or 15th century and houses a splendid collection of European arms and armour, tapestries and old musical instruments. The tower on the right may date from the 16th century and is joined to a gatehouse behind by a high curtain wall.

a valuable display of European arms, armour, tapestries, and musical instruments. There are often impressive and sometimes dangerous fords on the Kilmarnock Water (437391) and Craufurdland Water (451402). Craufurdland Castle (456408) is an old tower adjoining a 19th-century Gothic-style mansion.

Rowallan lies behind a high gatehouse on the B751 midway between Kilmaurs and Fenwick. Rowallan Castle is a 13th-16th century stronghold with a stairway entrance between twin conical capped towers. Its baronial successor to the north-west was designed by Robert Lorimer and built between 1903-06. Lorimer also designed the memorial cross to Alice Corbett (wife of the future 1st Baron Rowallan) which stands above her grave on Fenwick Moor at the junction of the A77 and B764.

FENWICK'S main street is long, winding, and wide, with a

gap between the lower and upper parts. Many of the older properties are grouped in terraces and step straight on to the street. Some show their weaving origins in the pattern of the windows with two to one side of the door and one to the other. High skews above the slates show where thatch was the original roofing material. Most properties have been modernised now but look for old detailing such as rolled skew putts, dated lintels, gables to the street, chamfered stonework and roundels. Notice the two doo-holes over the window of Rowallan smithy and the ploughman and horses represented above No. 81. The John Fulton Memorial Hall commemorates the Fenwick shoemaker who constructed the Orrery in 1832 which is now in the care of Glasgow Museums and Art Galleries. This is a working model of that part of the solar system which was then known to science.

Fulton is also commemorated by a headstone in the churchyard in Kirkton Road opposite the hall. There is also a splendidly-carved stone of 1727 showing a wright's square, dividers and axe, and two Angels of the Resurrection with trumpets; and some unusually wide headstones – one dated 1692, a double-size chest tomb, table stones and numerous Covenanting martyrs.

Fenwick Church was built in 1643 and attractively restored in the 20th century. Crow-stepped gables face outwards from the Greek cross plan. There is an outside stair to one of three lofts, with 1649 and the arms of William Mure of Rowallan on the ogee pediment. A belfry at the west end has an outside rope, and the jougs hang at the door as a warning to potential wrongdoers. Sentry boxes at both gates are dated 1828.

Waterside to the east on the A719 is a hamlet with a late 18th-century former mill and a one-time schoolhouse dated 1823. Moscow, farther south on the A719, has often-photographed name plates and a burn called the Volga. The road west from here to Kilmarnock passes the attractive Grougar primary school (1983), an octagonal farm building at Raws, and a 1799 lintel on a house beyond.

Lochgoin (530469) off the B764 is a moorland farm with a memorial and a museum (open to the public) commemorating the Covenanters.

KILMAURS has two towers which catch the eye – the St

This Martyr was By Peter
Ingles Shot
By birth a Tyger rather
than a Scot
Who that his monstrous
Extract might be seen
Cut off his head & kickit
o'er the Green
Thus was that head which
was to wear a Crown
A football made by clownfane
Dragoun.

Fenwick was a strong base for the Covenanters and a number of their martyrs are buried in the churchyard. James White's death was a particularly brutal affair if the inscription is accurate.

Maurs-Glencairn Church and the Town House. The church was extensively repaired in 1888 to plans by Robert Ingram. A Dutch bell of 1618 is still used and there are good stained-glass windows. One shows a representation of Rowallan Castle while there are rose windows on three sides behind the clock tower.

The vaulted burial aisle of the Earls of Glencairn, built in 1600, completes the cruciform shape of the church but is separated from it by a wall. This aisle contains an elaborate wall monument showing the 7th earl, his countess, and eight children together with their coat of arms. An inscription gives the sculptor as David Scougal of Crail. Two cavettos on the outside of the aisle bear the shakefork emblem of the Cuninghames, and a sundial on the south gable is dated 1753. There is a 17th-century lectern dovecote to the south-west of the churchyard. It can be seen better from a right-of-way path going between the two cemeteries and across the fields to the Crosshouse road.

Follow the A735 from the church towards the village, passing an old stone crest and inscription in the dip at Catherine Place. 'The Gleg Whittle' selling fancy goods reminds us of the former local industry in cutlery and sharp knives.

The Town House obstructs traffic at the junction of four roads, but is a unique attraction in the county for its middle-of-the-road position. Forestairs lead up to the former meeting place of the council. Underneath was the jail, and jougs for offenders still hang on the outside wall. The mercat cross stood to the north but was replaced by a more modern pillar.

Irvine Vennel to the west leads to Kilmaurs Museum in a 19th-century school (open Monday and Wednesday evenings in summer). The Fenwick Road to the east leads past the former Glencairn Church to Kilmaurs Mill (414414). A stone on the front depicts a sluice key, rope, pick and shovel. Mill Avenue to the south leads back towards the church past Holland Green on the right – birthplace of John Boyd Orr, first Director-General of the U.N. Food and Agricultural Organisation who was awarded the Nobel Peace prize in 1949.

At the summit of Morton Park on the right stands Kilmaurs Place, a restored 17th-century house of the Glencairns. The ruins of an older castle adjoin it to the west, with a fine war memorial nearby giving a good view over the Carmel Water to the village. The 'Monks Well' below was formerly the public water supply.

The A735 enters STEWARTON from the south under the impressive Lainshaw Viaduct. This has ten spans, curves across the valley of the Annick Water, and was opened in 1873. David Dale Avenue to the left leads past two lodges to Lainshaw House, now an old people's home.

At the roundabout beyond the viaduct, a lane to the right

The townhouse at Kilmaurs may have outlived its purpose as a meeting place and jail, but as the only example left in the middle of a street in Ayrshire it adds considerably to the character and tourist appeal of this small town. The mercat cross is a 19th-century replacement.

leads to the restored St Columba's church, built in 1696 and formerly known as the Auld Kirk. The churchyard contains some 17th-century stones, an obelisk to the uncle of Robert Burns the poet, headstones to labourers who fell from the Lainshaw Viaduct when under construction, and the mother of David Dale.

As you walk from the church to the town centre you pass Rigg Street at the Cross, where David Dale was born in 1739. In 1785 he started the New Lanark Mills where he practised enlightened policies regarding the welfare of his employees. The exact site of his birthplace is not known. The Social Club at the start of Rigg Street was originally a cinema.

The Main Street continues into High Street past the John Knox Church (1841). The Millhouse Hotel stands above the Corsehill Burn at the east end of High Street and carries the gable inscription 'No mill, no meal'. Opposite it is Sim's Mill, which supplied balaclavas to successful Everest climbers. Sim's Mill is a 19th-century complex with a cylindrical chimney and an engine house with Gothic arched windows.

Across the road, decorative iron gates lead into the Cunningham Watt Park where walks past a cairn lead up the Clerkland Burn to a bridge and steps leading south to Corsehillbank Street and then Graham Terrace. Robert Cunningham Graham, poet, traveller, nationalist, and gaucho was a frequent visitor to relatives in Stewarton and is commemorated by this street name.

Graham Terrace leads downhill into Avenue Street – which was planned and laid out in the 18th century, but never completed, as an impressive approach to an estate to the north. The Institute Hall dates from that time, while the small Congregational Church at the corner of New Street was built in 1828.

A short distance along Dunlop Street to the east brings you to the former Lainshaw Public School of 1876 with its pointed windows. Return to Avenue Street, go past the council offices which house a small museum, and you are back to Main Street again.

There are castle ruins at Auchenharvie (363443) and a fragment of a tower (417465) by the A735. East Pokelly (442458) carries an 1837 datestone showing a scythe and other farming tools.

The A735 enters DUNLOP from the south beneath a four-arch skewed rail viaduct. Dunlop roads are all bends and elbows and motorists are liable to miss the Glazert Burn passing beneath the viaduct and road, the former Lady Steps Mill to the west, the Hapland Mill to the east, and (in Netherhouse Road) Dunlop Cricket Club's ground – a very unusual feature in an Ayrshire village.

At the crossroads in the centre of the village, the former Free Church (1843) faces south as a church hall now. The road leading west to the Townfoot passes a former manse (1781) opposite the primary school; and Kirkland House, the splendid former manse of Dunlop, a crow-stepped greystone building with a capped stair tower.

The street narrows at the Townfoot with the church tower dominating the old terraced cottages. Marriage stones on the lintels are dated 1781 and 1782. A building near the church was restored in association with the National Trust for Scotland.

The church was rebuilt in 1835 and has some beautiful windows by Powell of London; and by Alfred and Gordon Webster. Near the session door a headstone erected in 1858 by John Frame, flesher, to his parents was the keystone of the former church.

Beside the front gate to the churchyard is the former Clandeboyes Hall with the burial vault of Hans Hamilton behind. Hamilton, the first Protestant minister at Dunlop, was created Viscount Clandeboyes by James VI and is depicted in marble with his wife facing each other in prayer inside the vault – known locally as 'the Picture Hoose' by those who have to peep in. The hall in front was built as the first school in the village in 1641.

Aiket Castle (388488) is a Europa Nostra award-winning restoration of a 17th-century tower house. This fire-gutted ruin was partly rebuilt in brick but harling hides all. Dunlop House (427493) is a Jacobean mansion designed by David Hamilton (1834) and is now in the care of Ayrshire and Arran Health Board. The Board also owns but no longer occupies Caldwell House (415542) designed by Robert Adam (c.1773).

Lugton is a hamlet at a road and former railway junction. It has limeworks and old kilns, and an eleven-arch former railway viaduct (399513).

CHAPTER 20
The Irvine Valley

The River Irvine flows west from Loudoun Hill through a distinctive valley until it reaches flatter land at Hurlford.

HURLFORD is a route centre with roads from the coast and from Lanarkshire and others from north and south meeting at Hurlford Cross, where the last propeller cast by Strang's Foundry rests on a paved area, bearing panels depicting aspects of working life in the community from the 19th century.

The two-span road bridge over the river was widened in 1905 and carries the A76 through Crookedholm past the war memorial, the Reid Memorial Church (1857 with spire added

Barr Castle at Galston dates from about the 15th century and has suffered some unfortunate additions. A plaque over the door records that George Wishart preached here in 1545 followed by John Knox in 1556.

in 1888), and Hurlford Parish Church (1875, James Ingram) in rich red sandstone with a south window by Sadie McLellan. A footpath goes down to the river (448373) and follows the north bank past a dam and under the seven-arch railway viaduct which carries the line from Kilmarnock to Carlisle. The modernised Riccarton Mill is seen across the river, then the path passes under the A77, then a branch railway bridge, before reaching playing fields on the outskirts of Kilmarnock.

Hurlford was a former railway junction with a second station, engine sheds, and workshops at Barleith to the south, where there is now a whisky bond only. The railway up the valley to Darvel was dismantled from 1964.

To the south of Hurlford Cross, the former U.P. Church in Mauchline Road is now just a hall. The two-storey school south-west of the Cross is an interesting red sandstone survival with a cupola-topped tower and richly carved symbols of learning above the windows. To the east of the Cross, Galston Road passes the two-storey Vulcan Foundry on the right and the yellow brick R.C. Church on the left, before passing into open country with Loudoun Hill a very prominent landmark ahead.

The A71 bypasses GALSTON on the north. Follow the A719 into Galston by Polwarth Street, and go through the crossroads to park under Barr Castle (502364). This is an impressive tower of red sandstone rubble with a hip roof above its corbells. Over a door at the south-west corner a plaque commemorates the preaching in this place of George Wishart in 1545 and John Knox in 1556. The building is now a masonic hall. An ancient tradition survived until recent years of playing handball against the castle wall in teams of three, with Galston challenging the world to take them on.

Walk back to the 'Four Corners', passing the Erskine Hall (1859) and the attractively detailed red sandstone Cooperative building. Turn left into Bridge Street, where the Burn Anne flows through the town centre. An even grander three-storey Co-op building on the left is dated 1901. Turn left along Brewlands Street, then right down New Road to Orchard Street, to see modernised terraces of sandstone cottages typical of this former mining town. The award-winning 1967 housing development between Brewlands Street and Orchard Street has added variety to the town. Turn back through Chapel Lane and enter the yard of Galston Parish Church by one of the back entrances.

The present church was built in 1809. It is rectangular in shape with a pedimented gable above its three front doors and round-headed windows. The red clock tower and spire are prominent above the roof-line of the town. A vaulted chancel was added in 1909 to the west side. The church contains a U-shaped gallery, a three-manual organ by James Binns of Leeds, a bell of 1696 by John Meikle of Edinburgh, and another of 1885. There is a memorial to Dr Robert Stirling, minister from 1824 till 1878, inventor of the Stirling Steam Engine. The churchyard contains two martyrs' monuments. One to Andrew Richmond carries sculptures of a Bible, a sand glass, and a dragoon shooting a Covenanter.

Leave the churchyard by the main gate opposite the baronial municipal buildings of 1926. Turn left then right into Church Lane. From a bridge the Burn Anne can be seen joining the River Irvine. Turn left into Polwarth Street past 'Blair's School' – a free school of the 19th century – and the former Brown's Institute of 1874, one of three given to the Valley towns by Miss Brown of Lanfine estate near Darvel.

Walk on to 'the Muckle Brig' for a different view of the confluence of the Burn Anne with the River Irvine just below a weir where salmon leap at the appropriate season. The three-span bridge built in 1839 bears a stone commemorating the original bridge built by Robert Legat in 1755. The ruins of Loudoun Castle (506378) are prominent above the trees to the north. The Castle, enlarged and embellished in 1811, was ravaged by fire in 1941. Loudoun Kirk (493374) is a picturesque ruin with some interesting gravestones.

Return along Polwarth Street past a number of interesting early 19th-century buildings and turn left into Henrietta Street. Opposite a former 19th-century lace mill turn right into Blair Street, and right again into Bentinck Street. The Templars Hall (1872) on the corner leads to St Sophia's R.C. Church which introduces a remarkably Byzantine prospect to Ayrshire. The church is in the form of a Greek cross, with a central dome 42 metres above the ground lit by eight windows. Doors, windows, and arches are half-rounded except for a circular window in the north gallery. The exterior is faced with red

The A71 curves its way through Newmilns alongside the River Irvine. The tall steeple of the church dwarfs the 16th-century Newmilns Tower to its left with the road climbing to Darvel beyond. The view is from 'Jacob's Ladder', a path rising from the A71 to the upper part of the town.

brick interspersed with masonry courses and rises to a drum tower under a slated conical cap. John, 3rd Marquess of Bute, commissioned the building as a memorial to his mother, Lady Sophia Hastings. It was designed by Sir R. Rowand Anderson and opened in 1886.

Leave Bentinck Street west, then south into Station Road. Opposite the fine war memorial, a path goes down past the 19th-century former Barr School to Barr Castle. Former S.C.W.S. blanket mills are in Garden Street at the south end of Barr Street. Just beyond is Galston Primary School, built in 1909, with detached and engaged columns at first-floor level and a heart-shaped motif in the boundary railings.

The Burn Anne can be followed upstream on the west bank from the bridge on the B7037 (507360), passing a low cave in the woods. Progress is barred towards Cessnock Castle, an ancient grey tower with lower additions which can be glimpsed from many points on the minor roads around it. There is a holy well on the stream (521352) and an extensive view from a Covenanters' monument on the ridge to the east (532354).

From Galston the A71 runs parallel to the River Irvine on its

209

north bank past Loudoun Gowf Club and enters NEWMILNS through several distinct phases of building – 20th-century council housing; Victorian villas; then continuous terraces of one and two-storey red sandstone dwellings. Look out for a car park on the right by the river. Walk from here along the main road on the north bank past the red-towered Cooperative building which stands on a gushet and commands the entrance to the town centre.

The old Town House (1739) on the right has a bellcote, crowsteps, and forestairs, and is now an information centre. A number of old buildings in Main Street are enriched with carvings and date stones. Behind the Loudoun Arms and easily missed is the 16th-century Newmilns Tower. The rubble walls are decorated above the entrance with two string courses. On a wall to the west is a plaque to a Covenanter slain here.

Continuing along Main Street, we pass Brown's Institute, then Loudoun Parish Church with a button-topped spire. During the American Civil War the weavers of Newmilns sent a message of support to Abraham Lincoln and received from him a U.S. flag as a token of appreciation. The flag inside the church was presented by the U.S. embassy in 1949 to replace the lost original. The church windows include the work of G. Maile & Son Ltd; and Gordon Webster. In the churchyard are several memorials to Covenanters.

Across the street is the Morton Hall, displaying an 1896 foundation stone and a sculpture showing the old Town House and a 'Weave Truth with Trust' motto. Beside it is another red sandstone building – the now-derelict Lady Flora's Institute, opened in 1877 as a girls' school in memory of the ill-fated Lady Flora Hastings. In front there is a civic garden and war memorial.

Main Street leads to Isles Street and the start of the climb out of town to Darvel. At the foot of the hill is a lace factory of 1898, built with yellow bricks and a red sandstone frontage. It was flooded by the Norrel Burn in 1954 causing considerable damage. Turn south before the factory into Union Street, go beneath the viaduct, then first left to a T-junction faced by an old crow-step gabled house. Turn right then right again into Ladeside past the modernised mill with a stone on its wall, 'No mill No meal JA 1914'. Pass the south end of Union Street,

The Irvine Valley towns have a high reputation for their skills in lace making, and many houses in the area display lace curtains in their windows. A lace darner is seen at work in the former Esco Mills at Darvel.

which has a three-storey mill on the corner, and on the other side of the road an unusual factory shop with white and grey enamelled brick walls, with red brick quoins, buttresses, and door and window arches.

Cross the Green and pass under the 26-arch viaduct of the former railway. Go past the back of the churchyard, climb the steps, and cross the early 19th-century Craigview Bridge. The road east provides an attractive riverside walk to Darvel. There is no through road for cars. Take the road west by the river to the two-span Bridgend Bridge, dated 1881 and carrying the inscription 'This arch destroyed by flood 1920. Rebuilt 1921'. The Royal Bank of Scotland on the corner is a remarkable building of red sandstone. Moorish windows combine with crow steps and other Scots baronial features to produce an unusual verticality for a bank.

At the far end of Brown Street a number of 19th-century mills and factories survive, with their functions changed. Vesuvius Crucible occupies an impressive range of buildings of two and three storeys. Notice the arches over the windows springing from sandstone piers, the sandstone cornices, curved pediments, sills, keystones and parapet contrasting with yellow bricks. The red-bricked range to the east is also decorated with sandstone, and dentil courses of brick. Farther west near the old railway bridge a two-storey sandstone-fronted factory has polyhedral finials.

Turn down to the river on the east end of that building and cross a footbridge – one of four which give access to the mills from the north bank. Shields Road and Riverbank Street lead back to the car park.

For the finest view of Newmilns, from the A71 at 533374 take the narrow path known as Jacob's Ladder up to Loudoun Crescent. The slope of the valley is used for a dry ski slope at 537376.

The A71 climbs from Newmilns to Darvel past Gowanbank. Now a hotel, this was the home of Alexander Morton who in 1876 brought to Darvel the first power loom for weaving lace curtains. A magnificent memorial to him sits by the road in front of Gowanbank. It was designed by Sir Robert Lorimer in 1926 and sculptured by Pilkington Jackson. The memorial contains a bust of Morton, two tablets showing the progress of the weaving industry, and statues of a boy with a sickle and a girl with a shuttle representing agriculture and industry. At the bottom of the valley is the old mansion of Waterhaughs, below the wooded estate of Lanfine.

DARVEL is a planned town, with straight streets and right-angled corners. The entry from Newmilns swings across the former railway line. On the right, at the corner of Dublin Road, the two-storey 'Lintknowe' is in Art Nouveau style. The 'Lang Toon' with its vista to Loudoun Hill is slightly reminiscent of Edinburgh's Princes Street and its Castle Rock.

Hastings Square in the centre of the town was laid out in 1815. A war memorial is flanked by the Dagon Stone and a

Darvel is a planned town with a long straight main street which opens out opposite the town hall at Hastings Square. A cenotaph dominates the square which also contains a memorial to Alexander Fleming, the discoverer of penicillin, who was born near the town.

bust of Sir Alexander Fleming by E.R. Bevan. Dagon is a basalt pillar around which wedding parties traditionally circled three times. Fleming the bacteriologist who in 1928 made the momentous discovery of penicillin was born near Darvel at Lochfield (583416) and attended his first school at Loudoun Moor (571409).

The Central Church on the south side of Hastings Square was opened in 1888 and contains a window, formerly in Gowanbank, celebrating the Diamond Wedding in 1923 of Alexander Morton and his wife. The Irvine Bank and Easton Memorial Church on the north side was built in 1885. The Town Hall (1911) to the east glows in red sandstone in contrast to the dark whin of its neighbour on the right. A number of buildings in Darvel show this dark stone which is sometimes, as here, used with red quoins for effect.

Ranoldcoup Road, to the east of the Square, leads past a fine

Co-op building and the former Irvine Bank Church to Mair's School of 1868 with an attractive classical frontage, and past Brown's Institute to Morton Park and the River Irvine opposite an entrance to Lanfine estate. You can walk along the south bank of the river from here to a footbridge opposite Waterhaughs and the west end of the Main Street, or continue all the way to Newmilns.

Darvel Old Cemetery in Causeway Road (566374) has a wall memorial to Alexander Morton and his family with two roundels by Pilkington Jackson. East Main Street nearby has more factory buildings along the River Irvine and Glen Water.

Loudoun Hill (316m) is a volcanic neck scoured by glaciers into a crag and tail formation. The hill has cliffs on the east and south sides but is easily climbed from the west or the north. A stone at the summit commemorates a battle in 1307 when Robert Bruce defeated an English force below the hill. Wallace had done the same in 1297. A memorial to John Jackson, a Strathaven climber, sits above the south cliffs. Sand and gravel are quarried south of the hill at the site of a Roman fort. A picturesque 13-span rail viaduct below the hill was demolished in 1986.

Distinkhorn (384m), the highest hill in the district, lies up the Avon Water past the heathery mound of Main Castle (612346). The Chair Stone (586332) is an erratic boulder with a smooth side to sit against.

CHAPTER 21

Irvine and the Garnock Valley

The Rivers Garnock and Irvine meet at Irvine which was designated as a New Town in 1966. This incorporates the old burghs of Irvine and Kilwinning, and smaller settlements such as Drybridge, Dreghorn, Springside, and Girdle Toll.

Irvine town centre is connected to the harbour by a covered shopping mall which spans the river, with a car park on its west side. The railway station is here also. Cunninghame House, the District Council headquarters on the north side of the car park, houses the magnificent Eglinton Trophy, made in 1842 and presented to the 13th Earl of Eglinton to commemorate his Tournament of 1839 (referred to later).

To see the harbour area, go under the railway and along Montgomery Street between the ship's bow-shaped flats. In Montgomery Place a shipyard worker's flat has been restored to the period of 1910 in a Victorian tenement and is open to visitors. This is one of the attractions of the Scottish Maritime Museum, which has a wedge-shaped Winch House and slipway to the river nearby, and its headquarters and workshops opposite in Gottries Road. Terraces of well-restored buildings lead along Montgomery Street to the museum's main attractions – its larger vessels moored at floating pontoons in the harbour. These include tug boat, puffer, and coaster. Other buildings at the harbour are the old Custom House and the Harbour Arts Centre.

The tower at the harbour mouth houses an out-of-use mechanism for warning approaching seafarers of the state of the tide. It was invented in 1904 by Martin Boyd, the harbour master, and involved twelve discs rising and lowering automatically by wires and pulleys as the water level changed. Sea World, in a Scandinavian-style building nearby, creates an underwater cavern-like environment for observing sea-living creatures housed in special tanks.

The Magnum Leisure Centre dominates the harbour area. It houses swimming pools, an ice rink, bowls hall, theatre or cinema, courts for a variety of sports, and many other facilities.

H

It is the focal point of an imaginative Beach Park which has a boating pond, trim track, fun fair, grass maze, wheelchair course, dragon sculpture, panoramic viewpoints and other attractions.

The walk through the covered shopping mall bridging the river passes a water-wheel sculpture, panels from Irvine Bridge and a fine view downriver past the Gothic-style Fullarton Church (1838), and the former Fullarton Free Church (1873) which stands by the river with its steeple truncated. The former contains a window by G. Maile, and a stone in memory of James Montgomery, poet, hymn writer, and journalist. At the eastern exit from the mall, the pastel-coloured and chequered stonework of Trinity Church towers above, with a window in the mall copying the rose window of the church and scattering colour attractively in morning sunshine.

The church was designed by Frederick Pilkington and opened in 1863. Its elevated site and high steeple make it the dominant landmark of Irvine. Redundant as a church, it was renovated for other community use.

An older Irvine reasserts itself as the narrow cobbled and flag-stoned Hill Street climbs southwards past some 18th and 19th-century houses of character, towards the wider Kirkgate and the parish church of 1774. Many of the windows are the work of local artists W. & J.J. Kier. A St Inan window by J. Blyth and W. Blair shows the emblems of Irvine trades and a scene at Irvine harbour. The churchyard contains some interesting memorials and leads by the back gate to the Kirk Vennel and the Golffields where the town built a powder house for its gunpowder in the 17th century. This was rebuilt in 1801 and survives as a harled octagonal building with a steeply-pitched cap roof (323385).

Return by the Kirk Vennel and cross High Street into Glasgow Vennel, which was once the main road to Glasgow. It has been beautifully restored as a cobbled traffic-free street and won a Europa Nostra Award in 1985. Robert Burns came to this street in 1781 to learn the trade of flax dressing and a plaque marks his lodgings at No. 4. The heckling shop where he worked can be reached through No. 10 which is tenanted by the Ayrshire Writers and Artists Society. The rubble-walled

The skyline of Irvine is dominated by the spires of Trinity Church and the parish church in this view from about 1960. Irvine Bridge was dismantled in 1973 and replaced with a covered shopping mall stretching across the river. Many regret the loss of what was probably Irvine's finest view.

Buchanite meeting house on the opposite side of the street is where the infamous Elizabeth Buchan and her religious sect met until their unorthodox and farcical beliefs and antics so scandalised the staid churchgoers of Irvine that they were banished from the town.

The High Street broadens out opposite the war memorial, designed like the mercat cross which once stood nearby on a site marked by cobbles. The Italianate Council Chambers (1861, J. Ingram) have a high octagonal tower which with the steeples of the Parish church and Trinity Church contrast with five multi-storey blocks on the Fullarton side of the river to make a unique but somewhat ungainly skyline when seen from miles around. The Royal Bank opposite the Council Chambers was designed by J.D. Peddie. Divert right from High Street along Bank Street for a look at Irvine Development

Corporation's prestigious Galt House office block on a redeveloped corner site. A few doors along, the *Irvine Times* occupies the former station building of the Caledonian Railway Company. Return to High Street and continue past the Eglinton Arms and the Kings Arms opposite. Notice the bronze plaque to John Galt the novelist outside the Bank of Scotland which stands on the site of his birthplace. Turn west down the Seagate. Seagate Castle is a three-storey fortified house built in the 16th century, with a vaulted pend running through the building to a spacious courtyard enclosed by a high wall. Bosses on the rib vaulting show the arms of Montgomerie of Eglinton (fleur-de-lis and annulets) and Drummond (three wavy lines) who united in the marriage of the 3rd Earl of Eglinton with Margaret Drummond of Innerpeffry about 1562. A substantial part of a rounded stair tower stands to the south of the pend. A plaque by the entrance records that Mary Queen of Scots visited the castle in 1563 – a doubtful tradition which allows the town each August to associate that queen with the older Marymass celebrations. At the foot of the Seagate there is a statue by John Steell of Lord Justice Boyle.

Turn right to Eglinton Street (a continuation of High Street) to visit 'Wellwood' identified by a provost's lamp-post. This is the home of Irvine Burns Club and has rare manuscripts; a valuable library; and a room in the style of the 18th century with murals by Ted and Elizabeth Odling of incidents in the life of the poet. The club also possesses a unique collection of holograph letters from renowned honorary members such as Dickens, Tennyson, Shaw, Fleming, Schweitzer, Menuhin, and Hillary. Upstairs there is a fine concert and assembly room with a mural of Irvine skyline; and a museum relating to the Burgh of Irvine. Burns is also commemorated by a statue on Irvine Moor (317398). Returning on foot, one can cross the river by a footbridge on the Low Green or follow the West Road past St Mary's R.C. Church (1875, Messrs Ingram) and the Mure Church (1850).

For a trip round some surrounding places, leave Irvine by Bank Street. Before bridging the bypass, notice the cairn to Burns re-located in McKinnon Terrace (331399). Knadgerhill

Cemetery (333401) has a stone at the gate commemorating the Scottish camp here in 1297 during the War of Independence. Stanecastle (338399) is a 16th-century tower house with Gothic windows added later. A fish sculpture revolves with the wind on the other side of the A736. Perceton House (354405), an 18th-century mansion, is headquarters of Irvine Development Corporation. Bourtreehill has an award-winning Church of St John Ogilvie (344392) with an octagonal pyramid roof and a dramatic band of red boarding wandering across the pale concrete walls. Dreghorn, at the junction of the A71 and B730, has an octagonal church (c. 1780) with a needle spire and windows by Gordon Webster and Susan Bradbury. The Dunlop Memorial Hall across the road contains a fine mural of road transport and commemorates John Boyd Dunlop who patented the pneumatic tyre in 1888.

Now to Kilwinning. From Dreghorn, via the bypass. From Irvine, past the attractive 19th-century villas in Kilwinning Road, and cross over the bypass to the Eglinton Country Park. It was here that the 13th Earl of Eglinton staged a mock-medieval tournament in 1839, attracting multitudes of spectators. Torrential rain ruined the three-day event, earning it a unique distinction in Ayrshire history – but not in the way the earl had planned.

Little remains of the Gothic Revival Eglinton Castle. An attractive reconstructed Tournament Bridge crosses the Lugton Water. The Georgian stable block, like the castle, was designed by John Paterson using the style of the Adam brothers. The buildings are used as offices and laboratory by Wilson's food processing factory – who through the Clement Wilson Foundation did much to restore the park before gifting it to the local authorities. The Park contains a Visitor Centre, Eglinton Loch, a bronze statue of Robert Burns, a starburst-shaped planting of trees, a restored dovecote, and other attractions.

KILWINNING's best known landmark is its ruinous 12th-century Tironensian abbey, or rather the buttressed clock tower at the west end of the abbey, which is a 19th-century rebuilding of one of the two west towers. There is a car park underneath this tower to the west. The abbey is best seen from the Abbey Green on the south side, which looks on to the south transept gable, the most substantial remnant of the abbey. This is pierced by a round window and four narrow windows. The three lower lancets are of unequal height and step down from west to east. The processional doorway from the cloisters under it shows fine workmanship in its mouldings, and human fallibility in its construction as the arch is asymmetrical. The Abbey Church to the north-east dates from 1774 and has windows by W. & J.J. Kier; Gordon Webster; J.T. and C.E. Stewart; Stephen Adam; and the Abbey Studio. A stone above an outside stair is dated 1593 and bears the arms and motto of the Eglintons. Table graves beside the church are pitted with the indentations of arrows from the annual papingo shoot. A papingo, or wooden bird on a pole, is set as a target projecting from the clock tower for the Ancient Society of Kilwinning Archers to test their skill. The magnificent Silver Arrow Trophy presented in 1724 is displayed in the town's public library.

Go east along Vaults Lane behind the churchyard and turn left from Church Street to the foot of Main Street. The River Garnock bridge to the east sends off footpaths to north and south on the west bank – the north one to a high and splendid seven-arch former rail viaduct in about a mile; the south one to join the B779 near the former Institute with its square clock tower.

Leave these for later and turn along the pedestrianised Main Street, from its three-storey corbel-cornered end development of recent date, past the wooden-topped Kilwinning Cross sitting outside the conspicuously quoined and lintelled No. 24, and the adjoining Crossbrae Tavern with its pediment at the eaves and rolled skew putts.

Walk on past the gable-end mural showing Kilwinning's major buildings. The street has been modernised – crassly at times – but some good stonework and detailing remain, and Art Deco flourishes at the north-west end. The red sandstone 'Mother Lodge' of freemasonry is numbered Lodge No. 0. The lane opposite leads to the Erskine Church (1838) which has a rope wheel in its bell gable.

Rejoin the traffic at the west end of the Main Street and continue west past the Mansfield Church (1861) to Caley House at the corner of Dalry Road, on the site of the

Cart-horses were a common sight in Irvine after they had disappeared from most other Ayrshire towns. The Carters Society plays a prominent part in the annual Marymass celebrations and an astonishing number of horses are mustered for the street processions and judging and races on the moor. A dignified champion is seen with his cup and proud owner after winning the best-dressed Clydesdale class.

Caledonian railway station. This is a group of young people's self-catering flats designed for the YMCA/YWCA by Irvine Development Corporation, incorporating a hall and glazed conservatory common room. The scheme was completed in 1984 and has won a number of important awards.

The Caledonian Railway's route to the south can be traced in the undeveloped parkland opposite Caley House. The path into this park and road to the left lead past Kilwinning Library where the papingo trophy can be seen. St Winning's R.C.

Church (1937, T. Cordiner) opposite the library has a fine interior. Follow St Winning's Road south then east from the church, crossing the B779 and following a lane past the rubble-walled 'Thrift Shop' back to the abbey clock tower.

The A737 from Kilwinning to Dalry keeps close company with the River Garnock and the Glasgow railway line. Dalgarven Mill (297458) has been restored as a Museum of Ayrshire Country Life and Costume. The three-storey high water-driven flour mill dominates a group of vernacular barns and byres, and a brick chimney at the side of the river. The hotel near it has unusual gate posts and an arch in the garden which is said to be from Kilwinning Abbey. Monk Castle (292474) is a 16th-century T-shaped building which belonged to the abbey and is now a ruin. To the north of it the road crosses the bed of a rope-hauled wagonway from a mine in the hillside to the former Douglas Firebrick Company's kilns – which now produce mushrooms commercially. The narrow tunnel under the road is still open to the west.

An attractive view opens out to DALRY, with the spire of St Margaret's Church dominant. All roads into Dalry drop to a water bridge, then have to climb to the town centre. Make for St Margaret's where there are parking areas to east and west.

This Victorian Gothic church is cruciform in shape with its spire 50m above the town square. The church, designed by David Thomson and completed in 1873, has windows by Guthrie and Wells; C.L. Davidson; and Rona Moody; a large Glasgow bell of 1872; a small Dutch bell of 1661; and an interior stone dated 1608 admonishing 'Remember Lot's Wife'. The churchyard contains a large horizontal sundial with a metal gnomon about 1½m high.

The square in front of St Margaret's contains a three-storey hotel; a crow-step gabled bank; and a fine pedimented former town hall of 1853 with a cupola bellcote and Ionic columns at first-floor level, which is to become a public library. The light sandstone Trinity Church (1857) along from it presents a spirelet-decorated gable to the street with a short broach spire above the bellcote.

Courthill Street beside it has a crocketed and gargoyled Gothic Mission hall, and a granite fountain – both 1876. A path goes down to the park, which contains a fine war memorial.

Go south from the Square along New Street past the red sandstone Bank of Scotland with curved and triangular pediments, and the bee-skepped swag of the Co-op. Pass the junction and the house gable-ended to the street, turn right along Garnock Street between the Royal Hotel and White Hart House. Turn right again up Aitken Street past the R.C. Church (1852), and some fine detached mid-19th-century dwellings, to the Renaissance public hall of 1883 with its hind-topped pediment and ironwork-crowned slate-hung roof.

Go left past the lancet-windowed post office (which was a school in the 19th century) and the attractive 1½ storey range opposite with narrow rounded windows and pedimented doorway. Turn right along the curving road west of St Margaret's Church, right again along the Main Street, and right at the Auld Hoose into North Street to return to the Square. This takes you through the main part of the town, with narrow street patterns and older stone buildings with shops at ground-floor level.

The three-storey Bridgend Mills at the foot of New Street (297494) date from the 19th century. The main building is an impressive industrial monument with segmental and half-round arched windows and hip-roofed tower.

The public are allowed to walk in the grounds of Blair estate, south-east of Dalry. The big house is an ancient tower extended into a T-shape plan with three and four storeys. Two entrances, side by side, carry an impressive display of armorial bearings, datestones, and an ogee-shaped marriage stone. An extensive wall surrounds the estate, with attractive lodges and a smithy decorated with lancet windows and ball finials. The stable block and other buildings, a 19th-century bridge, and decorative ironwork also add greatly to the interest of the area.

Cleaves Cove (318475) on the south bank of the Dusk Water is a secluded and remarkable series of limestone caves. Excavations in 1883 showed that humans had inhabited the caves in prehistoric times. Part of the system has collapsed, but about 80m of linked caverns are accessible from a central entrance – to those who can look after themselves. Small stalactites can be seen. There is a waterfall on the Dusk Water at the east end of the system. Montgreenan House (343445), now a hotel, has a collection of milestones within the estate. A farm is built around the ruins of Clonbeith Castle (339456). The Caaf Water south-west of Dalry has a car park at the Linn Bridge (288487). A plaque on this bridge commemorates 'Hughie's Field' and is a sister's tribute to a dead brother (1983). A path goes up the south bank of the stream past a fine waterfall where a lade and remains of a mill can be seen. Later, a bridge crosses to Pinnioch's Point, or Peden's Pulpit as it is popularly known – a huge rock sitting above the neck of the glen. The two-storey house at West Lynn (286488) was the home of George Houston, R.S.A., till his death in 1947, and has an example of his art above the door. North of the B780 the Cat Stone (257488) is a large boulder sitting in a field.

The B780 from Dalry enters KILBIRNIE past a garden city development. The Auld Kirk at the junction with the B777 dates from about the 15th century and is of special interest. A saddleback-roofed tower with a belfry stands at the west end. The Glengarnock Aisle was built in 1597. The Laird's Loft incorporating a private apartment with vault beneath dates from 1642, and carries splendid oak carvings and heraldic shields. The pulpit of 1620 is polygonal and has an unusual slanting sounding board which is also richly adorned. The boxed pews are starkly simple by comparison. Windows include the work of Sydney Holmes of Guthrie and Wells Ltd; and Gordon Webster. The kirkyard contains the Crawfurd Mausoleum (1594) which shows, through a narrow opening, the recumbent effigies of Captain Crawfurd and his wife – the captain who successfully ousted the English garrison from Dumbarton Castle in 1571.

The primary school at the junction is dated 1914 and is flanked by squat little towers. The florid swag decoration can hardly be missed but notice also the representation of children featured on the rainwater heads.

The road north to the town centre passes the war memorial gate opposite the former picture house (now a bus garage); a three-storey grey tenement which shows five storeys at the back to the river; and Lodge No. 399 which has an odd array of Doric, Ionic, and Corinthian columns side by side at the door. The Garnock Labour Club has a dignified headquarters with a chamfered chimneyhead above a central pediment. Chimneys over pediments are common features of this street,

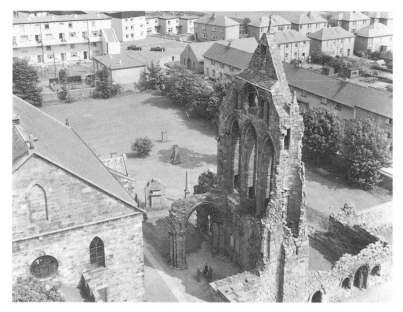

Kilwinning Abbey was founded in the 12th century by monks of the Tiron order. The much later Abbey Church and a clock tower occupy the site now and from this tower the view shows the most substantial remnant of the abbey – the south transept gable, with the cloisters and chapter house to the right.

along with other central decorative features such as datestones and sculptures. A large statue by D.W. Stevenson commemorates William Walker, M.D., who donated the halls behind to the town. There is a local museum next door.

The Cross is dominated by a three-storey Venetian-windowed block with a rounded oriel tower and balustraded roof parapet. It looks down on a former cinema and a rolled steel sculpture by John Henry White presented to the town by the British Steel Corporation. From the Cross you can see the impressive 19th-century Stoneyholm Mill just downriver, where brightly-coloured fishing nets are made and hung out in the yard.

The former West and East Churches (315546) face each other to the west of the Cross. The West Church is now the hall for the East – which dates from 1843, was restored in 1903, and is now called St Columba's Church. The restoration has produced an attractive and remarkable design, with a slightly tapering bell tower which has wide segmental arched openings. The Place of Kilbirnie (304541) dates from about 1470 and is now a ruin between two parts of the golf course. The prosperity of a mill started by William and James Knox in 1788 allowed them and their descendants to develop mansions at Place (303547). Moorpark (311551) and Redheugh (318555). Place is still lived in; Moorpark is being restored, with a nature trail; and Redheugh is a home for adolescents.

The Glengarnock Steel Works, on the south shore of Kilbirnie Loch, closed in 1985. The site is now an industrial estate, and is being developed also for water sports (327535).

Some trains stop at Glengarnock, but Kilbirnie and Beith have lost their stations. Work has started on turning an old trackbed between Johnstone and Kilbirnie into a cycle path which should eventually extend from the Highlands to the Ayrshire coast.

BEITH can be explored best from the town centre at the Auld Kirk (349541) which has a car park to the east. The Auld Kirk was built in 1593. What remains of it has been considerably altered and it now has a clock on the gable facing to the front. Eglinton Street to the south-west has numerous fine buildings – the Saracen's Head Inn, the post office of 1897 with its arched chimneyhead and royal coat of arms, the Bank of Scotland, and many dwellings with classical detailing. The Council Offices at the east end present a pedimented gable to the Strand beneath a prominent bellcote.

Climb the Strand past the fountain (1876) and the Clydesdale Bank with its conical-capped tower entrance. Go up Townhead Street to Kirk Road where a good view is had of the High Church. It is a T-shaped Gothic-style structure opened in 1810 with a bell and clock tower, windows by G. Maile and Gordon Webster, and an organ built by Harrison and Harrison in 1885.

Go round the church by the lane on the west, past the two-storey primary school with its four tiny lancet windows in the gable. Go downhill into Kirk Road past the Bethany Hall and turn east along New Street, then south-east along Head Street. The church here was built in 1784, has rubble walls, a hip roof and half-round windows, and is now used as a Boys' Brigade hall.

Return north-west and go on down Mitchell Street past the late 19th-century R.C. church to the Coach House with its arched pend. You are now at crossroads, with the slim-steepled Trinity Church visible to the north-east along Wilson Street. That church was built in 1926 and contains good local woodwork, and windows by W. Meikle and Sons. Go left from the crossroads along Main Street which has been neatly renovated. The Smugglers Tavern has a timpan gable with two small windows, and the public library next door is attractive. The Old Deer Inn round the corner has a similar gable to the Smugglers Tavern and brings you back to the Auld Kirk again.

Bigholm Road leads north-east from Trinity Church to the elevated golf course and good views over the district. Lochlands Hill (210m) and Cuff Hill (206m) have several features of interest. St Inan's Chair (373553) is a high-backed and winged stone seat with a foot slab in a line of crags above a road junction. St Inan's Well (372554) is beside the junction, where two modern spouts are more likely to catch attention. The Four Stanes (376551) are four large boulders in a group of two pairs facing Beith from the ridge. The Rocking Stone (383554) is a large boulder in a clump of trees but it no longer rocks. The Long Cairn (386550) has been uncovered and shows stone cists on the eastern slope of Cuff Hill. Coldstream Mill (385544) has a mill pond.

BARRMILL to the south on the B706 is a village which was once surrounded by railway routes from Beith, Glengarnock, and Kilwinning, to Lugton. There is a M.O.D. munitions depot to the south-west. Giffen Viaduct (367512) is an interesting skewed structure on which the seven arches develop from segmental to half round curves. Giffen limeworks (364508) closed in 1972, leaving behind a temple-like industrial monument with high battered walls of coursed rubble, brick and concrete, with two kilns at the base.

The River Garnock has its source near the highest summit of the hills above Kilbirnie – the Hill of Stake (522m). The river plunges over the spectacular Spout of Garnock (288607) and cuts for itself a deep valley before rounding the ruinous Glengarnock Castle (311574) and falling to Kilbirnie. The Hill of Stake can be reached via Lochwinnoch and the Muirshiel Country Park in Renfrewshire, then by a track to an old barytes mine (283650). The uplands are heavy walking, but the views extend from Fife and the Lothians to Islay and Jura, and from Wigtownshire to a vast array of Highland hills.

CHAPTER 22

The Cunninghame Coast

Cunninghame District meets Kyle and Carrick District south of Irvine. Irvine is a coastal town but it has been dealt with earlier and so is excluded from this chapter. Although it has a harbour, Irvine is not built directly on the coast like Saltcoats, Ardrossan, or Largs but lies behind the estuary of the Rivers Garnock and Irvine.

The Garnock flows from the north and almost parallel to the sea to the west of Irvine. The peninsula formed between this river and the sea is very sparsely represented on the O.S. map. Here among the sand dunes at Ardeer ancient peoples left behind a multitude of finds for archaeologists.

Then in 1873 at this site, the British Dynamite Company began the production of 'guhr' dynamite, the first safe commercial explosive incorporating nitroglycerine. In 1926 Nobel's Explosives Company Limited, as it was then, was incorporated into Imperial Chemical Industries Limited (ICI) as part of the Explosives Group of Nobel Industries Limited together with the other companies which formed ICI. After various restructurings, Nobel's Explosives Company Ltd is now a separate subsidiary company sharing the peninsula with other interests of ICI. The industry's importance to the area is shown by the exploding stick of dynamite on Stevenston's coat of arms.

As you approach STEVENSTON on the A78 from Irvine or arrive by train from Glasgow, the ICI works lie to your left and glisten with lights after dark like a town. The high cooling tower was a landmark but collapsed in a gale in 1973.

Motorists should take the B952 from the A78 for a closer look at this impressive industrial site. As you cross the railway bridge, the reedy course of the Master Gott lies north of the railway line. This is said to be part of a canal constructed between Ardeer and Saltcoats in 1772.

From the roundabout beyond the bridge turn right then left to the shore at the red sandstone octagonal-towered Ardeer Church. Go out on to Stevenston Point which juts into the Firth of Clyde but does not provide a harbour. Arran rises majestically across the water, as it does from many other viewpoints along the coast. Notice the high concrete sea wall topped with barbed wire stretching towards the estuary of the Irvine – a bad beach to be caught on by a spring tide!

Return along Shore Road past the church and the mural-decorated Ardeer Centre, cross the level crossing at the station, and go north up Station Road which once had a rival Caledonian Railway Station at the north end. Turn right into Moorpark Road East opposite the War Memorial Institute to Ardeer Park. This has been landscaped since its days as a quarry and coal pit area. A footpath circles the new loch but the embankment for a wagonway is still visible. Beyond the park the ground can be seen rising to upper Stevenston from a former shoreline of the firth. A high garden wall of the demolished Ardeer House stands at the foot of the slope, with a classical gazebo exposed to the westerlies.

Return to Station Road and continue north up New Street past the Livingstone Church, Glencairn primary school (with an arch of 1875 from the previous school), the entrance to the cemetery (with memorials to cholera and dynamite victims), the former Free Church (with bellcote), and Glencairn Lounge. This last contains a fine mural of Stevenston's history from Roman times to Nobel; local industries featured include spinning and weaving, coal mining, fishing, and making jews harps!

The High Kirk stands above the town centre and was completed in 1833 on a dominating site which has been in human use for centuries. A sundial below the tower window commemorates Dr David Landsborough, minister from 1811-43 who moved to Saltcoats at the Disruption. He was the author of books on natural history and Arran and is buried in the churchyard. A son, William, born in the manse adjoining in 1825, emigrated to Australia. In 1862 he led a search for the overdue explorers Burke and Wills and travelled from the Gulf of Carpentaria to Melbourne. In the same year John McDouall Stuart of Dysart travelled from Adelaide to the site of Darwin, both men becoming the first to cross the Continent, but in different directions.

The church contains a five-sided gallery in which is sited the

The remains of a beam engine house stand near the coast at Auchenharvie between Stevenston and Saltcoats. It was used for pumping water out of the mines in this area and is reputed to have held the second of Newcomen's engines to work in Scotland. The houses beyond Auchenharvie Academy sit on a raised beach.

organ. Four wall paintings by James Wyllie show the church in the four seasons. In front of them stands the pulpit with an unusual sounding board. Among the stained-glass windows are two by Oscar Paterson. There is a sentry box at the gate for elders on duty.

A path goes up the Stevenston Burn from the town centre, starting opposite the health centre and dignified baronial post office (1939). Beyond the A78 it passes the remains of a mill dam to Kerelaw Castle (269428). This is a curious ruin with rounded, squared, and pointed windows marking different periods of construction. A giant sequoia within the ruins indicates long neglect. Hayocks House to the east is now surrounded by council houses.

Stevenston has two sites of interest to Burns enthusiasts. Schoolwell Street (below the kirk on the south-west) runs uphill into High Road past Mayville – a fine house with a pediment bearing three urns, and a sundial in the garden. This was the birthplace of Lesley Baillie, who features in the song 'O saw ye bonie Lesley'. She is also commemorated on the family obelisk (263422) in Glencairn Street north of the A78.

Two roads connect Stevenston with SALTCOATS. On the sea side of Saltcoats Road is the Auchenharvie Engine House (257414). This is said to have held one of the earliest of Newcomen's steam engines in Scotland (c.1720), and other later engines used to pump water from the coal pits. The track of the former Caledonian railway to Ardrossan harbour crosses Saltcoats Road and is now a leisure walkway.

The existing railway runs close to the sea between Stevenston and Saltcoats and, with the promenade, can be drenched by waves when gales and tides combine.

Communities on the Cunninghame coast have good rail and bus services to the outside world. Saltcoats has a car park adjacent to the station, which makes a good starting point for a walkabout. The station buildings on both platforms are attractive sandstone survivals from another age. Leave the station by Countess Street, heading south past the town house. This has a tall square tower diminishing in sections to a final octagonal section from which springs a short spire.

Continue through Quay Street to the harbour. Betsy Miller was born in this area in 1793 and became the only female recorded in the British Registry of Tonnage to become a ship's master.

As the name indicates, Saltcoats developed a salt panning industry. Its harbour was built at the end of the 17th century. In the 18th century coal was brought from Ardeer by canal for export to Ireland. The development of Ardrossan harbour brought decline to the port of Saltcoats and only small boats are to be seen now. The Custom House (1805) became for a time a maritime museum. Tree fossils are to be seen halfway across the harbour at low tide.

Flat-roofed local authority housing behind the Braes does nothing for the town's image as a holiday resort. The Beach Pavilion at the west end of the harbour is a prominent landmark. Its function has changed from summer shows to amusements. A water sports centre is to be created out of three former bathing ponds.

Walk round the shore by Winton Circus for a view of Ardrossan across the South Beach, then turn right into Winton Street and right again at the roundabout into Hamilton Street. This is the main shopping thoroughfare running into pedestrianised Dockhead Street. The E.U. Congregational Church in Hamilton Street dates from 1863.

Turn left at the foot of Hamilton Street into the Kirkgate to visit the North Ayrshire Museum which has a good local collection housed in the former 18th-century parish church. Notice the sundial under the bell tower.

Leave by Manse Street to the north, going left and over the railway bridge in Caledonia Road to the lancet-windowed tower of St Cuthbert's Church. This is an impressive building of 1908 designed by Peter McGregor Chalmers. A model of a French frigate from the old parish church hangs under the north gallery. The three-manual Hill, Norman, and Baird organ was installed by Hilsden. Two windows are by Gordon Webster. A war memorial in the form of a lamp stands outside the door. Argyle primary school to the north is a fine sandstone building.

Recross the railway bridge and return along Manse Street passing the Erskine Church (1866) into Chapelwell Street and Dockhead Street. The Landsborough and Trinity Church on the left (1889) has windows by Ward and Partners; and Ballantine and Gardiner. Turn left at the east end of Dockhead Street back to your starting point.

St Brendan's R.C. Church (247430) in Corrie Crescent north of the High Road dates from 1965 and has a detached bell tower. Inside the church a big surprise comes as you turn to face the exit and are confronted by brilliantly colourful south windows on the gallery and roof.

Saltcoats and Ardrossan are divided by the Stanley Burn which curls round the Episcopal Church of St Andrew at the east end of South Crescent Road (239420). The church dates from 1875 and has windows by L.C. Evetts and J. and W. Guthrie. A number of impressive villas looking out to the sea over the South Beach have fallen victims to unsympathetic alterations with change of use. St Peter in Chains R.C. Church is a handsome brick building (1938, architect J.A. Coia). In front are sunken gardens with an 18th century sundial. Nearby the war memorial features sculptures of St Columba, Bruce,

Watt, Livingstone, Burns, and Admiral Wood.

Arran Place separates St Peter's from the Barony Church of 1843 which carries a ship weather vane on the spire. It has a window by Stewart Melville of W. Meikle and Sons. Arran Place turns into Princes Street running across a level crossing at the town station and across the peninsula of the harbour.

ARDROSSAN was planned by the 12th Earl of Eglinton at the start of the 19th century. Glasgow Street runs north-east from Princes Street and is a particularly wide and straight street where cars can be parked easily. Even though this is the main street there are few shops, as Saltcoats traders have captured the market – avenging the loss of their harbour trade!

Glasgow Street, Princes Street, and Harbour Street form a cross and have numerous interesting buildings. Walk along Harbour Street past the Winton Buildings and the bow-fronted Custom House to the Eglinton Dock. The late 19th-century brick-built Power House has arched windows and a square campanile-type clock tower. The Eglinton Dock and tidal basin to the west are connected to Montgomerie Pier to the north by a swing bridge. On the south side, trains from Glasgow run out to Winton Pier which adjoins the Ferry terminal to Arran.

Return to the cross roads and go along Glasgow Street past the columned post office and E.U. Congregational Church (1903). Just before the former Burgh Chambers climb steps on the right to Castle Hill where ruins of Ardrossan Castle stand above the ruins of the old parish church. The castle may have been dismantled by Cromwell to help build his citadel in Ayr but the church was blown down about 1691. An obelisk on the hill commemorates a local doctor.

The former St John's Church (231425) in Montgomerie Street and the Seafield School (228434) on the A78 are impressive buildings. Offshore from the Shell Refinery lies the bird reserve of Horse Island with its tapering stone tower.

There are a number of antiquities north of the three towns. Ashgrove Loch has the remains of a crannog (276443). There is a motte at Meikleaught (253451). At Montfode on the edge of Ardrossan there is a motte (227437) and a fragment of a castle (226441). Above the raised beach there is a fort at Boydston (219449) and a double fort to the north of it on the

The harbour at Saltcoats, and former Custom House and Harbour Master's House which was built in 1805. The building became for a time a Maritime Museum but the salt air was damaging the exhibits. The water recedes from the rocks in the middle of the harbour at low tide uncovering the remains of several fossil trees.

north edge of Kirkland Glen (215454). A narrow ridge at Coalhill above Busbie Muir reservoir has been fortified (245470) and gives an unusual view of the causewayed B780 crossing the Munnoch reservoir. Knock-Georgan (236473) has a distinctive dome-shaped summit fort, entered from the south over two ditches. There is a large cluster of cup and ring markings decorating a slab and facing the sky on the east slope of Blackshaw Hill (231483). They lie behind the west wall of an old 'drove road' which runs to West Kilbride north of Law Hill. According to tradition, dead monarchs were carried this way to be shipped from Portencross by Loch Fyne to Argyll for burial on Iona. Blackshaw farm (230491) is open to visitors in summer and offers tractor rides to the cups and rings.

WEST KILBRIDE has Law Castle (211484), a four-storey, 15th-century tower with gun loops and a rounded doorway.

The railway station below it was designed by James Miller.
Walk south-west from the station car park along Main Street.
Notice on the north side the 1623 stone rebuilt into a later
bridge above the burn; the 1½ storey row of vernacular houses
with dormers breaking the eaves line; and the lower cottage
with set-back dormer and gable crow-stepped to the front but
skewed to the cope at the rear. St Andrew's Church was built in
1881 and has a window by Wm. Meikle and Sons. Then on the
south side of the Main Street are the former Barony church of
1872 with a broached belfry; a fountain; the bank building with
geometric decoration; a higher building with a shaped gable;
and Kirktonhall House with a 1660 stone. This house faces
south to a multiple sundial dated 1717 and designed by
Professor Robert Simpson (1687-1768). He was born here,
became an authority on Euclid, and has a massive pepper-pot
shaped memorial in the local cemetery.

Main Street continues into Ritchie Street where the grey
stone Institute was built in 1909 and the red stone Overton
Church dates from 1883. This church contains windows by
Wm. Meikle and Son; C.E. Stewart; Gordon Webster; and
Towerlands Studio. The two windows by Webster include
Arran, Hunterston 'A' Power Station, Law and Crosbie Castles,
and William Wallace.

Yerton Brae leads down to SEAMILL and the A78. Seamill
Hydro Hotel is at the sea front, with the Sea Mill to the south at
the mouth of the Kilbride Burn – see it from the shore or look
over the wall and mill pond from the A78. A villa called 'The
Fort' opposite is built on an Iron Age site. A path returns to
West Kilbride past the Teachers' Centre and up the burn.
Tarbert Hill and Law Hill give good view points.

Portencross Castle stands above a tiny harbour at the farthest
west point of north Ayrshire. It is a rectangular keep with a
narrower but taller wing to the east. It is said to have been used
by monarchs journeying between the castles of Dundonald and
Rothesay. A cannon in front of the castle was recovered in
1740 from a Spanish ship wrecked off shore in 1588. There is a
hill fort and dun on the ridge above it, which rises over
Goldenberry Hill and forms precipitous crags on the west
called the Three Sisters. Northbank on the raised beach was
the scene of an unsolved murder in 1912. The pier was built in

anticipation of the railway coming this way – but it didn't!
Hunterston Castle (193515) is a three-storey medieval tower
restored by Sir Robert Lorimer (1913-15). It is now a Clan
Hunter centre south-east of Hunterston House (1799-1810).
The Hunterston coastline now has two nuclear power
stations (guided tours of Hunterston 'B' available), a fish farm,
an oil production platform site, a direct reduction steel plant,
and a deepwater ore terminal, while a plan for an oil terminal
at Portencross was rejected. These extraordinary developments
of the last 30 years sought to copy the success of deepwater
ports abroad – but the landscape has been marred, and the
expected benefits have disappointed.
A steep road from the A78 (205530) gives good views of this
area. The Glen Burn to the south can be walked past waterfalls.
Kaim Hill (387m) is easily climbed and gives superb views. The
west face, near the top, has outcrops of millstone grit which was
quarried in the past for millstones. The long rake of quarry
workings is worth seeing, and a half millstone sits to the north.
There are possible cup marks on a flat slab on Diamond Hill
(213539). The ruins of the 16th-century Southannan Castle
and its modern successor can be seen below to the west.
FAIRLIE station has a special siding and crane for the
transportation of nuclear waste. The tunnel to the north is over
half a mile long and opened the way to Largs and to Fairlie
Pier. The pier and its station have been demolished and the
area landscaped. The remaining pier is for a NATO mooring
and support depot.
Fairlie Church dates from the 19th century and has windows
by Messrs Powell; Heaton, Butler and Bayne; Morris and Co;
and Gordon Webster; and a plaque to Alan Boyle who flew the
first British monoplane in 1909. The Fairlie Stone in the
vestibule is an ancient sculptured stone showing a human and
animals. The church hall on the opposite side of the A78 was
formerly the rebuilt Free Church of 1879. The school higher
up dates from 1887. A walk up Fairlie Glen leads past a 16th-
century tower house and can be continued through the hills to
Dalry.
Kelburn Country Park between Fairlie and Largs extends
around a 16th-century tower which has extensive additions
from 1700 and the 19th century. Old farm buildings have been

converted into a visitors' centre and there are numerous fine walks among exotic trees and plants. The Kelburn Glen has waterfalls, high views over the Firth of Clyde, and an 18th-century classical monument. There is a splendid obelisk multiple sundial of 1707 near the castle.

LARGS faces straight on to the sea. It has a stony beach, is a very popular resort, and is best seen on foot. The pier is a good starting point with a car park, information bureau, ferry to Cumbrae, pleasure cruises, bus and rail stations, and a local museum close by. The setting is superb with the islands of Arran, Bute and the Cumbraes to seaward and a high green volcanic escarpment inland.

Moving south from the pier we pass the Moorings (1935, James Houston) designed in breezy nautical style; and the 1816 Bath House with rounded ends. The Clark Memorial Church (1892; T.G. Abercrombie), in Early Gothic Decorated style, has a complete set of chiming bells (now out of use). Large statues of Moses and St John look down from its lofty gable. It has a hammerbeam roof, an organ by Willis, and impressive windows by C.W. Whall; Stephen Adam; and Meikle and Sons – one shows Noah's Ark and its animals.

The Italianate St John's Church beside it was rebuilt in 1886 to plans by A.J. Grahame. Notice the Dunn Memorial Hall near the War Memorial, and cross the Gogo Water by the Brisbane bridge (1911). Sir Thomas MacDougall Brisbane, shown on a cast iron roundel, was born and died in Largs (1773-1860). In between he became Governor of New South Wales, catalogued thousands of stars of the southern hemisphere, and had a city and river in Australia named after him.

Continue along the front past the granite fountain, and the 19th-century Elderslie Hotel with its organ pipe-like chimney stacks. The Curlinghall Hotel has been demolished, but two ironwork arches depict curling stones and the name, at the site of the first indoor curling club in the world. A monolith stands opposite. Little Raith and the Picketlaw are fine bow-fronted buildings. Turn left up Anthony Road past Warriston to the main road back into town past the Douglas park or walk south to the Battle of Largs Memorial commemorating the defeat of the Norse invaders in 1263. The 'Pencil', as the memorial is known, was designed by J.S. Kay in 1912.

The 'Pencil' is a distinctive monument on the coast at the southern edge of Largs and was erected in 1912 to commemorate the victory of the Scots over Norse invaders in 1263. Storms scattering the Norwegian fleet and the failing health of King Haco their leader probably did as much to send the invaders home as did the Scottish forces. An annual Viking Festival is held in Largs to boost tourism.

The Douglas Park has a Robert Burns garden and extends up the steep hillside. There is a chambered tomb (209586) at the hill foot, and an Iron Age fort (215588) on Castlehill – above Cock-ma-lane, a high solitary cottage landmark.

Going north from the pier, the razzamatazz of the sea front has cheapened the Victorian Gallowgate. The spire of St Columba's Church is only slightly lower than the Clark Memorial to the south. Gothic in style and opened in 1892 also, to plans by Steel and Balfour, it has a fine interior with a Willis organ, a war memorial by Sir Robert Lorimer, an octagonal oak pulpit by M.S. Gibson, a marble mural Brisbane Memorial, and windows by Cottier and Co; Douglas Strachan; Alfred Webster; and Gordon Webster.

Continue north past Nardini's (1935, Davidson and

Partners), 'Brooksby' (designed by David Hamilton), 'Moorburn' (now council offices), St Mary's R.C. Church (1962) which has a large granite statue at the door of 'Mary and Child' by Hew Lorimer; and Barrfields Pavilion.

St Columba's Episcopal Church at the north end of the promenade was opened in 1877 (plans by Ross of Inverness) and contains a memorial to Lord Kelvin, the eminent physicist, engineer, and mathematician. The main road crosses the Noddsdale Burn on a modern bridge carrying a stone of 1824 from the first reconstruction. Netherhall gatehouse beside it carries a tablet to Lord Kelvin who lived here in the big house, designed by Campbell Douglas.

In the town centre, an entry off the Main Street leads into the old churchyard and site of the medieval church – now represented by a gable, and the Skelmorlie Aisle, built in 1636 as a Renaissance-style mausoleum for Sir Robert Montgomerie of Skelmorlie and his wife. They lie under an elaborately carved stone tomb housed under a timber-lined and splendidly-painted barrel-vaulted ceiling. The churchyard contains a Bronze Age cist, the burial aisle of the Brisbanes (1634), and a mound of unknown origin.

In the Main Street, notice the curved gable of the Royal Bank, the Tudor-Gothic offices at 72-74, and the light and airy concourse of the railway terminus, which contains a fine mural of the railways by Largs Academy pupils. The Academy in Flatt Road shows a mural of the Battle of Largs externally, while the Victoria Hotel on the sea front shows others internally. Flatt Road leads to a path into the hills above the Gogo Water and the splendid Halkshill House (212593). North of the Gogo Water in Waterside Street is Moot Hill, which has a cairn at its foot, and, on its top, three stone columns which were used as siting points from an observatory at Brisbane House.

Largs Cemetery on the Kilbirnie Road is well worth a visit. It contains many interesting memorials including a classical temple with mosaic floor to the Carswells and an Art Nouveau stone to the McNairs, designed by John McNair who worked with Charles Rennie Macintosh. Sir William Burrell who donated his fabulous collection to Glasgow is buried here.

A narrow inland road runs from Largs to Greenock up the Noddsdale Water. Brisbane House, now demolished, stood

Largs occupies a splendid coastal situation with green scarped hills behind and fine views to the islands in the Firth of Clyde. Groynes protect its pebbly beach from erosion, but despite its lack of sand the shoreline is very popular with day-trippers. The two tall churches were both erected in 1892. Nardini's and the Moorings beneath them are examples of 'white' architecture of the 1930s for a more leisured generation.

here (208619). Brisbane Mains (209622) is a courtyard farm with an attractive arched entry. A track goes past it from the road (212618) to the Knock (217m) which is crowned with a vitrified Iron Age fort defended by several ramparts and a gully to the north. The view from it is superb.

Back on the road, just before Middleton an iron gate leads west to 'the Prophet's Grave' where, as the inscription tells, Rev. William Smith died in a plague in 1647. Smith had stayed in Largs to tend the sick while the healthy moved away.

North of Middleton a track past a reservoir to Craigton gives access to the hills and more superb views. A ruined waterwheel stands on the burn south of Outerwards (234660). West of Outerwards, a Roman fortlet (232666) offers another great view to the coast and islands. A vehicular track has been laid along the crest of the ridge following the line of the Roman road. The Firth of Clyde narrows north of Largs. The coastal shelf is being reduced also as the Old Red Sandstone makes itself conspicuous in shore-line outcrops, cliffs inland from the road, and as building material for castles and mansions. Knock Castle (194630) stands above the cliffs. Skelmorlie Castle (195659) has an old keep on the north-east corner but was substantially rebuilt following a fire in 1959.

SKELMORLIE is unique among Ayrshire villages for the way its 30-metre cliff of conglomerate stands vertically over the Shore Road. The A78 can be lashed by sea waves as it enters from the south past substantial villas erected by wealthy businessmen in the 19th century. Where the cliff line pushed westwards, development switched to the sea side and the narrow road has to squeeze itself between a line of shops and houses and the bulging precipice. The pavement here must be the narrowest in the county and a number of householders have erected mirrors to help them join the hazardous road.

A hydropathic hotel was built on the top of the cliffs in 1868 and a lift added in 1941 from a small car park on Shore Road. The hydro has been demolished but the site of the lift and a gap in the buildings leading to a former pier can still be traced.

Skelmorlie and Wemyss Bay Church by the A78 was formerly the South Church and developed from the hall built in 1856 at the north end. The tower and present church were added by Honeyman and Keppie around 1895, with an Art Nouveau lamp free-standing at the door. The church contains some good stained glass, including a window by 'Morris, 1900' and two windows from St Andrew's Church, Greenock.

On the other side of the A78 there is a curious little round house at the entrance to Beach House. The former U.P. Church of 1874 has been converted into a dwelling and stands by the Kelly Burn at the county boundary. Wemyss Bay lies across the burn with its pier and railway terminus. Had the railway carried on to Largs it would have brought Ayrshire and Renfrewshire closer together but the landowners stopped it. A tunnel would probably have been required at Skelmorlie, for it would be difficult for a railway to find enough space along the coastal shelf.

Index

Illustrations, page numbers in *italics*

Kirkmichael 130-131
Kirkoswald 117-118; 23, 62, 65, 66, 74, 138
Knockdolian 124
Knox, John 28, 130, 206-207
Knox, W. & J. 78, 225, 226
Kyle 6, 13, 28, 34, 35, 39, 65, 86, 152-192
Kyle Castle 177
Kylesmuir 26

Ladykirk 27
Landsborough, David and William 230
Lanfine 208, 212, 214
language 10-11, 13, 59-60, 86
Largs 238-241; 1, 2, 4, 13, 42, 43, 48, 93, 94, 96, 97; *239, 241*
Lawson, Rev. Roderick 130
legends 34-41, 123
Leglen 67, 68, 152
Lendalfoot 122-123
libraries 7, 11, 30, 102, 120, 128, 129, 148, 154, 220, 221, 222, 227
lighthouses 103, 112, 116, 121-122, 234; *95*
lime and lime kilns 53, 73, 75, 108, 111-112, 124, 131, 136, 138, 164, 177-180, 205, 227
local government 6, 24, 104, 106, 112, 176, 198, 215
Loch Braden 133
Loch Doon 82, 133, 147-151; *11*
Loch Doon Castle 18, 150
Lochgoin 200
Lochlea 13, 62, 68, 157
Lockhart, George 8, 28
Logan, Hugh 84
Loudoun 28, 34, 35
Loudoun Castle 21, 37, 208
Loudoun, earls of 83, 87, 163
Loudoun Hill 2, 13, 30, 214; *99*
Lugar 176-177; 8, 76, 80, 180
Lugar Water 80, 159, 170, 174, 176-177; *180*
Lugton 205

McAdam, John Loudon 9, 45, 46, 50, 80, 104, 166
McKechnie Institute 119, 120
Maclaurin Gallery 108
Maclure, William 9
Macmillan, Alexander 9

Macrae, James 83, 182
Magnum Leisure Centre 98, 215
Maidens 86, 97, 116
Mair, John 88
mansion houses 20-21
Mauchline 157-160; 1, 12, 23, 26, 48, 62, 69-71, 74; *71*
Maybole 128-131; 26, 28, 65, 78, 88; *131*
Maybole Castle 129; *37*
Memes, John 88-89
mercat crosses 21, 101, 170, 175, 183, 202, 217, 220; *203*
Merrick 1, 133-134
milestones 223
Miller, Betsy 232
Miller, John, engineer 160, 174
mill rinks 56, 153-154, 170, 186, 200
mill stones 237
miners' rows 23-24, 146, 147, 153, 170, 176
Minishant 128
Ministry of Defence 134, 227, 237
Minnivey 147
monks and monasteries 26-27, 117, 157, 165, 219-220, 225
Monkton 27, 82, 184-186
Montgomery, James 216
Montgomeries, see Eglinton, earls of
Montgreenan 223
Morton, Alexander 212-214
mortsafes 30, 105
Mossblown 68, 153
Mossgiel 48, 62, 69, 157
mottes 18, 116, 123, 125, 140-141, 144, 148, 154, 177, 234
Mount Everest 109, 182, 204
Mount Oliphant 65, 144
Muirkirk 165-166; 16, 30, 36, 46, 50, 74, 75, 76, 77, 80, 84
Mullwharchar 150; *11*
Murdoch, William 8, 16, 80, 176-177, 180
museums 13, 16, 21, 23, 48, 58, 64, 68, 70, 71, 76, 80, 106, 108, 114, 118, 131, 137, 148, 158, 162, 173, 175, 197, 200, 202, 204, 215, 218, 222, 225, 232, 233, 238; *41, 71*
nature reserves 124, 154, 156, 188, 234
Neill, General James 104
Ness Glen 149; *147*
Newcomen steam engine 231-232